05/07

UNIVERSITY OF
WOLVERHAMPTON

ONE WEEK LOAN

International Relations

A Concise Introduction

Second Edition

Michael Nicholson

NEW YORK UNIVERSITY PRESS
Washington Square, New York

Published in 2002 in the U.S.A. by
NEW YORK UNIVERSITY PRESS
Washington Square
New York, NY 10003

Library of Congress Cataloging-in-Publication Data
Nicholson, Michael, 1933–
International relations : a concise introduction / Michael Nicholson.—2nd ed.
    p. cm.
Includes bibliographical references and index.
ISBN 0-8147-5823-1 (cloth : alk. paper) — ISBN 0-8147-5822-3 (pbk : alk. paper)
1. International relations. I. Title.
JZ1242.N53 2002   2002021921
327—dc21

10   9   8   7   6   5   4   3   2   1
11   10   09   08   07   06   05   04   03   02

This book is printed on paper suitable for recycling and
made from fully managed and sustained forest sources.

Copy-edited and typeset by Povey–Edmondson
Tavistock and Rochdale, England

Printed and bound in Great Britain by
Creative Print & Design (Wales), Ebbw Vale

To Christine

In memoriam

Contents

Foreword to the Second Edition

In the summer of 2001, while in the midst of revising this book, Michael Nicholson was diagnosed with cancer. He died in October of that year. Both the illness and his sudden death were unexpected and came as a shock to everyone around him, and not least to Michael himself. He had neither the time to complete the book himself, nor to advise me – who he named as his literary executor – on the status of the revisions.

Michael's publisher at Palgrave, Steven Kennedy, asked me if I would be willing to make final revisions to the typescript and also write some new sections that Michael had intended to add in the light of comments from a reviewer. Under the circumstances, he did not have an opportunity to produce these himself.

In the process I have tried to maintain the integrity of the text Michael left behind, I think successfully with one small exception. In his draft of a preface for the second edition Michael confessed his resistance to changing 'which' to 'that' for dependent clauses, as instructed by his computer's grammar-checker. I did not read this until the text had already been altered throughout in compliance with the grammatical rules of this computer program!

Michael himself had substantially revised and extended the book as compared to the first edition, in particular adding coverage on contemporary theories of IR and on globalization. Several further additions have been made to the text based on the recommendation of a very helpful reviewer's report. These include the sections on arms control, biological and chemical weapons in the chapter on security, the section on humanitarian intervention in the chapter on moral issues and several odd paragraphs throughout. The chapter on post-positivist theories was altered more significantly than others, and has benefited from the insights of John MacLean, who had provided Michael with comments before his death. Michael was perhaps least at home in the subject matter of this chapter. It is a great credit to him as an 'empiricist' that he would cover these theories, which represent a completely different perspective than his own and that are often ignored in textbooks. John and I have tried to introduce more clarity regarding the assumptions underlying critical theory, postmodernism and feminist theory, without altering Michael's original argument.

Michael had partly drafted a preface for the second edition while at Yale in the spring of 2001. Rather than try to complete it, I have carried forward the first edition Preface into this edition. His preliminary draft was very little changed from the earlier except for the addition of a note dedicating this book to his wife Christine, who died three years and three weeks before his own death. His draft also included the comment on 'which' and 'that', mentioned above, and a half sentence starting to thank those people who had contributed in some way to this second edition. As he had not yet inserted their names, this was a particularly difficult section to complete. It is not for lack of appreciation on his part that the rest of this remains unwritten, but for lack of opportunity.

One person who played a very large role in the completion of this text after Michael's death was Roisin McLaughlin. She updated the statistics and the reading lists as well as researching the background on various new examples that have been included. She has also done much detailed editing, updating of statistics and the index, proof-reading and liaison with the copy-editor for which I am most grateful.

As the first of his works to be published posthumously, this book is in many ways also a memorial to Michael himself. John MacLean's obituary, published in *The Guardian*, stated that Michael 'gave as much time and care to teaching first year students as he did to those doing research'. This book was written for them and for a broader public, to provide an easy and accessible entrance to a field that is too often bogged down in theoretical jargon and territorial debates. His ability to engage with subject matter across the spectrum of the discipline, as well as his willingness to dialogue with others representing very different views, was one of his trademarks, for which he was held in deep respect. My own connection to Michael emerged out of a dialogue over our two different approaches, those being constructivist and rationalist. Given these fundamental differences, it is a great honour that he has entrusted me with the task of keeping his work alive.

K. M. FIERKE

Preface to the First Edition

This book is an outline of the field of international relations as I understand it and interpret it. It comes from teaching international relations and related topics in various institutions but most recently at the University of Sussex. Former students will recognize a lot.

Everyone has their own emphases and everyone would make a somewhat different choice of topics. I have not hidden my own opinions but I have tried not to let them obscure the argument. I have tried to be fair in describing positions with which I disagree.

My debts are enormous and, of course, particularly to my students over many years who have forced a process of repeated reconsideration. I hope they do not feel that they have been excessively the victims of the errors in the process of trial and error which has resulted in this book. In some ways my debts are to everyone I have been associated with professionally.

However, many people have been directly concerned with this book. I thank particularly Libby Assassi for her research assistance and help in diligently searching out material with much ingenuity. Daniel Zander and Rebecca Beaven are students at the time of writing and have kindly read a late version of the manuscript in detail, resulting in some major, rather late alterations of a type which makes me grateful for the word processor.

Nancy Radcliffe disclaimed all knowledge of international relations and therefore proved a perfect guinea-pig. She read an earlier version of my manuscript in detail. My colleague, Stephanie Hoopes, who, on the contrary, knows a lot about international relations, also read it in great detail and I have made many alterations as a consequence. Similarly Christienne van den Anker read and commented on the whole manuscript. Fiona Robinson was kind enough to read the chapter on morals with comments which greatly improved it.

My family have read the manuscript. My adult offspring, Jane, Paul and Caroline have made many helpful comments as has Geoff James (who saved me from some unfortunate factual errors). For help in proof-reading I am also indebted to Jane. Christine Nicholson, as always, has read all versions and has frequently been responsible for making me turn one version into another. She has been a stalwart support, as ever.

MICHAEL NICHOLSON

1

Introduction: Aspects of Anarchy

The Nature of International Relations

Peace and war; imperialism and nationalism; the wealth of some societies and the poverty of others; nuclear weapons and the possibility of extinction; the environment and global warming; human rights across the world; the merging of states and the splitting up of states; the European Union; international organizations; religions and their political impact; trade and the development of the multinational corporation; race and gender around the globe; globalization and the information revolution.

Clearly these topics encompass many of the most profound political and moral problems that human beings face. They are what scholars of international relations study. We might accuse them of arrogance in approaching such a collection of fundamental problems but we can hardly accuse them of triviality.

Some of the problems studied under the rubric of international relations, such as the environment, are global. They affect everyone. Other problems concern only parts of the world, such as the relationships within the European Union, or the antagonism between Israel and the Arab world. Still others, such as those concerning nuclear weapons, superficially seem to concern only those who possess them or who may become their victims, but they are effectively global. If nuclear weapons were to be used on more than a few occasions, radioactive fall-out and climate change would affect everyone, and not just those who were the direct victims. Broadly, international relations concerns human relationships and interactions that cannot be looked at purely in the context of one state such as Britain or China.

Centrally, international relations is the study of social interactions in contexts where there is no higher authority to intrude or mediate and which is outside any single governmental jurisdiction. 'Interaction' is a central concept. Thus, as the chapter title claims, international relations is a study of aspects of an anarchy, though an anarchy which is not necessarily chaotic. Indeed, one of our aims is to search for patterns of behaviour in the international system, which lacks many formal rules.

A common view of international relations, though one that is much less popular than it used to be, regards states and their interactions as the central and perhaps exclusive concern of the discipline. By states, I mean entities like Belgium, Russia, Colombia, Nigeria, India and the United States. This state-centric view is normally associated with an emphasis on military security as the major goal of states.

This view of the relations between states provides a reasonable description of significant aspects of the European international system in the pre-1914 era, and in particular, of interstate war. However, since about the end of the First World War in 1918 it has become less and less adequate, and increasingly so since 1945. Issues of war are still valid and important but they are not confined to states, while a range of new questions now require attention. Governments seem as concerned with economic issues as they are with security issues, adjusting their foreign policies as much to guide lucrative contracts to their nationals as to further anything that could plausibly be regarded as security. Non-state actors in the international scene have grown remarkably in number, size and significance. The United Nations (UN) stands out, whatever its perceived shortcomings. The World Bank and International Monetary Fund (IMF) have a big influence on the global economic scene. Other organizations such as the World Health Organization (WHO) and the International Labour Organization (ILO) have significance in their specialist areas. Some of the international organizations are small but some are big and important. It would seem foolish to try to analyze the interaction of states without bringing them in. Somewhat differently, OPEC, an association of oil-producing countries, has periodically had great influence on the crucially important international oil market. Equally and perhaps more significant has been the growth of the multinational corporations (MNCs). MNCs are commercial corporations that are located in a number of countries and are only loosely tied to any single one. We shall have more to say about these throughout the book.

contrast, the Indian subcontinent, though poor, does rather better. Even Bangladesh, generally and properly regarded as a very poor country, has an income per head of $1530.

The incomes per head are average figures, of course. Rich countries can have many poor people whereas poor countries can have exceptionally wealthy élites. Unsurprisingly there are big discrepancies. As a measure of inequality, not necessarily poverty, we can compare the wealthiest 20 per cent of the population with the poorest 20 per cent to see how much more of the national income the wealthy get than the poor. Japan is the most equal country among the ones that were richest in the 1990s. There the richest 20 per cent get 3.4 times the income of the poorest. In the United States the figure is 9 while in Britain and Australia – two of the other countries in this group – the richest 20 per cent get 6.5 and 7 times as much, respectively, as the poorest 20 per cent. There is a much wider range of ratios between the poorer countries. Slovakia, where the rich 20 per cent get 2.6 times the income of the poorer 20 per cent, is the most equal of all countries, rich or poor. In Niger, on the other hand, the top 20 per cent receive 20.7 times as much as the bottom 20 per cent, a figure exceeded only by Guinea-Bissau where the figure is 28.0. The precise figures should be treated with caution but the general patterns are meaningful.

As figures indicating equality and inequality show, average income per head is only a crude indicator of well-being. A more complex indicator is the Human Development Index (HDI) used by the United Nations Development Programme and published annually. The HDI combines three central aspects of well-being: life expectancy, adult literacy and income per head. It produces a composite index of them, which indicates a lot about a society. Life expectancy is a good indicator of health; adult literacy a good indicator of how broad a range of people can participate fully in the economic, social and political aspects of society; and wealth, of course, is wealth. In 2001, to which all the following figures refer, Norway ranked the highest in the world followed by Australia, Canada and Sweden. The UK came in at number 14, while the United States came in at 6. New Zealand came in at 19. Despite its enviably high income per head, Luxembourg was ranked 12. Lower down came India, ranked 115, and Bangladesh, 132. At the bottom of those surveyed was Sierra Leone. Expectation of life is higher than one might expect amongst the richer countries, being 78.5 years in Canada, 78.7 in Australia and 77.2 in the UK. The Japanese live the longest. A Japanese baby can expect to live for

War and Peace; Poverty and Wealth

Two dominant themes in international relations, under which other aspects can be subsumed, are the issues of war vs. peace and poverty vs. wealth. Peace and wealth are the positive features of the world we seek to explore; war and poverty are the negative features. Inevitably the two are intertwined. Unsurprisingly, those parts of the world that have recently experienced violence, such as Somalia and the former Yugoslavia, have seen their incomes decline rapidly.

War and violence – and more frequently the threats of war and violence – are common between states. Many people regard war as legitimate between states. It does not mean that states are fighting each other all the time – there are many peaceful relationships as well as warlike relationships. Between 1946 and 1986, a state was at war on average only about 2.2 per cent of the time. However, it is horrific when it happens. Despite the horrors of the twentieth century the incidence of war does not seem to have decreased and it is still actively practised.

However, there has been a marked difference in the pattern of warfare. War within states has become more important and interstate war less, though this has not meant it has become less virulent. Even where interstate war is concerned, nuclear weapons and other weapons of mass destruction such as biological weapons have provided a major new dimension. Previously war was destructive and nasty but in general societies survived. Since 1815, when the Napoleonic Wars ended, about 1.3 per cent of the world's population have died as the direct result of war. This would be larger if the indirect deaths were also included. With nuclear weapons, the degree of mass destruction possible has vastly increased. A nuclear war that got out of hand could literally destroy the human race. This is something that has never been possible before. The persistence of war in the modern world requires some explanation. It causes immense suffering and is an inefficient means of settling disputes. Preparations for war are expensive even if no war follows. Yet war and preparations for war consume vast amounts of money, energy and talent.

Because not all warfare is between states, we must be careful not to elevate the significance of the state too much in this analysis. Lewis Fry Richardson coined the term *deadly quarrels* to denote all conflicts in which people try to kill each other. Interstate war is an important category of such deadly quarrels, though there are plenty of others.

There are civil wars like the American Civil War (1861–65) and the Spanish Civil War (1936–39). These were fought by armies and the mode of fighting was the same as for an interstate war. However, there are also acts of genocide such as the events in Rwanda in 1995 and ethnic cleansing as in the former Yugoslavia. There are acts of terrorism. These may have political goals such as the formation of a state, as in the case of the Palestinian Liberation Organization (PLO), or to alter the nature of a government, as with the Front Islamique du Salut (FIS) in Algeria. Many governments have turned on their citizens. In the former Soviet Union (also referred to as the Union of Soviet Socialist Republics or USSR), Stalin's purges of the 1930s killed about 3 million people, including those who died in camps. Overall the total casualties of Stalin's epoch may well have been in the region of 20 million deaths as Khrushchev claims in his memoirs. Rummell (1995) estimates that 170 million people were killed by their own states between 1900 and 1987. Though some of these acts are internal, they are rarely totally so, illustrating that there are no neat boundaries to the discipline of international relations. We move seamlessly from the totally global to the narrowly domestic with no clear boundary in between.

As we show on pp. 5–8, there are great disparities in wealth between different parts of the world as well as great disparities within states. It is possible that these disparities might be explained solely in terms of issues internal to the states themselves. However, it seems unlikely. The international economic system is very interdependent so the distribution of wealth is at least partially a global problem. The issues of poverty and wealth are not just economic; they are political as well. The relation of the international economic system to the political system, if, indeed, the two can be distinguished, is of clear importance on the global scale. It is generally studied under the rubric of *international political economy* (IPE) and *global political economy* (GPE).

A Brief Portrait of the World in Figures

Let us look at the world we are going to discuss in terms of some of the relevant statistics. Statistics can be treacherous assistants but there is no better way of getting a feel for the relative significance of things. As the new millennium began there were 6100 million people in the world. They are divided into about 190 states, though of radically different

sizes. The state with the largest population is China with well over billion (that is, 1000 million) people in the mid 1990s. The population of India is a little smaller but recently reached 1 billion. The US is smaller still with 280 million. In Latin America, Brazil has the largest population with 168 million inhabitants. Somewhat smaller but still substantial countries in Europe are Germany with a population of 82 million, followed by France and Britain which each have populations of about 59 million. Australia is smaller still with approximately 19 million inhabitants. There are also some very small European states, such as Andorra, which has 65 000 inhabitants. There are doubts whether such a small group of people can really function as a state without the tolerance and help of its neighbours – in this case Spain and France. However, several small states seem to be able to function perfectly well. Luxembourg has 432 000 people and the highest income per head in the world of $38 247. Iceland has a population of only 279 000 but, with an income per head of $26 283 in 1999, exceeded Britain with $22 220 per head. (All the income statistics in this chapter are for 1999.)

States vary greatly in wealth. We have to be careful, though, to distinguish wealth per head of population and overall wealth. Income per head is what matters as far as the individual is concerned. It is an index of prosperity, though only a rough one as it can conceal vast differences in wealth within a country. Aggregate wealth is what matters as far as international power and influence are concerned.

By far the richest country overall is the United States with a GNP of $8879.5 billion. It is also the richest per head at $31 910, except for the fortunate Luxembourgers. Following it, but a long way behind, Japan with a GNP of $4054.5 billion and an average income of $25 17 The third richest country per head is Switzerland, with a GNP per hea of $28 760, but there are only 7 million people, so its overall GNP low. Population seems unrelated to wealth per head. Both big countr and small ones can be rich (or, of course, poor). From this point view there seem to be no economies of scale as far as states concerned.

At the other end of the spectrum, much of Africa is desperately p Ethiopia's population of 63 million has only $600 each, a figure sh with Guinea-Bissau, which has a population of about 1.185 millio an annual income this is tiny and grotesque. There are several cou in Africa with incomes per head of well below $1000, such as M ($570 per head per year) and Rwanda ($880 per head per yea

80.8 years. In India this drops to 62.3, Bangladesh 58.1 and at the bottom Sierra Leone, with its appalling poverty, has an expectation of life at birth of 37.3. Though still a little rough and ready, as any index must be, the HDI gives a more meaningful picture of well-being than income per head alone. However, all comparative descriptions must tread a line between oversimplification and incomprehensible complexity.

Many statistics are collected using the state as the primary unit. However, we should not become over-absorbed with the state. In particular commercial corporations are major actors with vast wealth. Thus, the Japanese firm Mitsubishi earned $126.5 billion in revenues in 2001,which was $3.6 billion more than the Gross National Product of Finland, a small but rich nation (of 5 million inhabitants). Corporations do not challenge the larger states in wealth but they certainly do the smaller ones. However, the number of people involved is rather less. Wal-Mart with just over 1.2 million employees has the largest labour force of any corporation. There are a number of states with populations smaller than this but it still would rank as a very small state. However, from a financial point of view, the story is rather different. Wal-Mart's revenues are a little larger than the GNP of Turkey and about 5 times larger than the GNP of Nigeria. Corporations trade worldwide and are often located in several countries. Their wealth is comparable to many significant states, meaning that they are in a position to be very powerful actors on the international scene. More sinister is the vast amount of illegal money which is in circulation and available to subvert any system of law and social order. It is estimated that £500 billion in illegal money is made in any one year and is flowing about the international financial system. This is not far short of the GNP of Britain, though the figure is necessarily a guess and is imprecise even by the loose standards we are forced to accept in this area.

The consideration of issues of poverty and wealth makes us turn to the condition of women. Women are systematically less privileged in both rich and poor societies. In countries where illiteracy is a problem, it is almost always higher for women (and in no cases lower). Incomes for similar work are systematically lower and often very much lower. Property rights are never better than men's and usually worse. One disturbing and somewhat bizarre figure is that, due to premature mortality, there are 200 million fewer women in the world than there would be if women and men were treated equally as far as health care and general social position were concerned. (For comparison, the total population of the European Union in 2001 was about 376 million.)

The UN Human Development Index, discussed above, also provides pictures of gender issues on a comparative basis. It includes a Gender Empowerment Index, which is formed from the proportion of seats in parliament held by women, the proportion of female managers and the proportion of female professional and technical workers. On this measure, Norway again leads the world, with Australia coming second, the US fourth, the UK twelfth and New Zealand seventeenth. There is a clear overall pattern of the richer countries scoring better on the Gender Empowerment Index than the poor, though amongst the rich countries themselves the pattern is less clear.

This is a very broad-brush picture of the world we shall try and analyze. A list of facts just tells us what is the case. We would like to know why the world is as it is, though we are a long way from any satisfactory answers so far. Must the world be like this, or are there alternatives? If so, how do we achieve them?

Theory and the Search for Patterns

The facts and figures of the last two sections are not just collections of arbitrary data but describe things that have causes and are the consequences of various structures and events in the world. The world of international affairs may be anarchic but it is not chaotic. People do not behave in any social context in random and totally unpredictable ways whether they are engaged in trade, diplomacy or as spectators at a football match. There may be unpredictable elements to behaviour but there are also patterns and consistencies. We seek to find these causes and the patterns in the international context. That is, we adopt a *theoretical approach* to the analysis of international relations (see also Chapters 6 and 7, pp. 90 and 114). A theoretical approach stresses the consistencies in human behaviour. Thus, we ask what causes wars in general and not just the causes of a specific war such as the First World War. We want to examine whether trade promotes peaceful relationships in general and not just between Germany and Russia. We want to look at global poverty, asking what Malawi and Zambia have in common which makes them both poor, and how this relates to international and economic patterns. Conversely we might ask what has made some Pacific economies, such as Taiwan and South Korea, so successful (at least until recently). The degree to which we can find these patterns, make such comparisons, and even whether such patterns exist, is one of the many controversies in international relations (and indeed in the social sciences as a whole), though it would be extreme to assert that no comparisons at all were possible. Some scholars look to economics as an exemplar that should be followed in building a theory of international relations, though others are less enthusiastic.

This is not to downplay the analysis and explanation of particular events which is often a central feature of what we want to do. It is important to ask what caused the Second World War or the Korean War in 1950, looking for the specific factors rather than the general factors that led to these events. However, these specific factors are looked at in the context of more general factors. When historians discuss the origins of the Second World War they are not doing it in terms just of that instance alone, even if they might emphasize the particular. Thus, it is often argued that the appeasement of the Nazi regime in Germany during the 1930s was at least partly responsible for the Second World War. For this to be usefully analyzed, one has to have a more general theory of appeasement in which to interpret the particular instance, even if the general is downplayed to highlight the particular. Similarly, a historical study of the arms race before the First World War as a possible causal factor in its outbreak cannot be done totally in isolation. There must be some implied theory behind it.

It follows from this that international relations is not just an extension of international history, though a knowledge of international history is important for our understanding. Nor is international relations just an account of what is going on today – a sort of glorified current affairs. Though the present state of the world must concern serious scholars, there is much more to the study of international relations than can be derived from reading the newspapers, no matter how diligently this is done. Nor would you get it from reading history books, necessary though that is too. Both are necessary, but neither is sufficient. We need to go beyond them to expand our capacity to explain. For this we need theories.

Both the historical and the theoretical approaches above are based on the supposition that, if we try hard enough, we can develop some understanding of the world that will enable us to improve it. There is an implied (and sometimes explicit) view that the social behaviour of human beings can be studied objectively. This is sometimes contested.

In particular, some people, such as the postmodernists (of which more later), argue that we are always dealing with representations of reality, which are multiple. They argue that these representations provide the only possible point of access to social behaviour. If pursued to its limit, this view implies that we can say very little about human behaviour as a whole which, in its turn, means we can do little about it. This is obviously a very fundamental critique going to the heart not only of the discipline of international relations as conventionally understood but also of the social sciences as a whole. We discuss this further on pp. 117–19. Those tempted by the subjectivist critique should nevertheless see what it is they wish to destroy and spend a little while considering the arguments presented in the following pages.

The Structure of the Book

In Chapters 2 and 3, we consider the actors in the international system. In Chapter 2, we deal with decision-makers who are connected with the state. We also look at nations. These are interlinked with the state and are sometimes mistakenly thought of as being much the same thing. We show they are not, but the argument is not straightforward. States and their adjuncts, such as governments, are no longer considered the only, or even the primary, actors in international relations. We discuss actors other than states in Chapter 3. There are many of these and which ones we look at depends on the problem we seek to analyze. If we are concerned with poverty, we think partly of states but also of multi-national corporations, international organisations such as the IMF and so on. Part of our problem is deciding what actors are relevant and what sorts of decisions they can take. If we are concerned with war, we suspect that states are important actors, though probably not the sole ones. There are also the groups within a state participating in the violence that in its turn impedes economic development. Other actors which are significant in other contexts, such as the United Nations, are interstate groups though they may have a life of their own which is independent of the member states'. Many organizations transcend state borders and have a big influence on people's lives without having much to do with states. Religions cross boundaries. Even the differences between different forms of the Christian religion correspond very little to state boundaries any more than the divisions within Islam do.

Actors and the world they inhabit did not appear ready-made, all geared up to participate in the modern world. The world and its actors came from somewhere. The brief history of the last hundred years or so in Chapter 4 puts the problems of the present world into some perspective.

Chapter 5 describes the extraordinary expansion of the western European states in a rash of colonization which was a major characteristic of the nineteenth century, particularly the latter part. Huge areas of the world found themselves under the direct rule of foreign (usually European) powers. Failing direct rule, the dominant powers imposed puppet regimes that ensured their compliance with its requirements. The United States participated in indirect control, though it acquired few colonies in the formal sense. Much of this expansion happened within the space of a few decades. Yet these empires collapsed even more quickly. In 1945, immediately after the end of the Second World War, the empires of Britain, France, Belgium and the Netherlands were almost as big as they had ever been. Twenty-five years later they were virtually non-existent. This extraordinary phenomenon has left its mark behind, if only in the languages spoken. Formal empire may be at an end but many claim that the continuing informal, and largely economic, power of the rich states over the poor is effectively a form of imperialism. I describe imperialism and its legacies today as consequences of its past. However, it did not emerge randomly or accidentally. I stress some of the causes of imperialism in Chapter 5 and the theoretical structure in which a proper understanding must be embedded.

This leads directly to a more general discussion of theory in international relations in Chapter 6. This is the central chapter of the book. International relations scholars are not content just to give a list of events. They want to explain things. They see the world as consisting of patterns of events which they seek to explore. The search for patterns is still contentious and we discuss the various theories of international relations that have adherents today. In the following chapter we discuss the relationship of theories to change, and in particular the views of those who see themselves as dissenters from the orthodox who they perceive as conservative.

Issues of peace, war and security were outlined above on pp. 3–4. The issues as they are being reconsidered in the post-Cold-War world are discussed in more detail in Chapter 8.

The questions of poverty and wealth, and their connection with the global political economy are central, as we argued on pp. 5–8. They are discussed further in Chapter 9. We also examine why we need to integrate the study of economics with political issues and vice versa.

In Chapter 10 we consider *globalization* and its development. This is the account of how the world is becoming more and more closely interconnected – becoming the 'global village' with its good, bad, but undeniably important, consequences.

In Chapter 11 we discuss the global issues of the environment which are a central problem of both interest and concern in the modern world. Pollution ignores national boundaries. Smog and acid rain drift across the borders of states. Issues involving the control of both environmental degradation and the supplies of resources, particularly renewable resources such as fish, are international problems. What needs to be done to alleviate this? What agreements can be made and are states the appropriate bodies to make them? When do agreements hold and when do they not? All these issues relate in one form or another to wealth and poverty which themselves interconnect with issues such as social structure and gender. The overlap of issues is one of the characteristics of international relations.

The final chapter poses explicitly the moral problems in international relations. The central issues of war and poverty clearly involve moral issues. In international relations we investigate what can be done about them or, indeed, whether anything can. Perhaps they are inevitable and unalterable, but we need to know. If we can make choices, which ones ought we to make? It is the possibility of informed choice which raises the moral issues. Thus, is war ever justified? If so, when? Can the use of nuclear weapons be justified? What obligations do the rich of the world have towards the poor? Are the human rights of people in other countries our concern? These are all moral problems, most without easy answers. Moral paradoxes and conundrums abound in international relations. We raise some of these in Chapter 12.

In the Conclusion, we discuss some views about how the world may develop over the next decades. This is inevitably very speculative. Some of these views arouse a lot of passion despite the unreliability of any prediction. I also discuss my own views about international relations and what we can do about the obvious deficiencies of its working. Indeed can we do anything? It is my belief that we can, but only by recognising that it is a theoretical discipline based in fact.

An Invitation to an Argument

International relations is a very controversial discipline. The outsider could be forgiven for thinking that its practitioners are a quarrelsome set of people who disagree about everything. If so, some might argue, they should not be taken too seriously. They would be wrong. When there are disagreements about important issues, the sources of these disagreements should be explored to see the nature of the problem. This might lead to a resolution and a wider understanding of the issues raised in the discipline.

There are two different sources of controversy. First, there are the profound moral issues involved in international relations. These are acute in discussions of policy. Policies involve choices. Disagreements arise when there are differences in moral views about what is desirable. Differences over whether it was proper for the NATO countries to attack Serbia over the issues of Kosovo are bound to come about between people who have different attitudes to violence. Was it proper to kill civilians in Belgrade, however badly the government had behaved? These disagreements are moral. The facts are not seriously in dispute.

Second, international relations is still a very undeveloped discipline so we might also disagree about the theoretical propositions we make. There are arguments in every discipline as scholars get towards the boundaries of what is known. However, in physics there is at least a solid core of uncontroversial material. In international relations there is very little. Almost everything can be contested. There are those who hold that it always will be and that any analogy with any aspect of the natural sciences is inherently flawed. There are those, like myself, who believe this is unduly pessimistic, though it is hard to deny that there is very little secure theoretical knowledge at the moment. However, disagreements about theories are different from disagreements over moral values. Ultimately, theoretical disagreements can be settled by an appeal to the facts even though this resolution may be a long way away. Disagreements about moral principles cannot. It is important to distinguish between the two sources of controversy and to sort out, in any particular case, how the two are intermingled.

Because of the contested nature of so much of international relations, no textbook can be definitive in the way a textbook on chemistry can. The most one can do is show the outlines of the arguments. I invite readers to think their own ways through the themes, understand the approaches and debate the issues with those with whom they disagree.

Welcome, then, to an argument.

Further Reading and Sources

There are a number of introductory books that go into rather more detail than is possible in this short book. John Baylis and Steve Smith have edited *Globalisation of World Politics* (Oxford: Oxford University Press, 2001, 2nd edn), which is an excellent longer, multi-authored text. There are some rather longer American books such as Bruce Russett, Harvey Starr and David Kinsella, *World Politics: The Menu for Choice* (New York: W.H. Freeman, 2000, 6th edn); Joshua S. Goldstein, *International Politics* (New York: HarperCollins, 2000, 6th edn); Charles W. Kegley and Eugene R. Witkopf, *World Politics: Trends and Transformation* (New York and Basingstoke: St. Martin's Press and Macmillan Press – now Palgrave Macmillan, 2000, 8th edn). All provide good and detailed introductions to the subject.

Many important pieces that mark the development of international relations are published in John Vasquez (ed.), *Classics of International Relations* (New Jersey: Prentice-Hall, 1996, 3rd edn), which is a very useful reference. The development of international relations theory and approaches to the discipline are interestingly discussed by Tjorborn Knutsen, *A History of International Relations Theory* (Manchester: Manchester University Press, 1997).

Prominent in this chapter, and in international relations in general, are various national income figures. The Gross Domestic Product (GDP) figures in the text came from the *United Nations Human Development Report* (Oxford: Oxford University Press, 2001). In general this is a very useful source of data. Incomes per head come from *World Development Indicators 2001* (Washington: World Bank 2001), which is also helpful and vividly presented. Unfortunately – as ever! – not all sources agree.

The population figures quoted in the text come from *The Military Balance 1997/98* (London: Oxford University Press, 2001). This annual publication is valuable as a convenient source of basic figures about economies and a very detailed source of military information.

A very useful and well laid out source of statistics is Michael Kidron and Dan Smith, *The State of the World Atlas* (New York: Penguin,

1999). I warmly recommend it, partly because of the clear way in which it presents the material, making its study a pleasurable, or at least an endurable, task even for those who find statistics painful. There is the proviso that it came out in 1999 and things change. I have used it for the measure of inequality and other figures of poverty. I took the figures for the Human Development Index and the Gender Development Index from the *United Nations Human Development Report* (New York: Oxford University Press, 2001). The same source was used for illiteracy (particularly table 10).

On the number of women 'missing' in the world, Amartya Sen is more cautious than Kidron and Segal in his article 'More than 100 Million Women are Missing' (*New York Review of Books*, 20 December 1990). The figure of £500 billion for the proceeds of drug trafficking (that is, the profits not the volume of trade) was given by Ray Kindle, head of Interpol (reported in the *Guardian*, 10 September 1996).

Figures about war and casualties come from Oliver M. Ashford *et al.* (eds), *The Collected Works of Lewis Fry Richardson: Volume 2* (Cambridge: Cambridge University Press, 1993) and Bruce Russett, *Grasping the Democratic Peace: Principles for a Post-Cold War World* (Princeton: Princeton University Press, 1993). There are many formidable collections of statistics about peace and war. A readable description of one of the major ones is given in David Singer and Daniel S. Geller, *Nations at War: A Scientific Study of International Conflict* (Cambridge: Cambridge University Press, 1998), which gives further references. The figures of international violence are taken for R.J. Rummell, 'Democracy, Power, Genocide and Mass Murder', *Journal of Conflict Resolution*, Vol. 39, No. 1, pp. 3–36 (1995).

In general, an hour or two spent browsing through the annual statistical publications of bodies such as the United Nations is very illuminating. Another hour spent with an atlas is also much to be commended.

2

States, Nations and Governments

States

States are important in international relations, though just how important is a matter of controversy. The traditional view of international relations has been that the discipline's primary concern is the behaviour of states and their interactions with each other. These interactions were characterized by the fact that they took place in a situation of anarchy where there was no government to oversee and control them. Thus, war became a common feature of the system and security the dominant goal of foreign policy. States are regarded as *sovereign* in the territories under their jurisdiction, meaning that the state, or rather its government, controls what goes on within its borders. There is no overriding body in the world that rules over states and their governments and, legally at least, there is nothing anyone can do in the area of a state without the active or tacit consent of that government. Formally, in the state system, all states are fully sovereign in that no authority takes precedence over them in their territories (though this is modified in the case of the European Union, see pp. 42–3). In particular, the governments of other states should not meddle in the territories of a sovereign state. This view is known as the *realist approach* which is discussed in more detail in Chapter 6.

It can be argued that the realist view described the nineteenth century rather well from a political point of view, even if it rather neglected the economics. States ruled the roost. Industrial firms were clearly located in particular countries and could be controlled by the government of that country. Many countries were not disposed to leave economic life to the vagaries of the market but, like Germany and

France at the time, explicitly conceived of the control of the economy as a part of the security policy of the state. Realism also describes some aspects of much more recent periods. Thus the relationships collectively described as the Cold War can be seen in realist terms. It can be described as an instance of states pursuing security, though not everyone would describe it this way.

However, in the present period, to reduce everything to state behaviour leaves out too much. Even apart from the United Nations (though this, of course, is an organization of states), the whole growth of multinational corporations (MNCs) vitiates this position at least as far as economic matters are concerned. In any case, once there is significant international trade, a state's control over its economy is seriously limited. A slump in the economy of a trading partner quickly affects one's own economy. Trade is the partial relinquishment of sovereignty in the sense of losing control even if it is not so in the sense of surrendering it to another state. This was true even in the nineteenth century. Trade reduces the domain over which the state can take decisions. Even if the state still has dominion over such issues as security, the range of international relations is now much larger than it used to be and, for the most part, this enlargement has not been an enlargement of the state's domain but of other actors such as MNCs. Other actors gain their significance because they move in a mass, such as the buyers and sellers in a market. I shall call these mass actors *movements* and discuss them in Chapter 3. Markets such as stock markets are effectively uncontrollable, at least by a single actor such as a state and probably even by a group of states. However, they are a major influence on the behaviour of states.

States, Nations and Governments

States and *nations* are often confused. Both play an important part in international relations, as the very name of the discipline suggests. We are told, simultaneously, that the state is declining and that it is an age of burgeoning nationalism. Can both be right or is there simply a confusion about terms?

A few more careful definitions are needed in order to talk precisely about international relations. First let us consider *state*. A state consists of an area of territory which is under the single rule of a *government* (a term we shall come back to shortly). Broadly, the people who live in that territory are citizens of the state, something which confers both obligations and benefits. Citizens pay taxes. However, if they are lucky and the state works reasonably efficiently, they will receive benefits including roads and schools, internal security and, in richer countries, social security payments such as unemployment benefit and retirement pensions. They are expected to comply with the laws and their compliance can be enforced. In principle, at least, the laws are for the benefit of the citizens of a state as a whole and laws against, for example, murder and burglary are generally perceived to be for the general good. Only one government controls the area of the state at a time. Supposedly governments have the monopoly of violence in that state but clearly that is not always the case in practice. The lack of an overriding world government, or a government of governments, is held by many to be the distinctive characteristic of international relations and the source of the problems of the international system. It is an anarchic system.

Governments make and administer the laws which apply within the boundaries of the state. Governments are of many very different types. *Democracy* is the mode of government which most of the readers of this book live under and are likely to be familiar with. Broadly this involves voting for one of at least two parties which might form a government. There are many different forms of democracy but the core feature is that elections must be held in which most, if not all, of the adult citizens can vote. Further, the result of an election can genuinely mean that, on the basis of the voting, a government can be replaced by another one, consisting of different people. However, there exist many more despotic forms of government. In monarchies such as Saudi Arabia the monarch has absolute power, at least in theory. (In practice monarchs have advisors but these are chosen by the monarch who may or may not pay them much attention.) There are dictatorships in which an individual or small group control the government without much reference to anyone else. However, all are governments. We may disapprove of some governments and approve of others but, in dealing with the world, we have to acknowledge who in fact controls the state and not who we would like to control the state. Recent developments such as the indictments, at the international level, of former leaders, such as General Pinochet in Chile for human rights crimes and President Milosevic of Serbia for crimes against humanity present a challenge to the traditional assumption that governments are free to control their societies with impunity.

Nations are harder to define, though we shall try to do so. 'Nation' is often loosely and incorrectly used to mean 'state'. We shall start by enumerating some nations. The Scots are a nation. The Basques, the Catalans, the Hungarians and the Ukrainians are nations. Of these, only the Ukrainians and the Hungarians have states where most of the citizens are members of the nation; the other three nations are citizens of states that contain members of other nations. Most Hungarians live in Hungary but there are significant Hungarian minorities in several East European states. The Jews are a nation and were so before there was a Jewish state of Israel. Many Jews live away from Israel. Many of these would not really regard themselves as members of a Jewish nation, though many would. This raises some of the problems we have with the concept of nation. While we might recognize nations, it is hard to define them precisely and, partly because of this, the issue of nationality has caused a lot of trouble.

One attempt at definition is that a nation consists of those people who believe themselves to be members of it. Thus, there is a Welsh nation inasmuch as there are some people who think of themselves as Welsh and recognize as legitimate the claims of those other people who think of themselves as Welsh. However, the definition needs to be stronger than that, otherwise there would be a nation of Londoners or of New Yorkers. There has to be something, such as sharing a culture, that is not shared by anyone else. Unfortunately culture does not get us very much further. It is no more precise a term than nation. A shared language not used by others might seem an appropriate criterion and this works well for the Hungarians. It does not work very well for the Welsh. Though Welsh is used as a spoken language only by Welsh people, there are plenty of strongly committed Welsh people who do not speak it. For different reasons it is not very helpful for the English, whose native language is shared as a native language by many nations. The Basques (whose language is notoriously difficult to learn) have the same problem as the Welsh. The Catalans, fortunately, have a language more accessible to native Spanish speakers, so Catalans who are not native speakers of the Catalan language can achieve proficiency more easily than the Basques (or the Welsh). However, language can rescue us from the problem we faced in defining the Jewish nation. Hebrew is the language of Israel. It was not the living language of Jews for many centuries until it was revived with the creation of the state of Israel in 1948. (Yiddish, closely related to German, was closer to being a Jewish national language prior to that.) Jews who are not Israelis, and have no particular desire to become so, will rarely be proficient in Hebrew. In effect it is a good indicator of whether a Jew wishes to be identified as Israeli and part of a Jewish nation or not.

Hence, to define a nation is a difficult job. However hard it is to define, the reality is certainly there. Nationalism, meaning the sense of nationhood, appears to be a very strong form of self-identification in the modern world. Identity is a crucial aspect of it. A definition in these terms would be that the members of a nation are those who identify with the nation and are accepted as members by others who identify themselves as such.

We need another concept to add to our lexicon – *the nation state*. Taken strictly this would mean a state in which the overwhelming majority of the members were one nation. Unfortunately there are comparatively few states of which this is true. On one strict definition, there are only twelve genuine nation states. On a slightly more relaxed definition, we can get it up to 45. Even this is less than a quarter of the states in existence. Most states have several nations on almost any definition of nation. A few small countries such as Iceland are nation states in the strict sense but they are unusual. Of the major states, Japan has probably the best claim to be a nation state.

Nations are often spread amongst several states. The coincidence of state boundaries with nations is not a common phenomenon, though some states actively promote the idea of a common nation. Thus, the United States, which was built on an immigrant culture of people from many nations, explicitly promotes the idea that immigrants become American, that is, become members of the nation. Thus, the creation of a nation state was an explicit goal. Nation state is widely used in international relations to mean just state. Strictly, this is a loose usage of the term and it is as well to remember that, in its proper form, the nation state is something of a rarity.

There was a strong romantic movement in the nineteenth century, which carried on into the twentieth century, promoting the idea that the division of the world into a set of nation states was the ideal to be aimed at. At the Versailles Conference, shortly after the First World War, many people believed that one of the major causes of war was that nations did not have their own states. President Wilson of the United States was a strong advocate of this view. Once the world was divided into nation states, a major cause of conflict and war would be removed. Nationalism was held to be a very dominant form of identification.

There was a practical rather than a conceptual problem in the proposal to create a world of nation states. The different nations tended to occupy the same bits of land and be mixed up. The former Yugoslavia is a case in point. When Yugoslavia existed as a state, there were big areas where the different nationalities (or ethnic groups) were mixed. This is normal in large parts of Eastern Europe, and in many other places for that matter. Wherever one looks there is a minority. If one tries to make a partition such that the minority in the larger state becomes a majority in some smaller state or area, one finds that one has just created a new minority (Ireland and Northern Ireland are a good case in point). The task of creating a world of nation states is almost impossible.

Nonetheless, nationalism has been a very powerful force in the modern world. Human beings seem to have a powerful impulse to identify with a group and then invest that group with some moral standing, which makes defence of that allegiance a fundamental goal of life. Football teams, cricket teams, baseball teams and so on generate passionate loyalties amongst their followers that are out of all proportion to their apparent importance. When these are transferred to the political level they seem even stronger. The identification with a national group seems to be perhaps the most powerful of all. Marx believed that the basic groupings of society were class identifications, though this seems only rarely to be the case. Religious identifications are often powerful and are sometimes linked with concepts of nation. Even these seem less stable than national identifications which supersede all others and for which people seem perfectly willing to kill and die while totally convinced of the morality of doing so. There have been times when aggressive and assertive nationalism seemed to be waning. Any waning there may have been seems to have been reversed. Nationalism at the beginning of the twenty-first century seems a powerful and, at times, primitive emotion motivating many people.

The Structure of State Decision-Making

The *foreign policy* of a state is the general set of principles that its decision-makers adopt towards the outside world. Traditionally the external environment has meant other states and their foreign policies. Foreign policy is rather more broadly conceived these days than in the early part of the twentieth century. Foreign policy used to be concerned mainly with the political and strategic relationships between states. Now economic interactions, and not just those between states, have become a major feature of foreign policy activity, while issues such as human rights now appear on the foreign policy agenda, which would not have been the case until recently.

Quite apart from differences in size, wealth, population and so on, different states have different governmental structures and hence different forms of decision-making. Many argue that the different structures of decision-making affect the nature of the decisions taken; the degree to which this is so is yet another issue which is controversial. How states take decisions is something we cannot ignore. The analysis of this, and the differences between states, is the subfield of international relations known as *foreign policy analysis*.

The decisions of any organization are the decisions taken by a small group of individuals. In the case of a state it might be a cabinet. However, the individuals involved are able to influence things only by virtue of their role in the organization. Without the organization, the influence of the individuals would be very restricted. Suppose we say of Sweden, which joined the European Union in January 1995, that 'Sweden had decided to join the European Economic Community (EEC)'. We are using a dangerous but useful shorthand. It was not an entity 'Sweden' as such but the cabinet and the ruling party of Sweden that decided it. However, they decided only in their roles as cabinet and party members and in a context of approval. Many individuals were involved and none could have decided it alone.

We can divide states into two broad groups, the authoritarian and the democratic. Both types contain many subtypes and definitions must be rough and ready. Democratic states were defined above. Britain, Japan, Australia and the United States are instances of democracies. Authoritarian states are those ruled by a small group of people, perhaps even a single person as a dictator. I shall distinguish between two sorts. The first group are ruled by a dictatorship. This might be a literal, single dictator as in the Soviet Union under Stalin or a small oligarchy (or 'junta' to use the term popularized in Latin America). The second I shall call 'restricted states' such as the South African regime under apartheid. There was democracy as far as the white South African population was concerned. However, there was a large excluded population whose views and interests were ignored.

The British Case

Britain is a good example of a democratic state. There is universal adult suffrage and there is a realistic possibility of a government losing an election and vacating office.

The Foreign and Commonwealth Office (FCO) is the organization that is central to foreign policy decision-making. The Foreign Secretary is one of the senior members of the cabinet. Normally these days the Foreign Secretary will be a member of the House of Commons, though between 1960 and 1963 Lord Home sat in the House of Lords. The Foreign Secretary is answerable to the House of Commons. The basic work of interacting with governments is done by the FCO. Its members also staff the embassies around the world as well as the High Commissions, which are the equivalent of embassies in countries of the British Commonwealth. At any given time about two-thirds of the FCO are abroad in embassies and one-third is based in London dealing directly with the government. Major decisions are taken by the cabinet and in consultation with the Prime Minister who appears in all important meetings with heads of state. Historically the FCO, or its predecessor the Foreign Office (FO), was primarily concerned with issues of power and security. Concerns with such issues as the balance of power were central. A development from about the 1960s onwards has been the greater interest of the FCO in economic matters. In the interwar period, the commercial attaché at an embassy was not greatly respected. Today, one of an embassy's significant roles is the promotion of trade links with the host country – something that would have been regarded with horror by an earlier generation of diplomats.

The FCO does not act in splendid isolation from the rest of the government. Military matters, which are closely related to many foreign policy issues, are also the province of the Ministry of Defence and there is close liaison between the two branches of government. The intelligence services such as MI5 play a significant role here in ways which provide a good living for many writers of fiction, though often to the concern of outsiders who wonder just what goes on under the necessarily secret heading of 'national security'. Similarly, economic issues involve a range of other organizations from the directly economic, such as the Treasury and the Bank of England, to transport, agriculture and so on. Thus the whole apparatus of government is drawn into issues of foreign policy at certain times. The process of

forming foreign policy is not necessarily a quick one. Particular
decisions may be needed quickly but usually against a background of
decided policy. As so many organizations and individuals are involved
this can emerge over a considerable period of time. Further, if the
decision involves wider interests, such as policies with regard to
Europe, the process can involve a period of political debate which
can go on for years.

Though this is the formal structure of the decision-making process,
the informal elements can be equally important and interesting. Thus
there are many pressure groups and influences on the government that
can affect decisions. Commercial pressure groups object if some hostile
gesture towards a state with a profitable market will harm British
interests in those markets. Manufacturers of armaments prefer friendly
relations with rich regimes irrespective of the nature of such regimes.
On the other side, human rights groups will want some sort of
sanctions against those who violate human rights even if they do
provide good markets.

The Case of the United States

The United States is another example of a democratic state. There is
universal adult suffrage and elections are held frequently and fairly,
though in the Presidential election of 2000, there was some unease
about its fairness. An incumbent President, even if entitled to stand,
can be defeated in an election and have to leave office. Likewise the
membership of the Houses of Congress alters as a result of elections
and the configuration of parties can become significantly different.
Thus rulers and policies can be changed – and often are – as a result of
an election. This is the crucial characteristic of a democracy.

The President is a central actor in the formulation of the foreign
policy of the United States. He (all Presidents have been male so far)
and his advisors essentially take the initiative in foreign policy and are
the first to respond to major events coming from outside, such as the
outbreak of a war. The President appoints the Secretary of State who is
the person primarily responsible for Foreign Policy but who is not a
member of the legislature. The Secretary of State rules over the
Department of State, which is responsible for diplomacy and the
general mechanics of conventional foreign policy. Almost all states
have some equivalent of the State Department, which, in most states,
including the USA, is regarded as an élite branch of government.

Military issues are the concern of another central actor, the Assistant for National Security Affairs. The Department of Defense is likewise centrally involved as are the intelligence services such as the Central Intelligence Agency (CIA).

The role of Congress in foreign policy is considerable and there is frequently tension between the President and Congress, particularly when there are party differences between President and Congress. Congress can overrule the President. It controls such vital issues as the defence budget. It can declare war. However, as the President can order the movement of troops and has 60 to 90 days to get the approval of Congress, he can get very close to it in practice – though the restrictions on the President's power are still significant. The position of Congress distinguishes a democratic state in that an elected legislature has significant and not merely technical influence on foreign policy. The Senate Foreign Relations Committee can also make life very awkward for the foreign-policy decision-makers by making them account for their actions. Thus, the making of foreign policy is complex and comes out of an overall bargaining structure within the US government. What the President might want to do and what the President can in fact do are often very different things.

As in Britain, there are many pressure groups and influences on the government, such as commercial groups, which can affect the decisions. Political and ethnic groups lobby in the interests of a cause that particularly concerns them, such as Jewish groups in the interests of Israel and Cuban groups who wish to overthrow the government of Cuba. All these groups, with varying degrees of success, influence the formation of US foreign policy and make it hard to talk of the 'foreign-policy process' as if it were something easy to pin down.

Authoritarian States

Under authoritarian regimes, the government is all that really matters. However, even under a dictatorship, it is a mistake to think that it is just the will of the dictator that counts. There are constraints even on a dictator. The military were a significant pressure group even under the Stalinist regime in the Soviet Union. Under the slightly more relaxed oligarchies that succeeded Stalin, they were even more so. The Junta in Argentina up to 1982, likewise, had to keep the military happy. One motive for the invasion of the Falkland Islands (known to the

Argentinians as the Malvinas) was to increase the popularity of the Government, which was very unpopular at the time. What is significant is not just that the Junta did something for public support, but that it thought that public support was necessary in the first place. In Saddam Hussein's Iraq, the élite is flagrantly bribed with good living conditions. The mode of life of dictators is often determined by a situation of continuous, and usually justified, paranoia which itself is a tribute to the limits of dictatorial power. This argument can be broadened to include the government in general. In strongly religious states, religious groups have to be pacified, though there are splits within them, which makes the job of keeping them all happy rather difficult. In Iran, extremists want to cut themselves off from the West and the United States in particular. Modernisers want more contact. The leader, far from being an autocrat pursuing a self-centred agenda, may feel like the unhappy mediator between inconsistent interests.

Thus there is a sense in which all governments are coalitions of different groups with different emphases. Democratic governments have to please more people, or at least not offend them too much. Authoritarian governments can get away with a lot more than democratic ones, but all can find the constraints significant and often onerous.

Quasi States and Failing States

The governments of states vary very much in their ability to govern the territory that is under their nominal control. Some fail so disastrously that the state can hardly be said to exist. Such states are known as *failing states* and are often the vehicles for humanitarian disasters. They are seriously inadequate internally and sovereignty is accorded them simply because they are recognised as sovereign by outsiders and, in particular, by other governments. Called by Robert Jackson 'quasi states', they are particularly noticeable in Africa. Internally these states do not provide the basic services that they can be expected to provide. There is often little security and killings on the basis of tribal disputes are common. The basic underlying infrastructure that an economy needs (which, of course, includes security) is not being provided. Many of the African states are amongst the poorest in the world despite being reasonably well-endowed with natural resources. Colonialism and its successor, neo-colonialism, can be partly blamed but rapacious and corrupt élites can also be blamed. Further, as in Nigeria, the élites have often welcomed the multinationals, which are the neo-colonialists in Africa if this term can be applied to anyone. Together they have exploited the bulk of the population.

The very fact of recognition from outside, coupled with control of the means of violence internally, gave many élites the power to enrich themselves in a way any involvement in economic production would not. They can channel foreign aid in their direction, do favourable deals with multinationals for their own rather than their country's benefit, and tax their hapless compatriots on what little wealth they are able to accumulate in the dreadful political circumstances. Various periods in various countries can be described in this way and many, unfortunately, continue.

However, we can easily slip into the view that if a state is not failing in this rather extreme way, it is somehow succeeding. However, there are a number of states which have governments that are not failing in the extreme way, but where the government fails to provide many of the services normally expected of a government. Algeria, which has been immobilised by ongoing conflict between the fundamentalist Islamic Salvation Front and the secular government, is a case in point. This could easily become worse. Algeria may decline into a true failing state or reconstitute as a stable, but even more violent, dictatorship, either Islamic or secular. Algeria is not unusual.

Russia similarly is clearly failing as a state in a number of serious ways, though it would be a parody to call it a quasi state. It is beset by economic problems. Some of these at least, such as the widespread percolation of the economy by criminals and the inability to collect taxes, are the apparent inability of the state to carry out some of its necessary functions. The lessons of the market economy were learnt in stable societies. The background needed for social order and a functioning state was underestimated. The consequences of state failure in Russia, even the limited state failure at the start of the twenty-first century, might well be very serious outside Russia quite apart from the mass of the unfortunate Russians who are not members of the small élites. The effect of Russian economic collapse on the rest of the world economy might be severe both directly and because of the possible rise of new authoritarian governments with a great capacity for external disruption. It is ironic that a state that caused so much misery because its government was too strong is now causing misery because its government is too weak.

The primary concern is for the inhabitants of the failed states where poverty and insecurity are endemic and extreme. The citizens of failed states are amongst the poorest people on earth. A fairly strong state structure is necessary for economic growth and the other requirements of a reasonable existence. Further, the problems of a failed state can spread to its neighbours producing further civil unrest and economic insecurity. Whatever theoretical arguments there may be for anarchy, they are not exemplified in the present failed states. Apart from these ethical concerns, the richer states have more selfish worries. The uncertainties caused by the failed states impede the growth of the world economy, create refugees and cause instabilities within the richer states, such as those caused by the spillover of the Algerian disaster into mainland France.

In the case of Russia, the failure is partly a failure of its economic system, which is in part a failure of the world economic system. However, it is also in part because the state has lost its monopoly of the means of violence, which is an often-quoted characteristic of the government of a state. Russia is not alone in this. The Italian-based Mafia has long been effectively an alternative state, particularly in Southern Italy. The security of individuals has depended as much on not offending the Mafia as on the state that failed to provide them with adequate protection against the Mafiosi. Similarly in Colombia, the state is under siege. Though it is not failing in anything like the sense in which some African states are failing, the situation is precarious. To produce drugs, it is necessary to have reasonable tranquillity in various parts of the country. This can be provided by a sufficiently ruthless set of drug producers backed by an army which is sufficiently well bribed and which, in effect, provides an alternative state. But the situation can get out of hand, as it appears to have done in parts of Colombia, which has experienced high levels of political violence almost since its inception. The crucial failure here is that of the policing functions which, when extreme, is a central feature of state failure. The privatization of the means of violence, whether criminal or legal, should always be looked at with great suspicion. However, the international dimension here is also clear. Most of the drugs are exported to the United States where, as in most Western societies, there seems to be no very clear idea about how to deal with the whole social issue of drugs.

Thus, states do not fail according to clear-cut categories, but rather they do so in varying degrees and in different ways. A danger is that a weak state can quickly become a failing state. For the arms importer an increase in violence is always desirable. However, as violence increases, the weak state moves over to a failing state with catastrophic consequences for its inhabitants.

Crisis Decision-Making

Normally foreign policies, and even particular decisions, emerge over a considerable period of time as a result of a lot of analysis and debate. However, from time to time a crisis arises over some major issue where quick decisions are needed. In these situations, the decision-making process alters significantly.

There are many examples. In the few weeks before the First World War, the governments of Europe were faced with a major problem that fundamentally affected their security and a situation that could radically change overnight. This crisis resulted in war (see Chapter 4). In 1938, in what turned out to be the run-up to the Second World War, there was a big crisis over Czechoslovakia that resulted in the Munich Agreement by which Hitler and Germany more or less got their way. This resulted in peace, though only temporarily. A particularly intense crisis was the Cuban Missile Crisis in 1962. The Soviet Union installed missiles in Cuba, less than one hundred miles from the American coast. The United States objected vociferously and demanded their removal. For almost two weeks the world appeared to hover on the brink of nuclear war before agreement was reached and the crisis was resolved. In many people's view, this resulted in a more stable relationship between the two superpowers. Fortunately, the superpowers were led by two pragmatic and intelligent men – Khrushchev and Kennedy. We tremble to think what would have happened if they had been led by wilder or more foolish spirits.

International relations scholars have been very interested in international crises for many years and we have learnt quite a lot about them. The reasons for this interest are obvious. Most, though not all, interstate wars are preceded by crises. Many crises are resolved peacefully; a few are not. Why some crises develop into war and others do not is obviously an issue of great importance for us all.

Two characteristics stand out about crises. First, they are important events for the governments (and, indeed, the people) of the countries concerned. They involve fundamental issues of their security and possibly of their continued existence. Second, crises are rapidly unfolding events in which important decisions have to be taken quickly. Thus, it is not just a question of importance but the speed with which decisions have to be taken that matters. Which countries decide to join a single European currency is an important question for them and other members of the European Union, but the problem is hardly unexpected. By contrast, decisions about whether to go to war or not often have to be taken in the context of a quickly evolving situation. The speed with which crises evolve often means that a third factor becomes important – that of uncertainty. Often decision-makers are unaware of what other relevant states are doing, intending or even capable of doing. Thus, the consequences of their own decisions are unclear. For example, will a statement of solidarity with another state antagonize a possible opponent and make war more likely or, alternatively, frighten an opponent into caution, thus making war less likely? It is often hard to say.

Given the different nature of crisis decisions it is not surprising to find that the decision-making procedures in crises differ markedly from those adopted in normal decision-making. One characteristic of crisis decision-making is that the number of people involved gets small. In one way or another many people are involved in routine foreign-policy decisions, some of them indirectly. In crises, the decision-making group is small, rarely consisting of more than about twenty people and often much less. They may consult people outside the group, particularly if they need some technical information such as military capacities, but for the most part, the decisions are taken inside this relatively small group. This feature is consistently found in studies of crisis behaviour. Superficially this might seem surprising, I shall return to an explanation of why it should be below.

Clearly a crisis is a time of great stress for the decision-makers. The situation is one of high tension where errors can be very costly. The situation changes rapidly, which means that people have to work very hard to understand a situation which is complicated by the ambiguity of the information. Hard work, anxiety and coping with uncertainty are all very stressful and impose great strains on the decision-makers. This leads to a number of well-documented consequences. First, the decision-making group gets more homogeneous in its attitudes. Suppose the prevailing consensus is that firm action is required against a particular state. The position of someone who is sceptical of this becomes awkward. One of two things is likely to happen. Either the individual concerned keeps quiet and tries to accept the general consensus. Under the tension and pressure of the situation she may actually convince herself that she has genuinely adopted the position of the majority. Alternatively, however, the heretic speaks out. The group finds this very threatening and excludes the heretic from future discussions and confines such deviants to the margins of the decision-making process. This may not seem a wise thing to do as, on the whole, decisions are better made when a wide range of options are being discussed. There is not time to debate too many issues so it is easier to ignore solutions which are too far from the general view. Further, tired, overworked people are resistant to a careful debate on a wide range of issues. They want an answer and a decision in order to release them from the psychological stress they are under. As a second consequence, this stress leads to the simplification of the problems and the attitudes the decision-makers hold. Normally sophisticated people under pressure start to conceptualize problems in oversimplified ways. They perceive their enemies in stereotyped ways to be bad and duplicitous, invariably acting from base motives. They are blind to the more complex ambiguities of behaviour which they would normally take pride in recognizing.

The speed with which decisions have to be taken and the large amount of information that has to be considered suggests why crisis decision-making groups tend to be small. A small group can take quicker decisions than a large one. Once a problem gets enmeshed in a debate between different parts of a bureaucracy and between different divisions or ministries, sorting it out and formulating a decision becomes a slow process. Often this does not matter but in the case of a crisis it does.

This may seem an implausible account of the behaviour of the solid, reliable people who staff the foreign offices of the world, or even those who occupy high political office. And yet, there have been situations where the behaviour of such people appears to have verged on the bizarre. The beginning of the First World War is one. How did a group of sophisticated and, for the most part, humane men plunge the world into such a devastating war? The Suez Crisis is another where the behaviour of some people, conspicuously Sir Anthony Eden, the British Prime Minister, was, at best, deeply neurotic. The answer is that they were all human beings and that this is how human beings behave under stress. The view that leading decision-makers are immune from the normal frailties of the human condition is a consoling fallacy – but a fallacy nonetheless.

However, there are some more hopeful aspects to this. Because we have become aware of the problems of crisis decision-making, we know more about how to handle them. People are more conscious of such dangers as not considering a broader range of options. Also they are more conscious of the psychological effects of pressure. They may not always work to counteract them but they sometimes do. Being self-conscious about the situation can make people act more appropriately and avoid the irrational impulses to which they might yield if they were unaware of the dangers. Crisis decision-making procedures seem to have improved with the explicit awareness of the nature of what happens when crises occur. It is one area where systematic social scientific analysis of a facet of human behaviour of relevance to international relations has had an effect.

Further Reading and Sources

There has a proliferation of books about nationalism and ethnicity since the end of the Cold War. See, for instance, Craig Calhoun, *Nationalism* (London: Open University Press, 1997); John Hutchinson and Anthony D. Smith (eds), *Nationalism* (Oxford: Oxford University Press, 1995); Michael E. Brown, Steven E. Miller and Sean M. Lynne-Jones (eds), *Nationalism and Ethnic Conflict* (Cambridge, MA: MIT Press, 2001, rev. edn); Anthony D. Smith, *Nationalism and Modernism: A Critical Survey of Recent Theories of Nations and Nationalism* (New York: Routledge, 1998) and *Nations and Nationalism in a Global Era* (Cambridge: Polity Press, 1995); Adrian Hastings, *The Construction of Nationhood: Ethnicity, Religion and Nationism (Wiles Lectures, 1996)* (Cambridge: Cambridge University Press, 1998).

S. Ryan counts the number of nation states on a strict definition in 'Explaining Ethnic Conflict: the Neglected International Dimension', *Review of International Studies* 14 (1988), pp. 161–77. Fred Parkinson provides a more liberal definition in an essay called 'Ethnicity and Independent Statehood', in Robert H. Jackson and Alan James (eds) *States in a Changing World: A Contemporary Analysis* (Oxford: Oxford University Press, 1993). Robert H. Jackson wrote the central work on failed states in his *Quasi-States: Sovereignty, International Relations, and the Third World* (Cambridge: Cambridge University Press, 1993). A recently revised classic, which discusses foreign policy analysis in terms of the Cuba Missiles Crisis, but which has significance for a much broader range of problems is Graham Allison and Philip Zelikow, *The Essence of Decision: Explaining the Cuban Missile Crisis* (Toronto: Pearson PTP, 1999, 2nd edn).

I give an outline of the theories of crisis behaviour in my *Rationality and the Analysis of International Conflict* (Cambridge: Cambridge University Press, 1992). On the psychological aspects of crisis decision-making, see Irving Janis, *Groupthink: Psychological Studies of Policy Decisionmaking and Fiascoes* (Boston: Houghton Mifflin, 1992, 2nd edn) – one of the small number of books in international relations that is fun to read. For a recent study of crises, see Russell J. Leng, *Interstate Crisis Behavior 1816–1980 Realism versus Reciprocity* (Cambridge: Cambridge University Press, 1993).

3

Beyond the State: Non-State Actors in the Modern World

Actors and Movements

States have traditionally been the centrepiece of the study of international relations. In the classical realist view, international relations
focused on the interrelationships between states, particularly as they
related to security. Other issues were neglected or regarded as being
someone else's province. International trade, for instance, was for the
economists to study. There has always been some dissatisfaction with
this position but it strengthened in the last quarter of the twentieth
century. Other organizations are no longer regarded as either tools of
states or of minimal importance but rather as crucial to understanding
the behaviour of the international system.

It is useful to distinguish between *organizations* such as busines
firms or the International Monetary Fund and *movements* such as
stock markets or the spread of religions. Organizations take decisions
as units, though with the qualifications expressed in the next para-
graph. In the case of movements, what happens is not the result of a
single intentional decision but is the consequence of a large number of
decisions. Each decision-maker may or may not have foreseen, and
may well not have desired, the result of the set of decisions as a whole.
Let us start by considering organizations, where it is convenient to
distinguish between three major sorts. First, the multinational corporations (MNCs) are private business firms whose activities straddle states
and are not too readily associated with any single state. Second are the
organizations whose members are states. The United Nations is the

most prominent, but there are many others. Governments, not individuals, are the members and they are known as *international governmental organizations* or *IGOs*. Third are the range of actors known as *international non-governmental organizations* or *INGOs*. These are cross-national organizations, including campaigning groups, such as Greenpeace or Amnesty International, or larger and wealthier organizations, such as the Catholic Church (of which more below). Criminal organizations such as the Mafia rest awkwardly between the first and third of these categories. Their significance in international relations and in the global political economy has been recognised only recently. Organizations take decisions and act in accordance with them – or at least they try to. They have *policies*, which means they have sets of plans about what to do in the future. Thus, we can usefully say that 'Greenpeace decided to oppose Shell ' or 'Shell decided to invest in offshore oil' in the same way as, with sternly worded cautions, we say that 'France decided to increase its interest rates.' In all these cases a group of individuals within the organization took the decision according to some procedure. The individuals took the decision in their roles as members of the organization. The organization lays down what people in what positions can decide and the rules they must follow. The result is that these organizations are actors that take decisions.

In the case of movements no decision process is identifiable in the same way. Movements are poorly formulated in much of the older style of international relations and their categorization as 'movements' is my own. If one Turkish family decides to emigrate to Germany, or one Japanese family emigrates to the USA, it makes very little difference to the social and economic fabric of either the country they leave or the country they go to. When many families emigrate, it has a very big impact. The accumulation of individual decisions is large even though the effect of each individual decision is unimportant from the social point of view, however important it may be for the individuals involved. No-one makes the aggregate decision. It is simply the result of a lot of individual decisions and indeed the significance of the overall consequences of these decisions may go unnoticed for a long time. Markets are often social structures of this sort. No individual consumer of oranges has much impact on the market but the overall impact of consumers taken together in their usually uncoordinated behaviour is an important determinant of the orange market's behaviour. The more spectacular market phenomena are of this sort. In September 1992, the British government was forced to devalue the pound (that is, after the devaluation, more pounds were required to buy dollars or deutsche-marks). The day of the devaluation became known as 'Black Monday', though many commentators have argued that, in the long run, it was the best thing that could have happened to the British economy. The British government decided this, though under duress. The British government was an organization taking decisions in order to achieve a goal. However, the events that forced the British government to devalue were the result of many smaller decisions whose primary aim was incidental to the global effect that resulted in fact. These were movements as I have described them above. Movements are not just the rapid phenomena, such as the changes that occur in very volatile markets like money markets, but also longer-term movements such as the growth or decline of religions.

Decisions in the more orthodox sense have to be taken in the context of movements, as the Black Monday example illustrates. Governments often have limited control over such things as runs on the currency but they can and do try to do so. Sometimes they succeed. Whether something should be classified as an actor or a movement is often ambiguous. Some powerful individual financiers such as George Soros have significant influence on markets. Thus, we have a spectrum rather than a dichotomy but the distinction is still useful. In this chapter I shall mainly discuss actors though they are often operating in contexts such as markets. This is obviously true in the case of MNCs, but markets today are becoming an increasing constraint on the behaviour of states.

The United Nations

The United Nations (UN) was founded in 1944 as the Second World War drew to a close. It was intended as the organization that would preserve the peace in the postwar years. Its membership was to consist of all the states in the world, though the defeated powers of Japan and Germany were not invited to join for many years. Now the world has altered to such a degree that there is talk of them being permanent members of the Security Council, which is the central decision-making part of the UN. The UN is a grouping of states and thus it is premised on the notion that states are the primary units in the international system. It rests on an assumption that it is through the actions of states that we get both war and peace, although the assertion in the UN

War and Peace; Poverty and Wealth

Two dominant themes in international relations, under which other aspects can be subsumed, are the issues of war vs. peace and poverty vs. wealth. Peace and wealth are the positive features of the world we seek to explore; war and poverty are the negative features. Inevitably the two are intertwined. Unsurprisingly, those parts of the world that have recently experienced violence, such as Somalia and the former Yugoslavia, have seen their incomes decline rapidly.

War and violence – and more frequently the threats of war and violence – are common between states. Many people regard war as legitimate between states. It does not mean that states are fighting each other all the time – there are many peaceful relationships as well as warlike relationships. Between 1946 and 1986, a state was at war on average only about 2.2 per cent of the time. However, it is horrific when it happens. Despite the horrors of the twentieth century the incidence of war does not seem to have decreased and it is still actively practised.

However, there has been a marked difference in the pattern of warfare. War within states has become more important and interstate war less, though this has not meant it has become less virulent. Even where interstate war is concerned, nuclear weapons and other weapons of mass destruction such as biological weapons have provided a major new dimension. Previously war was destructive and nasty but in general societies survived. Since 1815, when the Napoleonic Wars ended, about 1.3 per cent of the world's population have died as the direct result of war. This would be larger if the indirect deaths were also included. With nuclear weapons, the degree of mass destruction possible has vastly increased. A nuclear war that got out of hand could literally destroy the human race. This is something that has never been possible before. The persistence of war in the modern world requires some explanation. It causes immense suffering and is an inefficient means of settling disputes. Preparations for war are expensive even if no war follows. Yet war and preparations for war consume vast amounts of money, energy and talent.

Because not all warfare is between states, we must be careful not to elevate the significance of the state too much in this analysis. Lewis Fry Richardson coined the term *deadly quarrels* to denote all conflicts in which people try to kill each other. Interstate war is an important category of such deadly quarrels, though there are plenty of others.

There are civil wars like the American Civil War (1861–65) and the Spanish Civil War (1936–39). These were fought by armies and the mode of fighting was the same as for an interstate war. However, there are also acts of genocide such as the events in Rwanda in 1995 and ethnic cleansing as in the former Yugoslavia. There are acts of terrorism. These may have political goals such as the formation of a state, as in the case of the Palestinian Liberation Organization (PLO), or to alter the nature of a government, as with the Front Islamique du Salut (FIS) in Algeria. Many governments have turned on their citizens. In the former Soviet Union (also referred to as the Union of Soviet Socialist Republics or USSR), Stalin's purges of the 1930s killed about 3 million people, including those who died in camps. Overall the total casualties of Stalin's epoch may well have been in the region of 20 million deaths as Khrushchev claims in his memoirs. Rummell (1995) estimates that 170 million people were killed by their own states between 1900 and 1987. Though some of these acts are internal, they are rarely totally so, illustrating that there are no neat boundaries to the discipline of international relations. We move seamlessly from the totally global to the narrowly domestic with no clear boundary in between.

As we show on pp. 5–8, there are great disparities in wealth between different parts of the world as well as great disparities within states. It is possible that these disparities might be explained solely in terms of issues internal to the states themselves. However, it seems unlikely. The international economic system is very interdependent so the distribution of wealth is at least partially a global problem. The issues of poverty and wealth are not just economic; they are political as well. The relation of the international economic system to the political system, if, indeed, the two can be distinguished, is of clear importance on the global scale. It is generally studied under the rubric of *international political economy* (IPE) and *global political economy* (GPE).

A Brief Portrait of the World in Figures

Let us look at the world we are going to discuss in terms of some of the relevant statistics. Statistics can be treacherous assistants but there is no better way of getting a feel for the relative significance of things. As the new millennium began there were 6100 million people in the world. They are divided into about 190 states, though of radically different sizes. The state with the largest population is China with well over a billion (that is, 1000 million) people in the mid 1990s. The population of India is a little smaller but recently reached 1 billion. The US is smaller still with 280 million. In Latin America, Brazil has the largest population with 168 million inhabitants. Somewhat smaller but still substantial countries in Europe are Germany with a population of 82 million, followed by France and Britain which each have populations of about 59 million. Australia is smaller still with approximately 19 million inhabitants. There are also some very small European states, such as Andorra, which has 65 000 inhabitants. There are doubts whether such a small group of people can really function as a state without the tolerance and help of its neighbours — in this case Spain and France. However, several small states seem to be able to function perfectly well. Luxembourg has 432 000 people and the highest income per head in the world of $38 247. Iceland has a population of only 279 000 but, with an income per head of $26 283 in 1999, exceeded Britain with $22 220 per head. (All the income statistics in this chapter are for 1999.)

States vary greatly in wealth. We have to be careful, though, to distinguish wealth per head of population and overall wealth. Income per head is what matters as far as the individual is concerned. It is an index of prosperity, though only a rough one as it can conceal vast differences in wealth within a country. Aggregate wealth is what matters as far as international power and influence are concerned.

By far the richest country overall is the United States with a GNP of $8879.5 billion. It is also the richest per head at $31 910, except for the fortunate Luxembourgers. Following it, but a long way behind, is Japan with a GNP of $4054.5 billion and an average income of $25 170. The third richest country per head is Switzerland, with a GNP per head of $28 760, but there are only 7 million people, so its overall GNP is low. Population seems unrelated to wealth per head. Both big countries and small ones can be rich (or, of course, poor). From this point of view there seem to be no economies of scale as far as states are concerned.

At the other end of the spectrum, much of Africa is desperately poor. Ethiopia's population of 63 million has only $600 each, a figure shared with Guinea-Bissau, which has a population of about 1.185 million. As an annual income this is tiny and grotesque. There are several countries in Africa with incomes per head of well below $1000, such as Malawi ($570 per head per year) and Rwanda ($880 per head per year). By contrast, the Indian subcontinent, though poor, does rather better. Even Bangladesh, generally and properly regarded as a very poor country, has an income per head of $1530.

The incomes per head are average figures, of course. Rich countries can have many poor people whereas poor countries can have exceptionally wealthy élites. Unsurprisingly there are big discrepancies. As a measure of inequality, not necessarily poverty, we can compare the wealthiest 20 per cent of the population with the poorest 20 per cent to see how much more of the national income the wealthy get than the poor. Japan is the most equal country among the ones that were richest in the 1990s. There the richest 20 per cent get 3.4 times the income of the poorest. In the United States the figure is 9 while in Britain and Australia – two of the other countries in this group – the richest 20 per cent get 6.5 and 7 times as much, respectively, as the poorest 20 per cent. There is a much wider range of ratios between the poorer countries. Slovakia, where the rich 20 per cent get 2.6 times the income of the poorer 20 per cent, is the most equal of all countries, rich or poor. In Niger, on the other hand, the top 20 per cent receive 20.7 times as much as the bottom 20 per cent, a figure exceeded only by Guinea-Bissau where the figure is 28.0. The precise figures should be treated with caution but the general patterns are meaningful.

As figures indicating equality and inequality show, average income per head is only a crude indicator of well-being. A more complex indicator is the Human Development Index (HDI) used by the United Nations Development Programme and published annually. The HDI combines three central aspects of well-being: life expectancy, adult literacy and income per head. It produces a composite index of them, which indicates a lot about a society. Life expectancy is a good indicator of health; adult literacy a good indicator of how broad a range of people can participate fully in the economic, social and political aspects of society; and wealth, of course, is wealth. In 2001, to which all the following figures refer, Norway ranked the highest in the world followed by Australia, Canada and Sweden. The UK came in at number 14, while the United States came in at 6. New Zealand came in at 19. Despite its enviably high income per head, Luxembourg was ranked 12. Lower down came India, ranked 115, and Bangladesh, 132. At the bottom of those surveyed was Sierra Leone. Expectation of life is higher than one might expect amongst the richer countries, being 78.5 years in Canada, 78.7 in Australia and 77.2 in the UK. The Japanese live the longest. A Japanese baby can expect to live for

Charter that 'War begins in the minds of men' also suggests a recognition of some deeper factors.

The UN grew up not just in the shadow of the Second World War but also in the shadow of the League of Nations, which had been founded after the First World War. The League similarly had ambitions to preserve the peace and, like the UN, also took the state as its basic unit. The League clearly failed – it took only two decades of its existence for the Second World War to break out. The founders of the UN tried to learn from the League's mistakes, the most serious of which they believed to be that it had failed to recognise the realities of power. Whether this diagnosis is right or wrong is contentious. What is not contentious is that it coloured the design of the structure of the United Nations.

The General Assembly of the United Nations has representatives of the states of the world as members. These representatives are nominated by their governments. Votes are held in the General Assembly, which can only make recommendations. The real power is vested in the Security Council, which consists of representatives of two groups of states. The first group is the five permanent members – the USA, Russia (formerly the Soviet Union), France, Britain and China – who were seen as the major powers in 1944 when the UN was founded. They were made permanent members on the view, derived directly from the realist theory, that if the big powers were not given a privileged position the UN would not work. The power of the permanent members was reinforced by giving each of them a *veto*. This meant that any one of them could stop a measure against the wishes of the other four. None of the powers has ever hesitated to use this veto when it thought its interests were at stake. The second group consists of ten further members of the Security Council who are elected by the General Assembly on a temporary and rotating basis. The Security Council can initiate action. The idea behind this structure was that the leading members of the United Nations had to agree for effective action in the world. This may well have been true. Unfortunately the main actors in the UN did not agree. The Cold War between the United States and the Soviet Union quickly came to dominate the international scene and made the work of the United Nations extremely difficult.

The Secretary-General of the UN is the person who makes the UN work. The Secretary-General is elected by the General Assembly but must have the support, or at least not the opposition, of the larger powers in order to function. Members of the Security Council can veto a particular candidate. Some, such as the first Secretary-General, the Norwegian Trygve Lie, took a relatively passive view believing that the role should be essentially that of a chairperson. Others, such as the Swede Dag Hammarskjöld, took a much more proactive view and became a significant international actor in his own right.

The end of the Cold War has made some things easier for the UN. At least it is not dominated by the hostility between the US and the Soviet Union, which paralyzed much of the possible activity of the UN, and certainly disappointed the hopes of its founders. The Cold War was so pervasive in the forty years after 1945 that many issues had a Cold-War perspective and thus excited the suspicions of either or both of the two superpowers.

The UN has been dogged by another problem, namely that it is chronically short of money. The UN gets its income from dues levied on its members, which are assessed proportionately to countries' wealth. Unfortunately many countries are seriously behind in their payments. These are not always impoverished states, as one might expect. The United States, for instance, owed over a billion dollars in dues to the UN, which it only began to pay after the 11 September 2001 attacks on the World Trade Center and Pentagon, as part of an effort to enlist that body in the fight against global terrorism. Though the USA can rightly point to inefficiencies in the management of the UN, these are now being addressed. Behind the reluctance of the US government to pay are some very mixed feelings about an international organization. While some of the UN's most enthusiastic supporters are American, there are also significant political groupings who are suspicious of a body whose first commitment is not to the USA's view of the world and might actually oppose it. The UN is accepted by many people, both inside and outside the USA, who are realists. They believe states are the dominant actors and that power is the ultimate currency of the international system. However, they argue that, in the long run, the stability and order that the UN might contribute is in the self-interest of the states themselves. It is worth putting up with some reverses to one's own short-run interests in order to attain this. Most countries have some groups who do not accept this view and are much more short-term nationalists. They are more powerful in the USA than in most places, which is particularly unfortunate for the UN because, as the richest and most powerful country, the USA is a major contributor of funds.

More positively in the post-Cold-War period, there has been a big growth in *peacekeeping operations*, though these have not all been an unqualified success. Perhaps the best-known operation is in the former Yugoslavia where the UN sent in a peacekeeping mission to try to keep some measure of peace in a situation where national and ethnic groups were fighting each other with great ferocity. The UN does not have armed forces of its own. The major military UN actions to counter aggression – as distinct from peacekeeping – notably the Korean War and the Gulf War, were carried out by national armies under national command and claiming UN approval. (Some cynics suggest that the United Nations' involvement was merely a fig leaf to cover the purely national ambitions of the major states involved; others argue that, though national interests were served, broader interests were served too.) Peacekeeping operations are somewhat different. Soldiers from member states who have no interest in the conflict come under United Nations command. They wear the distinctive 'blue helmet' chosen, presumably, because it would be a very bad colour to wear in combat as it can easily be seen. These troops are only lightly armed and can fight only if directly attacked. The troops can remain only so long as all the warring parties agree, which clearly puts them in a situation where diplomatic skills are paramount. Unsurprisingly the UN force in the former Yugoslavia ran into many difficulties, not least because there was no peace to keep. The UN force was succeeded by a NATO (North Atlantic Treaty Organization) force, which at least had better chains of command.

Peacekeeping operations are very expensive to run, which makes the financial crisis of the UN all the more difficult. If the UN is to have a significant role in the post-Cold-War world it is hard to see how it could decline to carry out such operations. UN peacekeeping or observing forces have existed since the early days, going back to 1948 when they observed the Arab–Israeli truce. However, they have expanded rapidly recently. As more experience is gained, expertise will grow both among the soldiers on the ground, who are doing something very different from conventional combat, and for the administration and command of these activities.

The UN has not been solely concerned with problems of peace and war, at least in its direct sense. There are a number of specialized agencies of the UN. Some of these are well-known, such as UNICEF which is concerned with the well-being of children, particularly in the Third World. It is largely financed by voluntary contributions. We discuss in some detail one of the activities of the *United Nations Environmental Programme* (UNEP) in Chapter 9. Some of these, such as the *World Health Organization* (WHO) and the *Food and Agriculture Organization* (FAO) are also well known. For the most part they have done important work and managed to avoid being overly inhibited by the Cold War. This was partly because much of their work is uncontentious, although the WHO occasionally runs into difficulties with religious lobbies, particularly over population control. The exception is the *UN Educational, Scientific and Cultural Organization* (UNESCO), which was accused of being under left-wing domination in the eighties to the extent that the governments of the USA and UK, both under conservative governments of Reagan and Thatcher, respectively, withdrew.

The World Bank and International Monetary Fund

Two particularly important and controversial IGOs are the *International Monetary Fund* (IMF) and the *World Bank*, the latter being more fully known as the *International Bank for Reconstruction and Development*. They have had a significant impact on the world economy. They are specialized UN Agencies which means that organizationally they do not operate under direct UN control. Originally they were set up at the *Bretton Woods Conference* held in 1944 towards the end of the Second World War. The organizations were funded by the member countries in proportion to their national incomes and received votes in proportion to their contribution. This meant that the USA has always had the dominant voice. These organizations were set up to help mitigate the economic chaos caused by the Second World War, which was still on, and in the vivid memory of the participants of the almost continuous international financial crises which had characterized the prewar years. The economic specialists, who dominated the conference, were anxious that monetary issues should not aggravate the inevitably severe economic consequences of the war. The initial aims were very much in this context. One can argue that the Bretton Woods System, as the postwar international monetary regime came to be called, prevented a repeat, in the postwar world, of earlier catastrophes amongst the capitalist economies. It survived, more or less, until the oil-price crises of the early 1970s. The Soviet Union and Eastern bloc stayed out of these arrangements.

The richer capitalist countries of the world for the most part experienced high rates of economic growth in the postwar years and thoughts of economic catastrophe receded. The main economic problem seemed more to be the persistent poverty of much of the Third World. The goal of the World Bank was to encourage international investment particularly in poorer parts of the world. The idea was that the World Bank would investigate projects for their economic and practical viability. The Bank would help poorer countries in drawing up various investment plans. If the World Bank found projects viable then it would provide capital, and in addition its approval would attract and encourage private capital as well. The Bank provides reliable information which gives investors confidence in countries and projects.

The IMF had a rather different task. Its goal was to help countries that were finding it difficult to export enough to pay for their imports. Such problems are known as *balance of payments problems*. It was generally believed that in the prewar years, countries were excessively affected by short-term balance of payments problems and that they should be helped over these by the provision of some generally accepted international credit. The IMF was to provide a more flexible credit regime. Its own funds were provided by the member states. However, help from the IMF was provided with conditions. Countries receiving assistance had to conform to policies indicated by the IMF.

The IMF has been criticized both for its conservative approaches to economic policy and its insensitivity to the economic problems of some of the states and in particular the poorer states. *Structural adjustment programmes* (SAPs), designed to bring economies back to some financial equilibrium, have often done so at the expense of grave social damage and cost. Probably any organization doing what the IMF was trying to do would find itself unpopular. However, there does seem some truth to the claim that it has required unduly rigorous regimes to be imposed as the condition of its assistance.

The World Bank has likewise been criticized for having an overly cautious and 'bankers attitude' towards investment, tending to take the financial community at its own valuation. It has also been accused of ignoring environmental issues when making loans. The World Bank has proved sensitive to these criticisms in recent years and, at least on environmental matters, has started to bring them into assessments. It also has become more sensitive to social and other non-financial issues than in its earlier days.

The European Union

In many ways, the European Union (EU) is a new sort of entity in the international scene. It is not an alliance, nor is it a customs union in anything like the conventional sense. It encompasses too broad a range of things for this. Nor is it a state that has emerged out of a coalition of states, such as the United States, which developed from a set of former colonies of Britain in the eighteenth century. It is something in between.

The EU has its origins in the European Coal and Steel Community founded in 1951 with France and Germany (but not Britain) as the central signatories. This was interesting enough in its own right. France and Germany were historic enemies who seemed forever doomed to fight each other. They were willing to come to some agreements over crucial aspects of economic policy only a few years after a devastating war. Further, the particular commodities were symbolic. In those days 'coal and steel' were central to armaments and had been even more so in the days of Franco–German enmity. This was a remarkable shift in attitudes. The Coal and Steel Community was always seen as a transitional step by many people and in 1957 the Treaty of Rome was signed which set up the European Economic Community (the EEC). The original six signatories were the governments of France, Germany, Italy, the Netherlands, Belgium and Luxembourg. Conspicuously they did not include Britain, which was invited to join but declined. It was not until 1973 that Britain became a member. By the mid-1990s, the EEC had broadened beyond the purely economic to become the European Union (EU) and consisted of fifteen broadly Western European states. Now there are active negotiations for an expansion of membership to the East, though there is also hesitancy, particularly amongst the electorates of member states, who are frequently less eager about the EU than the élites.

How far the European Union will expand, both in terms of more states and of extending the degree of integration between states, is an issue of intense political debate. Originally the EU was set up to coordinate economic policy between states, which was reflected in its earlier name of European Economic Community (EEC). However, there has always been a powerful school of thought urging closer unity potentially up to the creation of a 'United States of Europe', which would, in effect, involve the creation of a new state in a more traditional sense. This approach is in contrast to the more conservative view that Europe should be an association of individual states, retaining their individual identities. This would more resemble a traditional alliance, albeit a very close one. Which of these tendencies will prevail is hard to say. Integration may stabilize at some level or it may proceed until there is a federal state of Europe. The next few years will be fascinating to observe and participate in.

There are some features of the EU that go well beyond the normal concept of an alliance. Thus, the European Court of Justice can overrule the domestic courts of the constituent countries on various issues of European law. This means that European law is much more like domestic law than international law. Furthermore, individuals can take constituent states to court over such issues as human rights. What is perhaps interesting is that states accept this and accept the rulings of the European Court even when they go against the ruling government's wishes. This is a very fundamental issue. The states of the European Union have relinquished a basic element of sovereignty, namely the ultimate jurisdiction of their own courts, to a supranational body, though, admittedly, in only a few respects. A further development that puts the EU far beyond a mere association of states is the single currency. A currency, more than anything else, identifies an economy. The growing liberalization of markets has reduced economic sovereignty to a lower level than it has ever been before. However, the institution of a common currency takes this process even further. The most obvious definition of a single economy is a common currency. Both in its economic and symbolic implications it is much more significant than a free trade area.

Multinational Corporations

International economic actors are very important in understanding the broader field of international relations. However, states are still relevant actors in the international political economy and were even more so in the days of the communist regimes of the Soviet Union and Eastern Europe. These had *command economies* in which what was to be produced and how it was to be distributed was decided in the framework of a national plan, rather than being left to markets. Now the communist states have declined. Only China is left as a major but ambiguous communist actor, along with a few smaller states like Cuba and North Korea.

Business firms are also significant economic actors and at times political actors. We need to examine the way they take decisions more carefully. Some markets, such as currency markets, can be seen as a mass of impersonal actors where even the biggest, such as George Soros, can only have a limited impact on the market as a whole. However, this is often not true of firms that produce goods (such as aircraft), services (such as news services), or extract minerals (such as oil). One, or a few firms, frequently dominate the markets in which they operate and can do a lot to manipulate them.

If a firm produces, sells and buys its raw material largely in one country, then it is not of great interest to the international relations specialists. Few firms do this completely (though the building construction industry largely conforms to this pattern). Many firms engage in international trade, either as buyers or sellers or both. Some international trade has existed ever since anything identifiable as a state – or the even more amorphous concept of an economy – has existed. However, as we argued earlier, there has been a great growth in the multinational corporations (MNCs) active in many countries, since 1945. Though firms, and in particular multinational organizations, are major actors in the international scene, they are very different from states, whether democratic or authoritarian.

The primary goal of a business firm is to make profits. There are many subsidiary goals, such as the status of their leaders and, in some cases, power. Profit is an ambiguous concept. Large but speculative gains might be sacrificed for smaller but less risky profits. Short-term profits might be sacrificed for long-term profits (though there is the claim, particularly about British firms, that the reverse is true). The maximization of profits can mean many things. However, profit comes in to it somewhere and, as a broad-brush rule, it does not do too badly as an explanation of business conduct. This contrasts with the more complex and ambiguous goals of state decision-makers. The business decision-makers have a much less complex set of interests to satisfy than states. Pragmatically they may need to satisfy public opinion; otherwise a disenchanted public may work through states to curtail their activities. Oil companies such as Shell have run into difficulties with environmental groups and they will probably spend significant sums of money trying to pacify public opinion over the next few decades or so. Similarly tobacco companies have to be aware of the public concern over their lethal product and direct their marketing activities to countries where the state is unlikely to bow to the concerns of health activists. However, their main goal is to satisfy shareholders and the managers themselves whose incomes are often tied to the earnings and values of the shares and thus the profits of the firm.

A major difference between firms and states is the comparative instability of firms as compared with states. Occasionally states merge (as many did in the nineteenth century) and also they split into sets of smaller states, something that was once very unusual but has recently become more common (see pp. 61–2). However, firms often merge with, or take over, other firms. Their identity is less sharply defined than in the case of states and their employees are quite ready to shift their allegiance. Most major business executives change jobs and, over a lifetime, people often work for several different firms. There is no analogy to this in the way people serve states. That some large corporations have similar levels of wealth to some of the smaller states should not blind us to the many significant dissimilarities.

International Non-Governmental Organizations

Some of the non-commercial organizations in the world scene are not connected to governments at all. Indeed many are regarded with suspicion by many governments who find themselves the unwelcome subject of their work. Thus, Amnesty International is the human rights group whose main targets, inevitably, are states. Greenpeace works to raise concern about environmental matters both in general and in particular instances. Thus it finds itself frequently in conflict with MNCs over issues of pollution. Governments usually take the side of the companies in these matters. Governments also find themselves the direct object of Greenpeace's protests, as the French government did over its nuclear tests in the Pacific in 1996. One of the strategies of such organizations is to harness governments behind them, often because only governments can exert the sort of influence necessary to alter matters. The existence of the human-rights lobby can make states, particularly democratic ones, just that little bit more conscious of the more oppressive behaviour of some of their commercially-valued clients, even if this rarely makes much difference to their business behaviour.

Most successful international non-governmental organizations (INGOs) have rather specific aims that make their influence far out of proportion to their extremely modest resources. Issues, such as those of the environment, have been put on the global agenda, which many governments and MNCs would rather they had not been. It is hard to imagine that the environmental issue would be so prominent today without the activities, domestically and internationally, of the political environmental groups.

INGOs have also played a major role in some of the big developments of the last decade. After General Pinochet was arrested in 1998 on charges of human-rights crimes committed in Chile during his seventeen-year rule, INGOs promoted a campaign to build public support for Pinochet's extradition to stand trial in Spain. Among others, they were successful in requesting a judicial review of the British decision regarding whether he was fit to stand for trial, gave evidence at many extradition hearings in the UK, and kept the proceedings in the media and high on the public agenda.

The ongoing campaign against genetically-modified foods is another issue where INGOs have played a major role. In communicating the need to ban genetically-modified crops, Greenpeace has organised direct action campaigns, which included destroying a six-acre field of genetically-modified maize that was being grown for a seed company. Other tactics have also been used, such as working with food stores, restaurants and the public to raise consumer demand for organic food. Friends of the Earth also surveyed the top 26 food and drinks companies to find out their policy on using genetically-modified ingredients, in an attempt to hold companies directly accountable.

Basically Amnesty International and Greenpeace are campaigning groups. They seek to attract attention so that policies are changed. Compared to the organizations they are trying to influence their resources are minuscule. Other organizations, such as the International Committee of the Red Cross, are rather different. Their aim is to be independent of any government so that they can be trusted as impartial. However, in order to carry out their goals of humanitarian work they deal with governments (who are often in a position to facilitate or obstruct the work) but make no judgements about the governments' actions. As such, they are not trying to influence opinion but to achieve certain sorts of results directly.

Religions

Religious groups are clearly of great importance in the international scene. Their importance seems to have increased in recent decades.

However, the way in which they influence international relations is rather complex and does not fit into one single pattern. From some points of view, religions can best be seen as actors; from other points of view they can best be seen as movements. Thus, the spread of various religions is best seen as a movement. The increase in Islamic fundamentalism, which has taken place in the last few years in many parts of the world, was not a decision taken by an organization (though of course many organizations aided and abetted it). For example, in Algeria, the growth of Islamic fundamentalism came with the extremely high and increasing levels of unemployment and poverty, along with a total disenchantment with government corruption, and the apparent inability of the government to do anything. However, the Pope's frequently expressed opposition to birth control is a decision where the Vatican is in a position to influence events, though perhaps not as much as it would like. Thus the Pope and the Vatican are actors. Technically the Vatican is an independent state of which the Pope is the leader. However, his influence derives not from this, but because there are a large number of people who regard him as their spiritual leader and will obey him. Thus, the movement gives credence to the actor. One of the characteristics of the present time is that the degree of obedience to the Pope has dwindled among Catholics. Obedience is much more critical than in former times. This is a movement that affects the power of the Catholic actors.

A problem in assessing the power of religions is that people follow them with very different degrees of zeal. Almost one-third of the world is ostensibly Christian, a proportion which has varied only slightly since the beginning of the twentieth century. However, these include the intensely religious, for whom Christianity is the absolute centre of their lives, to those who feel nothing more than a vague cultural affiliation with Christianity. More significant from a political point of view are the intense believers, who may make up a small fraction of the total nominal believers. Impressionistically it seems that the intense believers, many of whom are fundamentalist, are growing in number today, but it is very hard to measure this.

Even ostensibly similar religions are frequently very divided. The Vatican is the centre of Roman Catholicism but the Vatican's authority is disputed by far more Christians than those who accept it. Similarly, there are several forms of Islam. The largest are the Sunni and the Shi'ite who represent about 84 per cent and 16 per cent respectively. Other Islamic groups are very small and together form less than 1 per cent of the total. Though many people would claim to speak for Islam, such as the former Ayatollah Khomeini of Iran, any particular leader's claim to authority is disputed. The same is true with Christianity. Indeed hostilities within religions are frequently much more intense and vicious than hostilities and rivalries between them. The perceived heretic, who is a deviant from the true faith and not a follower of another, has always been regarded as the most wicked of people. The Spanish Inquisition, often held up as the most extreme example of religious intolerance, mainly condemned other Christians. In this it both followed and anticipated the intolerance of many religions, Christian and other.

Religious representatives appear in all sorts of international meetings particularly on such matters as population and exert a very significant influence. The Roman Catholic Church is particularly involved in questions of population or, more precisely, birth control and abortion. Theologically it is opposed to contraception (though many Catholics disagree with the Vatican line on this) and it is even more strongly opposed to abortion. The Catholic Church played a large role at the 3rd International Conference on Population and Development, which was held under the auspices of the United Nations Fund for Population Activities in Cairo in 1994. There was a strange alliance between some fundamentalist Muslims and the Vatican to oppose any hint of support of abortion. In this the religions, in their organised form, are behaving as actors.

Religious movements often work through influencing states. Thus, the general support of Israel by the United States is heavily influenced by the electoral impact of Jewish groups in certain key electoral localities. Similarly Cuban Americans have a disproportionate influence on US policy with respect to Cuba. Religious groups in Israel itself also have major political impact, though there are also powerful secular groups. In Islamic states, conspicuously Iran, but also in Pakistan, Saudi Arabia and so on, secular groups are suppressed and the state is run on predominantly religious lines.

Further Reading and Sources

A good general book on international organizations is Clive Archer's *International Organizations* (London: Routledge, 2001, 3rd edn). Other books to be consulted on this general topic are Robert Keohane,

International Institutions and State Power: Essays in International Relations Theory (Boulder: Westview, 1989) and Paul F. Diehl (ed.), *International Organization in an Interdependent World* (Boulder: Lynne Rienner, 1997).

On the United Nations more specifically see Adam Roberts and Benedict Kingsbury (eds), *United Nations, Divided World: The UN's Role in International Relations* (Oxford: Clarendon, 1994, 2nd edn); David P. Forsythe, Roger A. Coate and Thomas George Weiss, *The United Nations and Changing World Politics* (Boulder: Westview Press, 2000, 3rd edn); Chadwick F. Alger (ed.), *The Future of the United Nations System: Potential for the Twenty-First Century* (New York: United Nations Publications, 1998); Louis Emmerij, Richard Jolly, Thomas G. Weiss and Kofi A. Annan, *Ahead of the Curve?: UN Ideas and Global Challenges* (Bloomington: Indiana University Press, 2001); and Ramesh Thakur and Edward Newman (eds), *New Millennium, New Perspectives: The United Nations, Security, and Governance (UNU Millennium Series)* (New York: United Nations Publications, 2000).

For further reading on the role of INGOs in world politics see Peter Willetts (ed.), *The Conscience of the World: The Influence of Non-Governmental Organizations in the UN System* (Washington DC: Brookings Institute, 1996); Paul Kevin Wapner and Lester Edwin J. Ruiz (eds), *Principled World Politics* (Maryland: Rowman & Littlefield, 2000); William Korey, *NGOs and the Universal Declaration of Human Rights: A Curious Grapevine* (New York: Palgrave, 2001); Julie Fisher, *Nongovernments: NGOs and the Political Development of the Third World* (Bloomfield: Kumarian Press, 1997); Terje Tvedt, *Angels of Mercy or Development Diplomats: NGOs and Foreign Aid* (New Jersey: Africa World Press, 1998); and Thomas G. Weiss, Leon Gordenker and Thomas J. Watson (eds), *NGOs, the UN, and Global Governance (Emerging Global Issues)* (Boulder: Lynne Rienner, 1996).

Studies of multinationals include Anne-Wil Käthe Harzing, *Managing the Multinationals: An International Study of Control* (Cheltenham: Edward Elgar, 1999); John Madeley, *Big Business, Poor Peoples: The Impact of Transnational Corporations in the World's Poor* (London: Zed Books, 1999); Volker Bornschier and Christopher Chase-Dunn, *Transnational Corporations and Underdevelopment* (Westport: Praeger, 1985).

4

A Brief History of the Twentieth Century

Introduction

The world as it is today did not materialize out of nothing. It developed from the world as it was, which in turn developed from the world as it was before. How one situation evolves from what preceded it is often what we are trying to find out in the social sciences in general, and in international relations in particular. To put the present situation in the world into context, we shall look, very selectively and inevitably rather superficially, at what has happened over the last century or so and pick out some significant developments. The present situation developed out of previous situations which, in turn, developed out of something previous to them. But we must start somewhere, however arbitrarily. In this chapter we shall start around the beginning of the twentieth century. In the next, on imperialism, we shall start a little earlier.

The First World War

On 1 August 1914 the world was at peace, or at least no-one was killing anyone else at the behest of the state. By 1 September, there had been half a million casualties. By the end of 1918 over 8½ million people had died in an orgy of violence.

The state system in Europe in 1914 was at its peak. States such as Germany, Austria-Hungary, Britain and France were sovereign in the sense that other states had little control over what went on within their

50

borders. Their economies were interdependent. According to Hirst and Thompson (1996), the British economy was more open in terms of trade and capital movements between 1905 and 1914 than it was between 1965 and 1986. However, the German government ruled in Germany, the British government ruled in Britain and so on. Furthermore, European governments ruled over many other parts of the world. India, much of Africa and many other scattered parts of the world were under the sovereign command of European governments. Even small countries such as Belgium had substantial empires. States, for the most part, viewed each other with suspicion. They were all well-armed and ready for war. They had formed alliances. Britain, France and Russia were in league against Germany and Austria-Hungary. Alliances were made for practical reasons of power and not for any great love of the allies. Indeed, there was much popular unease, particularly in France, about the alliance with the extremely reactionary Russia whose absolute monarchy provided a very different political system from those of its democratic allies. Germany perceived Britain as a particular enemy at sea and in the imperial field. The two had been involved in a competitive building of naval vessels since the beginning of the century, in what is often regarded as a classical arms race. The Germans saw Russia as a barbarian threat. The situation was fraught. From that fraught situation came the First World War.

Most of Europe entered the war and most of the land fighting was in Europe or around the Mediterranean. Initially it was predominantly a war of the European powers. The leading combatants were the so-called Allies of Britain, France and Russia on one side and Germany and Austria-Hungary on the other. Italy declared war on Austria-Hungary in 1915 and Germany in 1916. However, from the beginning, Australia, New Zealand, South Africa and Canada joined in and contributed disproportionately to the armed forces though there was very little self-interest in this. The empires of all the combatants entered the war with varying degrees of reluctance. Japan was a major non-European country to be involved on the part of the Allies, though it took no part in the European fighting and remained interested only in the Pacific. For some time the war was a stalemate and anyone could have won. However, in 1917 the Russians left the war as a consequence of the Russian Revolution, but the Americans entered on the Allied side. The American troops were fresh and backed by a huge industrial system. Though there were still to be some anxious moments from the Allied point of view, this nevertheless sealed the issue in favour of the

Allies. The fighting ended on 11 November 1918 at 11 o'clock, a day and time which is still celebrated as Remembrance Day in many countries, though the remembrance of past massacres has done little to prevent future ones.

What caused the First World War? There is still no consensus. Broadly there are three views; first it was accidental; second, it was deliberate; and third, it was inevitable. We shall look briefly at all three. According to the accident theorists, war came about because there was a general misperception of other people's intentions and motives. The Germans and Austro-Hungarians (that is, their governments, aided and abetted by their advisors such as their foreign offices) thought they could get away with a small war in the Balkans to improve their position *vis-à-vis* the Serbs. They did not think the Russians would enter the war. Though they expected a war with France at some stage they had not expected it to coincide with a war in the East. Indeed, the German High Command was particularly anxious to avoid a two-front war with France in the West and Russia in the East. Further, they had not really expected Britain to come into the war. As far as other countries were concerned, it seemed likewise to be a set of events which got out of hand. Armies were mobilized – efficiently but unstoppably in the case of Germany; inefficiently but unstoppably in the case of Russia. This added to the pressures towards war by increasing each adversary's fears of the rest while simultaneously providing a justification as militarist sentiments became widely expressed. No state, except perhaps Britain, was averse to a small war, but none wanted the sudden and unexpected arrival of a full-scale war throughout Europe. It was not possible to withdraw. Nationalist passions in all countries made this impossible. However, the entry of the United States into the war in 1917 was a considered act as a response to German submarine warfare. Thus, there was a miscalculation, if not outright misperception, on the German part. Greater restraint in submarine warfare might have kept the USA out of the war and made defeat less likely or at least less devastating.

The view that the war was deliberately started was particularly strongly held amongst the allies immediately after the war. The culprits, of course, were the Germans. The view was moderated as the years went by to be replaced by the view that it was everyone's fault or, alternatively, no-one's. However, in the 1960s, well after the Second World War, a German historian called Fritz Fischer (1967) argued in great detail that the German government had wanted war and deliberately provoked it. This created a great deal of controversy, particularly in Germany. Whatever the final verdict will be, Fischer has undoubtedly raised some uncomfortable points.

On the other hand, the inevitability school of thought argues that it was the structure of the international system that was at fault. There were a group of highly-armed states, many of which had grievances against other states. Some of these grievances derived from the later growth of some states in economic terms. Thus, Germany did not become unified until 1871 and had started its economic development later than Britain. A version of this stresses the importance of colonies and their role in Western economic development. Once the wealthier parts of the world had been colonized, the expansionary capitalist powers would begin to fight each other over the rest. The argument runs that, in such a tense world, a war of some sort would be bound to happen even if its precise nature would be hard to predict. The condition of Europe in 1914 was analogous to a dangerous bend in a road – an accident was bound to happen.

A variant of this structuralist argument is that Europe was going through a dangerous phase where a war was extremely likely. However, skill could have avoided it and perhaps steered the system back to a less unstable structure, where war was less likely to break out. Whatever its causes, the war itself was horrific in a way few had predicted beforehand.

The Interwar Period and the Second World War

After the First World War, the future of Europe and the world was defined by the *Treaty of Versailles* (1919). The victorious allies imposed serious penalties on the Germans who were in no position to object. It was supposed they could pay for the war by means of huge indemnities (scrapped in 1932) and their colonies were taken away from them. Despite the harsh treatment of the Germans, there was a lot of idealism to be found at the Versailles conference, even if much of it was sadly impracticable. President Wilson of the United States intended that the First World War should be the war to end wars and there is no reason to doubt his sincerity. He believed that a potent cause of war comes when nations are contained in states dominated by other nations. 'National self-determination' was the key to peace. Wilson was instrumental in redrawing the map of Eastern Europe so that state boundaries matched national divisions more closely than had earlier been the case when nationality had been often ignored. Unfortunately this was easier said than done as national groups do not live conveniently in clearly demarcated areas. He also pushed strongly for an international body, consisting of the major states, which would be a forum for discussion and the prevention of war. This was to be known as *The League of Nations*, and which was a new social institution of a sort never experienced before, though the philosopher Immanuel Kant had suggested something like it at the end of the eighteenth century. Unfortunately, though Wilson was its prime advocate, the United States Congress refused to join, which in itself was a serious blow to the League's credibility.

Thus was the path of the international world laid out in 1919. People hoped that the war would prove to have been an aberration, and a more benevolent version of the state system would continue. It was taken for granted that the state system in a fairly strong form would exist. Moves for world government or other systems remained on the political and intellectual periphery, where they remain to this day. People's hopes for peace proved ill founded. The succeeding years were appropriately characterized by E.H. Carr as 'The Twenty Years Crisis' in one of the most famous (and readable) books about international relations.

The situation in Germany was dreadful. The battering of the war accompanied by the burden of reparations was enormous. There was widespread poverty presided over by a weak but still democratic government. However, the condition of the economy improved some-what and by 1929 life was beginning to be bearable. Then came the world economic collapse, which hit Germany particularly badly, resulting in 4.4 million people being unemployed by the end of 1931. The number of unemployed grew to 6 million in the winter of 1932/33. This was not a recipe for political stability, nor was political stability achieved. From immediately after the First World War, right-wing nationalists, resentful at the provisions of the Treaty of Versailles, organized and prospered in the context of poverty and international humiliation. The Nazi party under Adolf Hitler became dominant amongst the nationalist right and in 1933, despite mixed electoral success, came to power. From then on it ruled as a harsh but probably popular totalitarian party which was totally ruthless towards its enemies. The Nazis believed in a doctrine of the superiority of the white Anglo-Saxons over everyone else. They were particularly hostile to the Jews and only slightly less to the Slavs. Black races were similarly deemed inferior but this was less of an issue as, in those days, there were very few black people in Europe. This was combined with an aggressive expansionism, which sought not merely to regain Germany's influence in the world but to make it the dominant power.

Germany was not the only, or even the first, regime of the authoritarian right to be dominant in the interwar years. Mussolini's Fascist party had come to power in Italy in 1922. Until late in the 1930s, many saw Mussolini not Hitler as the greatest threat, though the greater power of the German armed forces justifies the later picture of Hitler as being the dominant partner.

Even before the end of the war, the situation in Russia had altered dramatically. In 1917 there was a revolution against the authoritarian, monarchical regime. Strictly speaking, Russia had been replaced by the Soviet Union, which took in territories of the former Greater Russian Empire. This extended far beyond the boundaries of where the ethnic Russians, speaking Russian, lived. Initially the more moderate revolutionaries, called the Mencheviks, wanted a democratic monarchical system something like the British. They were also prepared to stay in the war. However, there was a second revolution later in the year which installed the Bolshevik or communist regime under Lenin. The Bolshevik government withdrew from the war on the grounds that it was an imperialist war and doing a lot of damage to Russia. (This last could hardly be denied.)

The Bolshevik regime had a very difficult start and, several times, was on the point of being overthrown. However, it survived and by 1922 was securely in power. Stalin came to power on the death of Lenin and the regime became more and more authoritarian. It imposed its rule harshly to the point of causing a severe famine in the interests of the collectivization of agriculture. The regime was detested by most other governments while the Nazis saw it as the primary enemy. However, there were many people, ignoring or ignorant of the regime's excesses, who saw it as the hope for the future. Though in the light of hindsight this may seem naive, given the alternatives which were on offer in the 1930s, some wishful thinking was understandable. Many people were no less naive about the Nazi regime. In its first twenty years, the Soviet Union was not expansionary, which distinguished it markedly from the Nazi regime. Given the hostility of much of the world, Stalin was extraordinarily reckless in his distrust of the military. He executed large numbers of senior and less senior officers for largely imaginary acts of treason which made the subsequent performance of the Soviet armed forces in resisting the German invasion all the more impressive and unexpected.

Hitler managed to violate many of the conditions of the Treaty of Versailles to the accompaniment of protests, but little else, from the rest of the world. As the 1930s progressed, Germany invaded in turn the Saar Land, Austria and Czechoslovakia. At each step it succeeded and the rest of Europe did nothing. Finally it invaded Poland for which there was practically no excuse. This brought Britain and France into war. In September 1939, just over twenty years after the end of the First World War, the Second World War started. This was to result in an even greater number of deaths.

Criticism of the so-called appeasement policy and the reluctance to stand up to Hitler earlier is more or less conventional wisdom. It is often argued that an earlier confrontation with Hitler would have prevented the war. This is hard to determine either way though it is undeniable that one can make good arguments for the view. However, it is also understandable why there was little enthusiasm for a strong anti-Hitler policy. The population of Europe was still suffering from the effects of the First World War and had little enthusiasm for a repetition. It is surprising that so many of the Germans were enthused by the concept of war, though perhaps resentment and poverty could give even the First World War an air of spurious romanticism. Further there was some feeling in Britain and France, not totally irrational, that the so-called *appeasement policy* might work. Germany had had a bad deal at Versailles. If it could be appeased by granting its legitimate demands, then all would be well. Germany would be a barrier against the now-Communist Soviet Union while many Europeans on the political right outside Germany looked fondly at the martial practices of the German Nazis and the Italian fascists. Thus, both the political left and the political right lacked enthusiasm for a strong anti-German policy until very late.

In the case of the First World War, the move to war came over the preceding years but the actual war itself started abruptly at the beginning of August 1914 with high casualty rates immediately. There was little violence prior to that. The Second World War was rather different. The first month of September 1939 saw heavy fighting and 150 000 casualties but after that the fighting dwindled. There were very few casualties until the middle of 1940 and the really major killing did not come until 1941 in the Soviet–German battles. However, for the whole decade prior to 1939 there had been a build-up of violence. Traditionally it is argued that it started in 1939 when Britain and France went to war with Germany and Italy, the *casus belli* being the invasion of Poland. In fact, there was little fighting at the beginning once the Germans had occupied Poland. There was a confused period when the Nazi–Soviet Pact between the two arch-enemies meant the Soviet Union acted in its own interests in Eastern Europe, though it did not actively fight the allies except ambiguously in Finland. In the Far East, Japan attacked the European colonies and linked up with Germany and Italy in the Axis bloc. Initially the United States was neutral and there was a lot of feeling there that the USA should keep out of the war. In 1941 Hitler attacked the Soviet Union in a surprise attack. Five months later the Japanese also carried out a surprise attack against the American navy at the American naval base of Pearl Harbor. By the end of 1941, all the combatants were involved.

The slow move to war, however, characterized the interwar period for many years. Japan was restive in the Far East. In 1931 it withdrew contemptuously from the League of Nations and proceeded to invade Manchuria, which, like Germany's expansionism, led to international protest but no action. This can be regarded as the beginning of the violence that developed into the Second World War. Actual violence in Europe started a little later. In Spain in 1936 some right-wing officers led by General Franco staged a revolution against the democratic government. The Fascists won in 1939 after a brutal civil war. Against expectation, however, the Franco regime did not join in the Second World War but remained neutral throughout. In a move to become an imperial power, the Italians invaded Abyssinia in 1935. There was an attempt to put pressure on the Italians by means of economic sanctions but these failed. All these can be seen as part and parcel of the Second World War, which was not so much a single war as a set of wars going on together, in which the allies were more or less accidentally thrown together. The war between Japan and America in the Pacific was not very closely related to the war between Germany and the Soviet Union in Eastern Europe. The United States and the Soviet Union were always suspicious of each other. Like the Second World War, the First World War can also be seen as a composite of many loosely related wars, but it differed from the Second in having a clear beginning and a clear end. Scholars differ as to whether this is a significant issue or not.

The dropping of two atomic bombs on the Japanese cities of Hiroshima and Nagasaki signalled the end of the Second World

War. The decision to do so was made by the new President of the United States, Harry Truman, who accepted the responsibility for what is still a controversial act. The war undeniably ended shortly afterwards, but the Japanese were about to sue for peace anyway, though it is not clear whether Truman knew this. In any case it was argued that a demonstration bomb could have been dropped perhaps at sea or at least that, having dropped the first, there was no need for the second. More lives were lost in at least three air raids using conventional bombs – on Dresden, Hamburg and Tokyo; however, the awesome destruction caused by a single bomb had a powerful symbolic effect quite apart from the potentiality (to be achieved in the next few years) of greater levels of destructive power. Nuclear weapons were to dominate the postwar period (see Chapter 9).

The Post-1945 Era

Contrary to people's hopes, the end of the Second World War did not herald an age of peace any more than the end of its predecessor had. The modern era provides a catalogue of war as depressing as any previous period.

Tensions between the Soviet Union and the United States, always present, became evident almost immediately the Second World War was over. America and the Western European countries viewed the Soviet dominance over Eastern Europe as expansionism. The Soviet Union, as well as many other critics, regarded the American dominance in other parts of the world, such as Latin America, as American Imperialism. The Cold War began shortly after the hot one had ended; its beginnings can be detected in the war itself and, indeed, back to the Russian Revolution of 1917.

Briefly, Western Europe was freed from German rule by an army of Americans, British, Australian, Canadian and many other contingents. Virtually all European countries of both West and East had their representatives. This army got about halfway through Germany when it met the Soviet troops who had driven the German armies from the western part of the Soviet Union and Eastern Europe. Broadly, the West retained control of the areas it had conquered and likewise with the Soviet Union. Berlin, which was to be a constant source of tension, at times very acute, was divided by the victorious powers. There were elections in some Eastern European countries, such as Poland, but the resulting governments were supplanted by communist regimes sympathetic to the Soviet Union and were of doubtful legitimacy. The last to become communist was Czechoslovakia where there was a coup in 1948. The so-called 'iron curtain' divided Europe and continued to do so for the following four decades.

The Second World War left a world which was dominated by the two superpowers of the USA and Soviet Union. There were big differences though. The USA was the only major combatant not to have experienced fighting on its own soil nor to have experienced bombing. Many European countries such as France had been occupied by the Nazis as had large parts of the Soviet Union. Europe, Japan, China and the Soviet Union were devastated and impoverished. Despite the enormous costs of fighting the War, and the distortions imposed on it by a high level of military production, the US economy was in good shape. The Soviet Union, in contrast, was badly damaged and struggling to be a superpower. Further, the USA had the atomic bomb whereas the Soviet Union did not. This did not stop the Soviet Union retaining large armed forces and keeping a firm military control over Eastern Europe.

The hostility between the Western powers and the Soviet Union grew. Each became deeply suspicious of the other (and in neither case without some justification). In 1949 the Soviet Union exploded an atomic bomb and the US nuclear monopoly came to an end. This came just a few weeks after the Western countries had formed the North Atlantic Treaty Organization (NATO) consisting of the USA, Canada, Britain, France and other Western European states. The Alliance was founded to combat any further expansion by the Soviet Union in Europe. The East responded in 1955 with the Warsaw Treaty Organization (WTO) more commonly referred to as the Warsaw Pact. The British acquired their own nuclear bomb in 1952 and the French in 1964. Both had a desire to appear major powers; a motive which they deplored in others.

The Cold War was not only a European phenomenon. In 1949, after a long civil war against an increasingly corrupt government, the Communists took control of China and proclaimed the People's Republic of China (PRC). It had barely done so when a major conflict arose in Korea. Like much of Europe, Korea was divided into two parts, the North under Communist and the South under American control. The North attacked the South. Quickly many countries under the leadership of the USA and under the cover of the United Nations joined in on the side of the South. The fortunes of war changed from time to time and the Chinese came in on the side of the North. It was not until 1953 and after 1.6 million people had been killed, mainly Chinese and North Korean, that an armistice was signed leaving the border where it was and where it remains to this day. It was a major war and is often referred to as a 'proxy war'. The United States fought directly but the Soviet Union carefully kept out (though it provided armaments) and fought by proxy.

The Cold War remained cold, at least between the superpowers, even in the Korean War, and American and Soviet troops never directly faced each other in combat then or in the future. It is probable, though not certain, that no American killed a Russian in combat or vice versa. We know this now, in retrospect, but there were various times during the course of the Cold War when people thought that some time a hot war would break out, not least at the time of the Korean War itself. The worst occasion was the Cuban Missile Crisis in 1962 (see p. 29) when nuclear war seemed imminent to many people.

There were great fears in the West that China and the Soviet Union, as ideological allies, would also be military allies. No doubt many in the Soviet Union had hopes that this would be so. However, it proved incorrect. Tensions between the two communist giants appeared quickly and there were times when they seemed more likely to go to war with each other than with any Western power.

The Chinese were involved in another major proxy war with the United States in the Vietnam (or Indochina) War. France had been the colonial overlord of Indochina but withdrew after a series of military defeats in 1954. Vietnam was also divided into North and South which proved a very unstable solution. It seemed that the whole of Vietnam would become communist. Unlike many other cases of communist control, the communists had a lot of support and would probably have been able to form a legitimate government. The USA stepped in where the French had left off and the infamous Vietnam War resulted. This did not end until 1975 when the communists and nationalists took over. It is the only war the United States has unambiguously lost. This, along with the persistent unpopularity of the War, had enormous impact on American attitudes. In the meantime, China became the fifth nuclear power by exploding an atomic bomb in 1964.

In the early part of the twentieth century, Europe and the countries surrounding the North Atlantic dominated the world arena, at least in the eyes (and history books) of their inhabitants. As the century progressed, this perspective became harder to maintain, helped, course, by the fact that the USA had a large Pacific seaboard as well as the one on the Atlantic. China looks towards the Pacific. Japan is a major Pacific country and, despite blemishes such as the excessive corruption and a severe slowing down of its economy, has been one of the success stories of the last half of the century. Devastated in defeat at the end of the Second World War, it has had remarkable economic growth and become one of the world's leading economies. It has stayed out of the arms races which, until recently, have hampered the other industrial economies. Initially the USA, which was afraid Japan would again become a militaristic power, imposed disarmament. Subsequently, the Japanese found it very much to their economic advantage and were happy to remain a largely non-military state. The Australians and New Zealanders see themselves more and more as members of a Pacific community rather than as an overseas branch of a European, primarily British, community. Australian republican sentiment and a coolness to the British monarchy preceded similar movements in Britain. A less vivid, but perhaps more significant sign was that, by the 1960s, Australian trade with Japan exceeded trade with Britain.

Not all the military activity of the states involved in the Cold War was to do with the Cold War. The Western European countries ended the Second World War with their very substantial empires largely intact. Over the quarter of a century following 1945, these empires became independent with varying degrees of bad grace on the part of the imperial powers. The British, French, Dutch and Belgians all used their armies to try and resist this. The most violent war was in Algeria where the French resisted Algerian independence for a long time and almost at the cost of a civil war in France itself. Decolonization, one of the most significant developments of the postwar era, is discussed in greater detail in Chapter 5.

Decolonization resulted in the creation of many new states. This made the world a very different place in 1995 from 1945. In 1945 there were 70 independent states, in 1990 there were 168, by the millennium there were almost 200. Most of these came from formerly colonial territories. Earlier expansions in the number of states had come through decolonization. In 1800 only 22 of today's states existed in any recognizable form. By 1850 this had expanded to 45 with most of them being the states of Latin America, then newly independent from Spain and Portugal.

Since 1990, the number of states has expanded further but for different reasons. Several states have now broken up into smaller states. Thus the former Soviet Union has broken up into its constituent republics calling themselves the Commonwealth of Independent States (CIS). Yugoslavia has broken up in a particularly violent way. Czechoslovakia has broken up more peacefully into the Czech Republic and the Slovak Republic. Until recently, the break-up of states has been a rare phenomenon. States have tended to amalgamate rather than disintegrate. The ones that broke up did so for rather special reasons. Germany divided in 1945 because the victors in the war insisted. Bangladesh split from the rest of Pakistan in 1972, but it is doubtful whether the original Pakistan was viable in the first place. However, in the last few years, states have split up more readily. Quite what the long-run significance of this will be, and which other states will follow them, is still unclear and may well prove to be one of the fascinating problems of the next few years. We should, perhaps, try and find out why some states split up relatively peacefully whereas others, as is the case in the former Yugoslavia, seem to do so with the maximum of acrimony.

The Collapse of the Soviet Union and the End of the Cold War

The Cold War seemed as though it would never end. The USA and Soviet Union seemed to be stuck in a stalemate of perpetual rivalry. Then, under Gorbachev, the Soviet Union started to liberalize its political system and endeavour to get its ailing economy moving. The change got out of hand and the whole edifice of the Soviet Union quickly collapsed and the Cold War with it. This was very remarkable as the Cold War had been the centre-point of international relations during the whole of the post-Second-World-War period. This centre-point had suddenly become a historical curiosity. Few analysts predicted this dramatic change, which is an embarrassment to the profession.

By the 1980s, the economy of the Soviet Union was in a bad way. Though successful in a handful of militarily-related projects such as space research, it was poor at providing consumer goods. The level of economic efficiency was low. It operated a so-called *command economy* in which the production of goods was specified in a complex central plan rather than being decided by market mechanisms. This was not working well and many socialist economists were concerned at the lack of flexibility and concern for any sort of pricing system. Several East European states were getting restive. This was particularly true of Poland where the anti-government trade union movement, Solidarity, became prominent in 1980, making the life of the Communist government very difficult. Also in 1980, the Soviet Union had sent troops into Afghanistan to support the communist government of the country. It found itself caught in a difficult and costly war with guerrilla troops who had been well-armed by the USA.

It is tempting to say that, in this situation, something had to happen though this is easier to say with the wisdom of hindsight. Certainly few were prepared for the scale of what happened.

In 1985, Mikhail Gorbachev became General Secretary of the Soviet Communist Party, which meant he held the central power in the Soviet Union. He was a keen reformer. He not only realized that the present situation in the Soviet Union was intolerable but he wanted change. It was not something forced on him. He embarked on a path of drastic reform, not only of the economy but also of the political system which he sought to open up and make more genuinely democratic. He was more successful politically than economically. The command economy, which, for all its inadequacies, provided the basic means of life, broke down and the market systems replacing it were chaotic. In the winter of 1989/90 the standard of living fell dramatically. At about the same time, the communist regimes of Eastern Europe also abandoned the struggle and became more pluralist in their political complexion. As the Soviet Union descended further into both political and economic chaos, opposition mounted. A 'coup' by the old guard removed Gorbachev in 1991. Another reformer, Boris Yeltsin 'rescued' Gorbachev and in doing so replaced him. By now, and rather suddenly, the various constituent states of the Soviet Union were demanding independence. Russia was the largest of the republics and historically had always been dominant, so independence often meant independence from Russia as much as independence from the Union. This desire for independence, and the vigorous and at times extreme nationalism which went with it, emerged very quickly and was another of the many unexpected features of this whole dramatic situation. The independence of the constituent states was quickly achieved. In 1991, the former Union of Soviet Socialist Republics was replaced by the Commonwealth of Independent States (CIS) with the stress on 'independent'. The reality was a collection of independent, not always very friendly, states espousing a not very successful form of capitalism. The ideological battle of the Cold War had ended. Further, the power of the former Soviet Union was vastly reduced. Russia was generally recognized as the central actor in the former Soviet Union. It occupied the permanent seat on the Security Council of the United Nations, which had earlier been that of the Soviet Union, and still had the lion's share of the nuclear weapons. However, it was no longer a superpower and the military tensions of the previous decades were seen, for the moment at least, to be over. It is hard to exaggerate the difference in attitudes that this had led to as this long episode drifts into history.

The Middle East since 1945

The new states, even in the earlier period, were not just the result of the end of colonial regimes. A very important case, which is *sui generis,* is that of Israel which formally came into being as an independent state in 1948. The Jews, though originally coming from Palestine, have been a stateless nation for many centuries though there was always a tradition that one day they would return to a state of Israel. Thus the prayer at the religious festival of Passover that they would all meet 'next year in Jerusalem'. A few Jews had always remained in Palestine and there had been some Jewish immigration throughout the twentieth century, accelerating in the period after the Second World War. The political doctrine of Zionism, viewing a Jewish state to be something to be aimed for as an achievable political goal, became significant from the late nineteenth century. By the end of the Second World War this looked like being a practical possibility. There were now many Jews in Palestine. Further, the horrendous experience of the Holocaust, where the Nazi regime massacred 6 million Jewish people (and many others beside), created great sympathy for the Jews in general and for the notion of a Jewish state. The late 1940s was the one time when the notion of setting up a Jewish state would be greeted with much sympathy. It had its opponents. The Soviet Union was not enthusiastic. Ernest Bevin, the British foreign secretary, accepted the creation of Israel but hardly welcomed it. However, given the anti-Semitism which is sometimes active and seemingly always latent in many societies, both

East and West, a Jewish state had probably as popular a start as ever such a state was likely to get.

Unfortunately the creation of a Jewish state neglected the Arabs who lived in what was Palestine and which became Israel. In their anxiety to gain friends in the First World War, the British who were dominant in the area had made sets of inconsistent promises to the Jews and the Arabs about the future of Palestine. Both sides could and did appeal to Britain, which managed to gain the hostility of both. The Arabs of the area gained the support of the Arab world, and to a considerable extent the non-Arab Moslem world such as Iran as well. There has been tension at best and war at worst between various Arab states and Israel from the beginning. Jerusalem has the misfortune of being a Holy City for three different religions – Islam, Judaism and Christianity. Though ostensibly religions of love, this seems to have guaranteed that it be a centre of dissension and violence.

Today the dissension is as acute as ever. Crucial on the one hand is the desire of Israel to be guaranteed its survival against many in the region who want to see it destroyed. Crucial on the other is the desire for a genuinely independent state of Palestine. The positions seem irreconcilable. On both sides there are extremists, mainly religiously motivated, who want to exacerbate the conflict. Hard-line Jewish settlers have built provocative settlements on the West Bank, against all agreements, which they justify on biblical grounds. Hard-line Islamic zealots believe that by carrying out acts of terrorism they will somehow destroy the Jewish state. The extremists make intolerable the position of the moderates on both sides who might be interested in compromise.

The Middle East was the scene of a curiously anachronistic set of events in 1956 known as the Suez War. The British and the French were at that time pro-Israel or, perhaps even more pointedly, anti-Egypt. In Egypt a group of moderately modernizing army officers had replaced the docile and compliant ruler of Egypt. As nationalists, they wished to transform the formal independence from the western states, in particular Britain and France who, between them, had dominated Egypt for the previous century or so, into something more substantial. The British Government in particular had rather implausibly identified Nasser, the President of Egypt, as some future Middle-Eastern Hitler. The Egyptian government nationalized the Suez Canal, which ran through Egyptian territory. This was the last straw for the British and the French. In secret bargains, they arranged that the Israelis should attack Egypt and that the British and French should then 'rescue' the Israelis and give the British and French the excuse to topple Nasser. Unfortunately the Israeli's military success made the idea of rescue implausible, though the British and French tried it nevertheless. The whole war came to an embarrassing end when the Americans, annoyed at the whole business, refused to let the World Bank bail the British out of the foreign-exchange crisis which the war had imposed on an already fragile British economy. The whole thing petered out with a United Nations force to spare the British and French blushes. The incident seemed an outdated return to the days of gunboat diplomacy, which the British and French could no longer sustain. Though it was very controversial in Britain at the time, it is now regarded almost universally as either, at best, embarrassing or, at worst, wicked.

Further Reading and Sources

An overview of the century which is witty and controversial is by Eric Hobsbawm, *The Age of Extremes: the Short Twentieth Century, 1914–1991* (London: Abacus, 1994). To emphasise the controversial nature of these topics, G. Arrighi calls his book *The Long Twentieth Century: Money, Power and the Origins of Our Times* (London: Verso, 1994). Covering a broad sweep, but spending about two-thirds of the time in the twentieth century and speculating beyond, is Paul Kennedy, *Rise and Fall of the Great Powers* (London: Unwin Hyman, 1988). He does so very readably. The figures regarding the British economy were taken from Paul Hirst and Graham Thompson's *Globalisation in Question* (Cambridge: Polity Press, 1996).

Immanuel Kant's *Perpetual Peace*, translated by Lewis L. Beck (New York: Bobbs-Merrill, 1957), originally published 1795, is unexpectedly easy to read.

For the origins of the First World War, see James Joll, *The Origins of the First World War* (London: Longman, 1992, 2nd edn), from whom statistics of unemployment in Germany come. Also Gordon Martel, *The Origins of the First World War* (Harlow: Longman Paul, 1996, 2nd edn); Hew Strachan, *The First World War – Volume 1: To Arms* (Oxford: Oxford University Press, 2001); Gerard de Groot, *The First World War* (Basingstoke: Palgrave, 2000); and David Stevenson, *The*

Outbreak of the First World War: 1914 in Perspective (London: Macmillan – now Palgrave Macmillan, 1997).

On the Second World War, A.J.P. Taylor provoked just about everyone with *The Origins of the Second World War* (New York: Scribner, 1996). A later assessment by various scholars is edited by G. Martel, *The Origins of the Second World War Reconsidered: The A.J.P. Taylor Debate after Twenty Five Years* (New York: Routledge, 1999). E.H. Carr, *The Twenty Year's Crisis* (Basingstoke: Palgrave, 2001, 3rd edn), originally published in 1946, can be read in this context (see Chapter 6). Statistical information comes from *Demography of War: Oxford Companion to the Second World War* (Oxford: Oxford University Press, 2000).

For a general and detailed picture of the post-1945 period, Peter Calvocoressi's *World Politics 1945–2000* (London: Longman, 2001, 8th edn) is very scholarly and gives a good factual account though very much from the point of view of states. It is very useful for reference. An analytical collection of essays edited by Ngaire Woods, *Explaining International Relations Since 1945* (Oxford: Oxford University Press 1996), takes the task of 'explaining' seriously.

There is a vast literature on the Cold War. Its origins are discussed in M. McCauley, *The Origins of the Cold War, 1941–48* (London: Longman, 1996, 2nd edn). A collection of essays is edited by M.P. Leffler and D.S. Painter as *The Origins of the Cold War* (London: Routledge, 1994). For origins and the earlier part of the Cold War, see Michael Dockrill, *The Cold War 1956–63* (London: Macmillan – now Palgrave Macmillan, 1988). John Lewis Gaddis, who wrote influentially on the Cold War when it was in progress, has written the best account of its end to date in John Lewis Gaddis, *The United States and the End of the Cold War: Implications, Reconsiderations, Provocations* (Oxford: Oxford University Press, 1994). See also his more recent book, *We Now Know: Rethinking Cold War History* (Oxford: Oxford University Press, 1998).

5

Imperialism, Post-Imperialism and Neo-Imperialism

Empire and Colonies

A conspicuous feature of the nineteenth and early twentieth centuries was the way in which several of the Western European countries such as France, Britain, Germany, the Netherlands and Belgium took control of large parts of the world. Thus, at its peak, the British Empire alone consisted of more than one-fifth of the world's land surface. Some states such as France and Britain had earlier imperial ventures, though Germany, as effectively a new state, was a new comer. However, the burst of expansion in the nineteenth century was remarkable. Little remains today of formal empire in the sense of territory directly ruled by a foreign power. However, there are those who hold that empires exist as much as before but that now imperial control is more insidious and circumspect. Whether this is true or not, recent imperial history has left such a mark on the present world that an awareness of it is necessary in order to understand present structures.

Imperialism is a recurring theme throughout history. Some societies have expanded far from their boundaries and ruled over populations vastly larger than their own domestic populations. The Roman Empire, the Greek Empire, the Spanish and Portuguese Empires are well-known instances. Clearly, very different sorts of societies embark on these adventures. These were not just marginal increases of neighbouring territory but involved the domination of territory much vaster than the domestic territory and of societies which were far from the metropolitan state in both distance and culture.

Imperialism does not come in a standard form. There are different ways in which societies expand. I use the word 'society' and not 'state' or 'government' deliberately. While the state is associated with formal imperialism, it is only loosely associated with other forms of expansionism, some of which are not normally referred to as imperialism. The tightest form of imperialism is *colonialism*. A colony is a territory ruled directly by the imperial power. The laws are laid down at the centre and administered by its agents in the colonial territory. The more senior agents are usually nationals of the imperial state. In the case of the British colonies in Africa, the Colonial Office was involved. This ministry was directly responsible to the British parliament which, of course, included no members from colonial societies. Other colonial powers were similarly organized. The Roman Empire was governed by Roman Governors with great local power.

Control can be exercised without overt colonialism, though such control is usually weaker. Many Indian princedoms in the late nineteenth and early twentieth century, were ostensibly independent, though they had British residents who advised the Princes. The Princes usually found it prudent to accept this advice. There are still weaker forms of control today, most commonly referred to as *neo-colonialism* (or new colonialism) though, in fact, the general nature of the institution is far from new. The central power does not exert overt political control over another territory though it exerts influence over the government whenever its interests are threatened. These interests might be either military or economic, as in the relationships of Britain and the United States to nineteenth-century China. The relationship between the United States and many Latin American states is a twentieth-century example.

The prime characteristic of imperialism is asymmetry. There is an asymmetric relationship between the imperial power and its client. The imperial power can control aspects of the client's behaviour in its own interests where there is no reciprocal influence by the client. However, the degree of control by imperial powers varies enormously according to the nature of the imperial structure. Imperialism is not a phenomenon that exists or does not exist. There is a spectrum which ranges from centrally-run colonialism to loose influence over an economy.

The expansion of societies, which becomes entangled with the expansion of states and hence imperialism, is a major feature of the international scene when viewed over the years. We shall attend to three questions. First, why do states become imperial? Second, how do they survive and why do some survive very much longer than others? Finally, why do they decline? It is important to stress the long history of empire. It is not a recent phenomenon. However, we shall concentrate on recent manifestations from the nineteenth century onwards with glances back.

Imperial Expansion

The expansion of Europe during the nineteenth century was spectacular when the orgy of colonialism was one of the most conspicuous features of the international scene. Most of the Western European powers quickly expanded their dominion such that most of sub-Saharan Africa was under their control and much of North Africa as well. The British rule in India was strengthened, while the Far East came further under the domination of the Western countries, though less in the form of overt colonialism. Some of the colonial powers were no novices in this. France and Britain, in particular, had a long history of colonial adventure, while the Netherlands had a long interest in trade and occasional conquest. The vigorous expansion of the nineteenth century appeared to some to be just a new, if a rather energetic, move in an old dance. However, the speed and extent of the new burst of imperialism suggests that it may have been stimulated by some features of the nineteenth century.

Spain and Portugal, two of the oldest of the still active Imperial powers were, perhaps oddly, going into decline except for some small incursions by Spain in North Africa. Latin America had been dominated by natives of the Iberian peninsula from the end of the fifteenth century onwards. Columbus, though probably an Italian from Genoa, was a servant of the Spanish monarchy. However, the nineteenth century was marked by independence movements. The Latin American countries disentangled themselves from Spain and Portugal who showed little interest in the nineteenth-century expansionism.

Given that the states in question started their expansion within a few decades of each other, we should look at the characteristics of the nineteenth and possibly eighteenth century for hints as to what led to the release of so much energy. The obvious thing is the Industrial Revolution. This started in Britain in the late eighteenth century and was quickly followed in several West European states and, of course,

North America. Capitalists, it appeared, quickly tired of their home markets as a source of supplies, of industrial capital and of markets.

The English economist, Hobson, formulated one such theory in 1902. Lenin was influenced by Hobson's work and reinterpreted it in a Marxist form. Briefly, the theory went like this. In the early stages of an industrial revolution, there were plenty of lucrative profit opportunities close to home. As the economy developed, these became less profitable and higher profits could be earned by investment abroad where industrialization was less developed. Consider the case of railways. In their early days there were plenty of British cities which could be linked up, and building railways was a profitable if highly competitive and risky business. However, there are limits to this. Only so many railways are required and, owing to the competitive building of two rival railways between important towns, there had been a high failure rate in the industry. The next step, then, was for entrepreneurs to look for countries without railways and build them there. Financiers could make big profits building them while engineering companies could do well from their actual manufacture. Railway lines need to be bought as well as large supplies of rolling stock. In general, the virgin territory was more profitable than the now well-stocked home base. In the case of railways, it was not only the less developed countries that were the object of railway building. British companies were heavily involved in the building of French railways in the middle of the nineteenth century. The Argentinian railways were largely built, owned and run by British companies. Africa, India and most of the Far East acquired railway systems financed in Western Europe and with material bought and manufactured there. Railways are just one case. The vigorous Western European economies expanded rapidly all over the world, and in particular to the poorer parts of it.

Investors were anxious to keep as much control of their investments as they possibly could and in particular they did not want to lose them. Though profits were generally good, severe losses were also experienced, either because the investment failed or because the borrowers defaulted. An obvious way to reduce the risks of investment was to take political control of the area it was in. This was neither possible nor necessary when the investments were in places with stable political structures like France or the USA, which imported vast amounts of British capital. However, it was easily possible in areas that were not ruled by modern forms of governments, such as most of Africa. Thus imperialism developed to defend and promote economic activity in

general though, particularly in the Leninist version, it was to protect
capital in particular. The desire for direct political control to protect
investments should not be exaggerated. In fact, between 1815 and 1880
only one-sixth of the financial credit accumulated by Britain was in the
Empire. However, the desire for political control was a factor, particularly in parts of the world where there was not a well-organized state
system.

The British led the imperial rush. This could be expected. As we
noted above, Britain was the first with the industrial revolution but
most of Western Europe followed. They were going through a phase of
vigorous industrialization at much the same time which, as Lenin's
theory would suggest, led to a vigorous imperial expansion shortly
afterwards. This explains why Spain and Portugal were not conspicuous imperialists at this stage. They were also laggards in the industrial
revolution.

Lenin went further. Imperial expansion by several states could carry
on simultaneously provided that there was plenty of lucrative and
easily conquered territory available. At some point this would be used
up and at this point the imperial powers would grow hostile to each
other and eventually fight. In Lenin's view, this was a major factor
behind the First World War.

The cases of Russia and the United States can be explained in this
context even if neither joined in the rush for colonies, at least in places
like Africa. The United States had a very dynamic economy and should
have been an imperial power according to this theory. In effect it was.
Within the United States and associated territories there was a vast
expanse of land for immigrants to develop. While the Europeans were
compelled to move South, the Americans simply moved West. By the
end of the nineteenth century, even this was proving inadequate. Along
with many European states, the United States developed a strong
interest in China. Though direct political rule was impracticable due to
the strength of the Chinese political system, at least compared to
African tribal ones, considerable control and influence were exerted
on the Chinese government. The United States was also constantly
interested in Latin America, which at least in the twentieth century,
involved greater degrees of control, though there was no mass colonization.

A related tale can be told about Russia. There was a vast expansion
of Russia proper to other areas such as the Ukraine, which came under
Russian domination. As with the United States, it was a case of

internal expansion. The nineteenth century was the era of 'Greater Russia,' beloved by Russian nationalists but less eagerly welcomed by other parts of the growing state. Greater Russia roughly coincided with what later became the Soviet Union. The Russian industrial revolution came late and its linkage with the internal expansion is less clear than with the other states we have considered – ironically, perhaps, given Lenin's role in formulating the theory.

To try to explain even nineteenth-century imperialism purely in terms of economic expansionism conceals many other features. The theory presupposes the states were willing to be a part of the acquisition of colonies for purposes of economic expansion. In fact, the political will was often weak. In Britain, imperialism was not always very popular. It seemed to many that a lot of money was being spent on an empire that was of doubtful value to the average Briton. If merchants wanted to trade abroad, so be it, but there seemed no need to acquire an empire in the process. Indeed, imperialism became a word of abuse (as it was to become again a century later). Only towards the end of the century did it become a popular cause and then as much for nationalist reasons as anything else. The governments were not always the passive servants of the investing classes as the more extreme versions of Marxist theory would have us believe. In the end they became enthusiasts but it took some time. It started with trade, quickly followed by the missionaries while the state came afterwards, often reluctant converts to the doctrine of imperialism.

Just as economic expansionism did not necessarily involve colonialism or even much political control, so not all colonialism can be explained in economic terms. The initial motive might have been economic, which remained a continuing factor, but in due course colonialism became an issue in its own right. Power political factors came into play and the motives tended to be to keep another country out of an area as much as to be in it oneself. Thus, throughout the nineteenth century Britain made intermittent and largely unsuccessful attempts to gain control of Afghanistan. It did not particularly want Afghanistan for its own sake, but it was most anxious that the Russians should not get control and thus be able to threaten India. The imperial wars in Afghanistan are more readily explained strategically than economically. In Africa the economic factors were always significant but, for the British, stopping the French or the Germans was always a factor and had a distinct strategic motive. The other powers, of course, thought analogously about the British.

The missionaries should not be ignored in any attempt to describe imperialism. Many religious organizations were enthusiasts for converting the heathen, something the nineteenth-century imperialists shared with sixteenth-century Iberian imperialism. In many places they were not very successful. In 1931 only 1.3 per cent of Indians were Christian and many of them were descendants of early Christian groups, which long predated the British. The numerous American missionaries in China fared little better. Nevertheless, the hope of making religious conversions inspired many imperialists and was a source of support for imperial ventures from a wide section of the population.

The Stability of Empires

A remarkable characteristic of many empires, from the Roman Empire to the British, is how a very small number of members from the imperial state controlled large populations in the dominated society. There were only about 1500 Englishmen in the Indian Civil Service (ICS) (women were not allowed). Even after the Indian Mutiny (not a name Indian nationalists favour) of 1857, which badly shook British self-confidence, there were only 65 000 British troops in India (many of whom were Scottish or Irish), making up less than a third of the army of 205 000. The rest of the troops were Indian. They ruled a population that was estimated at that time to be around 200 million. In the case of the Roman Empire, a handful of Romans controlled Western Europe for centuries as well as substantial parts of the Mediterranean area including North Africa. How did they manage it? One charitable interpretation is that the benefits of colonial rule were so clear that the ruled gave their consent to the situation, a consent which legitimized the political structure. One does not have to be very cynical to have some doubts about this interpretation. Nevertheless, it was probably believed by most people in Britain prior to the Second World War.

One method of imperial domination is by direct rule, in a way which destroys the original political structure of the colony. This effectively happened in many, though not all, African societies. It was more obviously the case with the European settlers and the native America Indians. Another form of control is structural. One account of this is known as the *structural theory of imperialism*, which runs as follows.

Within all societies the distribution of power and wealth among people is unequal. Those with power tend to have wealth and those with wealth tend to have power, though the correlation is not perfect. There may be some altruists who use power for the benefit of the powerless, but, for the most part, states are run primarily in the interests of the powerful and wealthy. While it masks many finer distinctions, it is convenient to divide a society into a *core* of the powerful and a *periphery* of the powerless. Similarly, states can be divided into powerful, or core, states and the less powerful, or peripheral, states where the former dominate the latter in an imperial or semi-imperial relationship. If we go back to the late nineteenth century, when imperialism was at its peak, there were core states such as Britain and France, and peripheral areas such as Africa or the Indian subcontinent. The peripheral states also had their core and periphery. In a peripheral state, the core had traditionally ruled over the periphery and the methods of social control were well established.

In many cases the approach was more subtle. The élites in central society made common cause with élites in the peripheral society giving them major benefits while taking ultimate control of the society. However, the underlying structure of the society remained the same. By controlling some central nodes in the social structure, the society, at what one might call the nuts-and-bolts level, was left intact. The procedures of social control often remained much the same. If they were altered, they were supported by the native élites of the peripheral society who could see that there were many benefits to be enjoyed under imperial rule. The masses were not always greatly affected. Thus, in the eighteenth century, Southern India had been occupied by Muslim invaders from the North, who were replaced by the British. Their rulers became paler and spoke yet another language, but not much else altered as far as the Southern Indians were concerned.

The common interests of the élites were reinforced by vigorous socialization of certain key groups. The many Indian troops in the British army in India, largely officered by British officers, were quickly socialized into disciplined loyalty to the regiment and other groupings, which detached them from their religious and latent national loyalties. In this manner the British could control India. By seizing the focal points of social control, they did so remarkably inexpensively. The mystery of the few controlling the many is thus quite easily explained.

India was not the only part of the Empire where this form of social control was imposed, though it was the place where it was most thoroughly applied. Lord Lugard, the Governor of the then British Colony of Nigeria from 1912 to 1919, explicitly adopted this policy (it is perhaps relevant to note he was born in India).

The British and other Europeans were not the first imperialists to use this form of social control. The Romans were adept at something similar. They had also socialized key élites and had largely native armies doing the work of control. A high honour for a native of, say, Britain was to achieve the status of Roman citizen, which was given to those particularly loyal to the Roman cause. When the British in their turn became imperial conquerors, an occasional knighthood was bestowed on especially distinguished members of colonial territories.

This model adapts well to circumstances beyond that of strict colonial domination. Thus, the asymmetric power relationships, which existed for many years between Britain and France, on the one hand, and Egypt, on the other, were of this sort. On a larger scale, many of the Latin American states were clearly dominated by the United States. The states involved were certainly independent in a formal sense. However, there were undoubtedly dependency relationships between the powerful and less powerful states. The élites in, say, Chile, strongly identified with those of the United States and were unlikely to take any action seriously detrimental to the United States. The virtue of this approach is that imperialism can be seen as a spectrum from high to low dependency rather than an all or nothing affair.

The Decline of Empires

During the late nineteenth century and up until the Second World War, the Western empires flourished. In 1945 the British Empire still covered a larger area and ruled over more people than any previous empire in history, though its peak had been passed when southern Ireland achieved Home Rule in 1922. Within a quarter of a century it was virtually extinct, as were the empires of the other European powers. On some interpretations (such as that of Edward Gibbon in *The Decline and Fall of the Roman Empire*) it took the Roman Empire a thousand years to fade away. Why did the twentieth-century empires collapse so quickly? In Africa, many of the colonies lasted barely a generation. Northern Rhodesia was annexed, or taken under formal political control, by the British in 1889. It gained independence in 1963. Nyasaland (now Malawi) was annexed in 1893 and became independent in 1962. Uganda was annexed between 1890 and 1894 and also became independent in 1962. Admittedly the British had been prominent in the areas beforehand but rarely for more than a few years. For much of Africa, formal empire came and went in well under a century and in less than the lifetime of some people.

The story of the British Empire was never one of unequivocal growth. The colonies which became the United States gained independence in the War of Independence as long ago as 1784. Colonies dominated by a white, English-speaking settlers class became 'Dominions'. These were self-ruling, though acknowledging the British monarch as Head of State. Thus, Canada, Australia and New Zealand became independent without wars. Canada became a dominion in 1867, New Zealand in 1907. Australia preferred the word 'Commonwealth' in 1901. Ireland was always a special case. The Irish were Catholic and, in the rural areas in the nineteenth century, spoke their own language. The culture was Celtic and very different from the Anglo-Saxon English. The British had always regarded the Catholic Irish with deep distrust and Irish independence as equivalent to treason. Ireland, it was felt, was a part of the United Kingdom. Perhaps because of this, British behaviour in Ireland was especially brutal and one of the least defensible aspects of British imperialism. The problem was complicated by the Protestants in the North and the dominance of the Protestant ruling class in the South. These, for the most part, had little sympathy with Irish Gaelic nationalism (though, ironically, many of the Irish independence leaders were from the Protestant élite). An attempted solution to the problem came in 1922 with the partition of Ireland. The Republic of Ireland became independent of the rest of Britain, but the Protestant northern counties remained part of the United Kingdom. It seemed a good attempt at a solution but, as is generally known, much discontent still exists, though mainly in the North. Independence, in any case, was a white privilege. The nineteenth century was a time when the black and brown members of the human race found themselves increasingly the subjects of white rulers.

The European empires contained some of the seeds of its own destruction, as we can illustrate again with the example of India. The élites of India, perhaps more than any other parts of the Empire, had come into close contact with the British élites and had absorbed many aspects of the culture. Pandit Nehru, the first Prime Minster of India, was educated at Harrow, a leading British private school (or 'public school' as these very expensive fee-paying schools were oddly known at the time). He followed this with a university education at Cambridge. Nehru spoke English with the authentic patrician accent of the English upper classes. When he was Prime Minister, he is alleged to have commented ironically that he was the last Englishman to rule India. Nehru was not unusual amongst wealthy Indians. Many of the richer Indian intellectuals spent some years in Britain. Krishna Menon was a Labour member of the St Pancras Borough Council in London from 1934 until 1947, when he became the first Indian foreign minister. While this indicates a close association of the Indian élites with Britain, it could and did have mixed consequences. The Indians tended to associate with the political left, but it was on the political left that there were growing doubts about the legitimacy of Empire. The Indian intellectuals both influenced and were influenced by this debate. After the First World War, a major theme at the Versailles Conference was the legitimacy of nationalism and the desirability of the nation state. But if the nation state was the core of legitimacy in Europe, why not elsewhere – such as India? Thus, nationalism and the desire for independence were fuelled by the linking of élites in India and Britain, one of the strongest features of imperialism. The close association of many of the Congress Party politicians with Britain – and the Congress party was the ruling party for many years in independent India – was conspicuous. The linking of the independence movements with anti-imperial sentiment was most pronounced in the case of the Indian subcontinent but the other colonies were not immune. If nationalism was good in Europe, it was only a matter of time before people realized that it should be good for the rest of the world also.

The disenchantment of the metropolitan élites with the colonial system might be a partial explanation for the rapid decline of the European empires, but it is inadequate as a total explanation. Empires were becoming costly. The relationship between the Indian (and other) élites and the élites of the metropolitan powers did not make the task of the nationalists one of polite debate. Harrow and Cambridge did not preserve Nehru from prison for political offences. He was typical. A period in jail was almost a requirement for high office in the post-independence governments of the former European colonies. However, even peaceful protest was expensive for the colonial powers and nationalist protest was often not peaceful. Riots are costly. In some cases, there was all-out war, as in Algeria. The military burden of maintaining colonies was becoming enormous, particularly in a world in which a third world war loomed ominously in the background. The costs of empire were escalating as its benefits declined. The extreme impracticability of empire was demonstrated by the occupation of France, Belgium and the Netherlands by Germany during the Second World War at a time when their empires were still intact.

A further explanation for the decline of the colonial empires was that they were ceasing to be profitable. Even apart from the costs of keeping disaffected populations under control, the gains of European rule were becoming more and more uncertain. Trade with, and investment in, independent countries can be profitable also. Even in the high noon of imperialism, much investment went outside the empire, as we showed above. As multinational corporations were developing, they were more interested in a flexible trading and investment system and became less concerned about maintaining direct political control. Influence could be as effective as formal political control and was normally less expensive.

The colonial powers of the post-1945 era were Western European countries who had suffered badly from the Second World War. The United States was the ally of them all, but itself was not a colonial power, at least in the sense of overt political control. The Americans regarded colonialism with distaste. Its own origins were colonial and its own war of independence was the first of the modern wars of independence. The United States pressed its allies to get rid of what it saw as the colonial embarrassment, which could only serve to justify the Soviet gibes of Western imperialism. It is unlikely that the American pressure would have caused the West European states to abandon their empires if they had remained lucrative. However, this was not the case. The former colonies were not, for the most part, grateful to the United States for any pleading it may have done for the cause of independence. National independence movements tended to be left-wing, at least in formal ideology if less so in deeds. They distrusted the United States and what they saw as the aggressive capitalism it seemed to promote. The Soviet Union was a more congenial model to the leaders of many newly independent states. Many of the leaders of colonial independence movements viewed the United States as hypocritical. While its objections to colonialism were sincere enough (though cynics attributed this to its own lack of colonies), the American enthusiasm for less formal imperial ventures seemed to be as vigorous as anyone's. Further, the barriers to American trade implied by other people's empires were felt by many to be as important an issue as any concern for the liberation of the colonial peoples. It is perhaps not surprising that many leaders of the Non-Aligned Movement, which sought to tread a path between the Soviet Union and the United States without being allied to either, were often people such as Nehru from the former colonies.

Settlers, Immigrants and Native Populations

A colony is ruled by the imperial power from the centre. However, this characterization conceals many variants, depending on the role and significance of settlers who had emigrated from the imperial power. In some cases the settlers have totally dominated the colonial territory, numerically and economically, and pushed the original population to the margins of society. North America, Australia and New Zealand are the leading cases of this. Such colonies quickly rid themselves of colonial status, but under the control of the immigrant, not the native population. The Latin American states became self-ruling though mainly under the control of the descendants of the original immigrants (though, in this case, of many centuries' standing).

In the case of some of the African colonies, the number of settlers was relatively small but they nevertheless completely dominated the economic and social structure. The colonies were run primarily in their interests. However, in the Indian case, there were few genuine settlers. The soldiers, the administrators, the tea-planters and the traders went out to work, often for a lifetime, but nevertheless did not regard themselves as settlers. They dreamt of an affluent retirement in Britain where the children of the wealthier ones had been educated. Few intended to live and die there, expecting their children to follow their example.

Algeria provides an extreme example of the problems created by settlers. Algeria, on the Southern coast of the Mediterranean, has been a French colony since 1834. Its settler population, which was largely French, was proportionately larger than that of most African colonies and it had arrived earlier. After the Second World War, the tension in Algeria was acute and there was a particularly brutal civil war. The settlers, or *colons*, believed they had as much right to live there as anyone. Their families had been settled in Algeria for generations. The Arab population saw them as intruders who had manipulated the society in their own interests. There was a further complication. France declared some of its colonies as *départements* of France and thus legally and governmentally a part of metropolitan France. Thus, at the height of the Algerian war, France excluded all discussion of it at the United Nations, on the perfectly legal if morally dubious grounds that it was an internal matter. Legally, Algeria was a part of France. This, of course, is what the nationalists particularly disputed.

Settlers were common in sub-Saharan Africa. While some of the administrators expected to return to Britain at the end of their careers, many of the farmers had immigrated permanently with their families. They regarded themselves as extensions of the imperial power and looked to it for protection and general support. They certainly did not regard themselves as fellow citizens of the native population who were simply a source of cheap labour with few, if any, rights. A crude and extreme racism was the norm. The South African regime, both as formalized under apartheid and before, was the most conspicuous of these. Some of the settler groups, mainly of Dutch origin, had been in South Africa for centuries rather than years, and had little contact with the original homeland. Even the language (Afrikaans) had gone through significant changes from the original Dutch. However, though of shorter duration, regimes such as those in Southern Rhodesia (now Zimbabwe), Kenya or Tanganyika (now a part of Tanzania and, before 1918, a German colony) were similar in both structure and practice.

Whether the dominant élite were settlers or not must have seemed a technicality to the native population during the period of colonial rule. However, the presence of settlers complicated independence when it became an issue. The settlers regarded themselves as citizens of the colony with a perfect right to stay there. There was a serious sense in which, for them, it was 'home'. In itself, this would not have mattered, but, in most places, they wanted to maintain their extremely privileged positions. Thus, the white population in Rhodesia wanted a white-dominated state. The settler government announced an independent state but one in which the whites' privileges were strictly preserved. These were not terms that were acceptable to the vast majority of the population, which was black, nor to the British government which, by the 1960s, had been converted, at least in principle, to the notion of racial equality. In the end, the white government fell, but not for a number of years. Rhodesia was extreme but the general phenomenon was typical in the settler colonies of all the European powers. It was perhaps the major problem to dog the whole process of decolonization. It did not really afflict the Indian subcontinent where, at least by the time of independence, the white population accepted that the Raj had ended. Psychologically it was very different. With a few exceptions, the white population in India left to go home to Britain. They did not feel they were abandoning their homes. They simply took early retirement. The major problem to dog Indian independence was the communal conflict between Muslim and Hindu. This cast a dark shadow over independence but it had nothing to do with European settlers.

Though the African colonies had immigrant settlers who gained enormous powers, the settlers were small in number compared with the native population. There was nothing to rival the big movement of population to North America in the nineteenth century. The early colonists to North America were refugees from religious persecution. However, they were quickly followed by people in search of a better standard of living. The native population was comparatively small (probably no more than a million). The immigrant population and their descendants rapidly overwhelmed them. This was partly by sheer numbers but also by a deliberate use of more advanced military technology to kill or push them to the margins. The native population was virtually irrelevant to the mainstream society. They had no major role in the settlers' economy, unlike the native population in the African colonies who, in the late nineteenth century, provided crucial cheap labour. The propriety of this indigenous displacement was rarely questioned until recently, though now the morality has troubled many people in the United States, New Zealand and Canada. The situation was similar in Australia, with a major difference being that many of its earlier immigrants were involuntarily transported as convicts.

The Latin American case was somewhat different again, even apart from being earlier. There were large numbers of immigrants from Spain and Portugal who gave Latin America a profoundly Catholic and Iberian culture. Brazil became a Portuguese-speaking country and the rest of Latin America became Spanish-speaking, in much the same way as North America became mainly English-speaking. The countries of Latin America remained under the colonial control of Spain and Portugal until the early nineteenth century. The native population was much larger in South America than in the North. The natives were brutally treated and very many were killed. They were pushed to the margins of the dominant society. However, the indigenous population was too large to be totally sidelined as it was in the North. One estimate (and emphatically a rough and ready estimate) is that the native population of what became Latin America at the time of the conquest in 1536 was around 14 million, many more than in North America. As in North America, now there are feelings of guilt about their earlier (and in many cases continuing) bad treatment.

Neo-Colonialism and Informal Empires

We have discussed empires where states have formal political control over territories beyond the metropolitan area. On this definition, imperialism declined dramatically during the quarter of a century after the Second World War with the collapse of the European empires. However, this was a period when both the Soviet Union and the United States were widely accused of being imperialist. Neither was imperialist in the sense of acquiring formal political control of territory. However, they acquired effective control of states either by bullying or by the insidious process of the structural management of societies. Many of the accusations were a part of Cold War rhetoric. However, behind the words, designed to persuade rather than describe, there is a genuine phenomenon that should be examined.

The Second World War in Europe concluded in 1945 with the armies of America, Britain, France and other Western States occupying Western Europe, while the Soviet Red Army occupied Eastern Europe. Broadly speaking, the areas that had been conquered by the respective armies remained within the respective blocs, though with varying degrees of consent by the inhabitants, as we outlined in Chapter 4. There is little doubt that the Communist regimes were not very popular during the forty years or so in which they were in place. The various states were not under the formal control of the Soviet Union and so were not colonies. However, the degree of effective control was high. The states were not able to act independently of the Soviet Union on any serious issue. This was then a 'Soviet Empire'. 'Soviet Imperialism' was also the cry when the Soviet Union sponsored and supported communist movements anywhere in the world, though its success was limited. Indeed, there were doubts about whether the government of the Soviet Union was seriously interested. Many in the West thought that any communist movement must be Soviet-supported, and they failed to see that there might be genuine indigenous communist sentiment, as was clearly the case in Vietnam.

The domination of Eastern Europe was a real phenomenon. Probably none of the communist parties would have been elected or remained elected in a genuinely free election. Why was the Soviet Union so interested in its mini-empire? In this case, it was primarily a state issue. Any economic issues were under the sway of state-controlled firms and any commercial interests were channelled directly through the state. The Soviet Union did well out of reparations after the war. Also it was able to impose, or at least acquire, favourable trade agreements with the East European countries. The first could probably have been had anyway, while the second, though useful, were not sufficiently beneficial to go to too much trouble over. A more convincing explanation is that the Soviet Union wished to have a set of buffer states around it to act as a defensive ring. As the inheritor of the government of the old Imperial Russia, the Soviet Union also inherited its paranoia about attacks from the West and, in particular, Germany. The idea of hostile governments, perhaps of a right-wing inclination and possibly in alliance with the feared capitalists of the United States, was an anathema to the ruling groups in the Soviet Union. They reacted as the custodians of great powers tend to do – they dominated their near-neighbours. Given their relative strength, this was not difficult. Like all imperial powers, they firmly asserted it was for the good of the inhabitants.

The Soviet Union was severely criticized for its imperial policy. The obvious counter-attack was that the Western states of Europe were under the control of the United States, whose élites viewed the Soviet Union with the same degree of distrust and dislike as they themselves were viewed by the Soviet élites. The symmetry of the argument broke down in that the Western European states, such as Britain and France, for the most part had genuinely free elections. Probably most of the population preferred an alliance with the United States to one with the Soviet Union. Further, there was relatively little control exercised by the United States on the internal policies of the Western European states, even though many were developing welfare states and mixed economies, which were ideologically unappealing to the more capitalist-inclined American élites.

However, the situation regarding Latin America was rather different. Though there was no formal colonial control over the Latin American states, many Latin American economies were dominated by US economic interests. *Dependency theory* was largely worked out in the context of Latin America (see Chapter 7, p. 115). Dependency theorists argue that the operation of one economy can be essentially subservient to that of another such that the more powerful one becomes increasingly powerful in relation to its poorer neighbour. This can be done by economic control, perhaps with some sort of political backing, but with something short of colonial control. This form of control is thus very close to the structural theory of imperialism, though now applied to apparently independent states. Thus, part of the explanation of the relatively poor performance of the Latin American economies, and the continuing serious poverty there, has been that the economies have been run primarily for the benefit of the United States. When one of the Latin American states stepped out of line, as Chile did with the election (in a genuinely free election) of the Marxist government of Salvador Allende in 1970, the United States government had no qualms about getting rid of it by force in 1973. Thus, the United States had effective control over Latin America. The control was more flexible than overt colonialism but it was also cheaper. It replaced political and military power with economic power as the dominant mode of imposing acquiescence on smaller states in the international system.

Similar arguments can be made about the former colonial territories. This neo-colonialism is the continued dominance of former colonial powers (or sometimes another power such as the United States) over the life, and in particular the economic life, of the former colony. This varies from place to place. The French have traditionally exerted greater control, albeit informal, over their former colonies than the British.

The Post-Imperial World

The former colonies of the European powers achieved independence amid great optimism that they would develop into free and politically-developed societies, with good levels of economic growth and development to eliminate the poverty which had so far appeared to be endemic. The record has so far been mixed. Much of what is called the Third World is ex-colonial but much of that is still poor. As we showed in Chapter 1, there is extreme poverty in very many of the ex-colonial states of Africa. Political stability is rare. Most African countries and many others have had at least one political coup, usually a military coup. The military who have carried these out have ranged from those who were genuinely despairing at the hopeless mess the civilian governments were making to simple opportunists who were after power. Algeria, whose struggle for independence from France was warmly applauded by many, and whose independence from France was seen as a triumph in the movement away from imperialism, has been a sad disappointment. Corruption, economic incompetence and religious revolutionaries have combined to put it in a desperate state. Even India, which claims without irony to be the world's largest democracy, has had some moments of nervousness, particularly in 1975 when the government of Indira Gandhi announced a period of emergency because her power was being threatened. Despite this, the Indian record is good. The facts are clear, though the ex-colonies are not alone in having major disturbances. As Eric Hobsbawm convincingly argues (Hobsbawm, 1994, Chapter 15), long-period political stability is a rarity. The regional instability that ensued following the collapse of communist regimes in Eastern Europe and the former USSR at the end of the twentieth century exemplified this.

The ex-colonies of the West European imperial powers did not have a very good start in all this. The imperial powers behaved casually and often totally irresponsibly toward the colonies that were coming up for statehood. As far as Africa is concerned, the whole independence movement seems to have taken the western countries by surprise. The extreme was the Belgian Congo which became Congo and which was granted independence almost without any preparation or warning. It is scarcely surprising that this led to some serious troubles. The lack of preparation meant that there had been very little attempt to educate people and even literacy levels were disastrously low. More advanced training, such as medical or engineering training, was virtually non-existent and few of the newly independent states had more than a small handful of people who had any significant administrative experience. The states of Africa, moreover, were based very closely on the old imperial boundaries of the colonies. These bore little connection with African nations (or tribes as the Europeans preferred to call them). It appeared to be a recipe for disaster. It is a surprising factor that the boundaries of the states of Africa have remained comparatively stable. One would have expected them to collapse or at least be changed fairly frequently. The development of the very poor states has not always been helped by their former imperial rulers or the multinational corporations that stepped in to take their place. In principle, the development of less developed countries (LDCs) requires capital from outside. However, it also requires that a substantial part of the profits or surplus is reinvested within the country to promote further economic growth. This happens far too infrequently. The multinationals, partly anxious to get the best profits they can and partly fearing political instability, tend to take short-period views about the economies in question. When they can make a good profit from short-term operations, they are unlikely to want to take a very long-term view which, in an uncertain world, might or might not pay off. Thus we have a situation where poor and unstable states have remained poor and unstable. The situation reinforces itself.

There is no glib answer as to how poor states can jump out of these vicious circles and into virtuous circles of political and social stability and economic growth. This is a problem which development specialists struggle with.

Cultural Imperialism

Though the normal definitions of imperialism are in terms of political and economic control, it has become increasingly common to talk of more general forms of imperialism and, in particular, of cultural imperialism. It is hard to get a precise definition of this. In rough terms, it means that the culture of one society is imposed on another to the detriment of the weaker society.

In the case of formal colonialism, the cultural component is clear. The Europeans imposed legal systems, language, educational systems and so on in the colonial territories. Religion is an important component of culture, but there was often disagreement amongst the imperialists about this. Obviously the missionaries were anxious for conversion, seeing it as a matter of truth not culture. Many administrators were reluctant to interfere with religion believing it to be a matter for the people concerned. In any case, interference tended to provoke social unrest. Nevertheless, the religious motive was a powerful source of imperial enthusiasm. The imperialists of the nineteenth century took it for granted that the European culture was superior to any other. Even Karl Marx, who is not normally associated with a positive view of imperialism, thought that the destruction of what he saw as primitive cultures was a positive aspect of capitalist expansion. Today, people are less sure of European or Western cultural supremacy than they used to be. All cultures are deemed to be 'valid' in some sense. There are some problems whichever view one takes. For example, though the British in India were reluctant to interfere directly with religious practices, they prohibited the practice of *suttee*. This was the custom amongst some Hindus of burning a widow on the funeral pyre of her late husband. If one believes in leaving cultures totally alone, it was improper to prohibit suttee. However, if one believes that there are some moral issues which transcend a particular culture, then this is not only legitimate but morally required.

The current concerns about cultural imperialism are rather different. They are vigorously expressed in countries which, by any normal definition, are not under any form of imperial domination. Nonetheless, there is concern that many aspects of American culture seem to proliferate around the globe, making it a world safe for McDonald's hamburgers. American or American-style pop music is everywhere and American television programmes can be seen in all parts of the world where they are not specifically prohibited (and furtively in many parts where they are forbidden). The French, in particular, are concerned that aspects of their culture, such as the film industry, are being swamped by Hollywood. They worry especially about the purity of their language in the face of the apparently unstoppable adoption of English words and phrases.

While this is often referred to as imperialism, it can be seen just as readily as an aspect of globalization. When cultures come into contact, there is going to be some mixing. Normally the bigger, dominant culture is going to influence the smaller more than the other way round. Whether we want to call it imperialistic or not, it undoubtedly shares the quality of asymmetry with imperialism. Thus, the French watch the American cinema to a much greater degree than the Americans watch the French. The asymmetry with the British cinema is much less marked. However, the Americanization of French life is a characteristic of the latter part of the twentieth century and the start of the twenty-first, as communications and travel have vastly increased. It was not a feature of nineteenth-century France. Broader sets of imperial-type relationships have developed than were previously the case.

Cultural imperialism is a form of mass behaviour which cumulatively becomes a cultural act. If McDonald's can make a living in Paris, this is because the Parisians want to eat their burgers or, at least, the visiting tourists do. If this is an imperial relationship, then the Indians, Pakistanis and Italians are voracious culinary imperialists. Similarly, if people want American cinema, then it is up to them. They are not compelled to watch American films. Globalization involves a homogenization of culture throughout the world. American culture dominates because it is very prolific and operates in an international language. However, it is accepted voluntarily by people in a way other imperial relationships are not.

On this definition, cultural imperialism is less obviously imperialistic than other forms. If one defines imperialism purely as asymmetry, then it is imperialistic. If imperialism implies coercion, either military or economic, then cultural imperialism falls outside this definition.

Further Reading and Sources

Mentioned already in Chapter 4, Eric Hobsbawm, *The Age of Extremes: The Short Twentieth Century 1914–1991* (London: Abacus, 1994) provides a lot of information and an always fascinating analysis of imperial issues both before and after independence from the perspective of an open-minded and scholarly Marxist.

Charles Reynolds gives a very interesting account of different ways of explaining imperialism in *Modes of Imperialism* (Oxford: Martin Robertson, 1981). The classic statement of 'structural imperialism' is by Johan Galtung, 'A Structural Theory of Imperialism', *Journal of Peace Research*, Vol. 8, No. 2 (1971). The expansion of Europe is discussed in W.D. Smith, *European Imperialism in the Nineteenth and Twentieth Centuries* (London: Nelson-Hall, 1982) and in some essays edited by H.M. Wright, *The 'New Imperialism': An Analysis of Late Nineteenth Century Expansion* (London: Heath, 1964). Jack Gallagher, *Decline, Revival and Fall of the British Empire* (Cambridge: Cambridge University Press, 1982) is interesting and controversial and the source of some figures about investment flows. Dates of annexations and so on of colonies are taken from James Joll, *The Origins of the First World War* (London: Longman, 1992, 2nd edn).

Figures for India's population are taken from Robert M. Cassen, *India: Population, Economy, Society* (London: Macmillan – now Palgrave Macmillan, 1978). Other information about India comes from *British Rule in India: An Assessment* (London: Asia Publishing, 1963: printed in Delhi). Early figures for Latin American population come from the *Encyclopaedia Britannica*, Vol. 17.

6

Theories of International Relations

The Nature of Theory

Scholars have developed various sets of conceptual tools in order to make sense of the international system. It is assumed that there is some sort of pattern in the world and that the international system is not just 'one damn thing after another'. For example, in Chapter 4, we discussed briefly the causes of the First World War about which there are many different views. The disagreements are not, for the most part, over facts, which are largely known, but over the interpretation of facts. In other words, people have different theories of how international relations operate. Therefore we need to consider these theories if we are not to regard such things as the First World War as one of a series of haphazard if unfortunate events.

Ideally we would have a theory of the international system to which all scholars would give their broad assent, in the same way that virtually all physicists accept the theory of relativity. Such levels of agreement are rare in the social sciences and unknown in international relations. I refer to 'theories' in the plural because of this lack of agreement. There are various approaches to international relations which, at least on the surface, appear inconsistent with each other. I shall describe some of the more important of these approaches and then compare them.

Some theories concentrate on the actors in the international system, though followers of different theories disagree on which actors are important and what the goals of the actors are. The *realists* concentrate on states as the main actors and hold that the major goal of each state is the pursuit of power. Related to these are the *neo-realists* (the new realists) and the *structural realists*, but there are no clear demarcation lines between the different subschools. All three agree on the central importance of the state. In contrast, while the *pluralists* agree with the realists that, to understand international relations, we must understand the behaviour of actors, they disagree with the overwhelming significance given to the state. They think of states as one of many actors, albeit important ones. Not only do they stress the importance of other actors such as multinational corporations (MNCs) but they are sceptical of the central role that realists give to state power and security within the international system. The *structuralists* (of whom the structural realists are one form) approach the matter in a different way. Instead of concentrating on the actors they concentrate on the structure of the system and the constraints which this puts on actors. Thus, they see states and other actors as being severely circumscribed in their actions and with much less freedom of action than decision-makers like to think. To understand the international system we must concentrate on these structures rather than the behaviour and choices of the individual actors.

We shall now look at these different schools of thought in greater detail.

Realism

Historically, the most important approach has been realism. It has been the dominant way of explaining international behaviour until recently and still has many adherents. Realists argue that states are the most important actors in the international system, to the virtual exclusion of all other actors. The security of the state is the primary motivation for a state's actions (or, to express it more carefully, the actions of the government of the state). Many states also have predatory aims. If a state lies unguarded such that its neighbours can take advantage of it by military or other means, then the unguarded state will find itself attacked. There is, at least latently, a war of all against all. The human condition is one of potential insecurity where predators take advantage of the weak. Sometimes this view is known by the German word *realpolitik* or by the English phrase *power politics*.

Realism is a beguiling and seductive theory, though pessimistic in both its assumptions and conclusions. It stems from the view of society that was most clearly articulated by the English political philosopher

Hobbes in the seventeenth century. He argued that, if there were anarchy, life would be 'nasty, brutish, and short', not because human beings are necessarily aggressive, but because they fear the possible aggression of others and are thus in a state of armed insecurity which would overflow into violence. Government is necessary within a society in order to provide order and security, including basic physical security against violence. However, the international scene is still without a world government and there seems little reason to suppose that one will appear in the foreseeable future. Hence the international system is anarchical and security must be the dominant goal of any state. The members of a state may wish to be moral, and not pursue tough-minded security based policies. They may wish to be more peaceful. Similarly they may wish to pursue some ideological or religious agenda. To do so, however, will be self-defeating. They will be overrun, or at least dominated by some other power with less altruistic aims. The realists do not deny that there are other forms of international behaviour, such as trade. However, they regard them as subordinate to the issues of military power and security. Thus governments permit trade and even encourage it, but only inasmuch as it does not threaten the hierarchy of interests in which security is dominant.

Realism derives its name from its adherents' belief that they are being realistic and looking at the world as it is, warts and all. However much we may deplore it, they argue, we have to recognize that this is the way the world is and accept it as such. Indeed, if we are going to work for a more peaceful international society, we must recognize how people really behave rather than maintaining some idealized version. The doctrine of realism can be traced far back in political analysis, at least to Thucydides' realist account of the Peloponnesian War in the fifth century BC.

After the First World War there was some disenchantment with realism. In the nineteenth and early twentieth century, states were governed by people who followed realist principles. The First World War followed. If the war was a consequence of realism, it was clearly a disastrous doctrine. The *idealists* then became more influential. They, likewise, thought the state was the central actor and recognized that there would still be states operating on a power political principle. However, they thought that the League of Nations, founded in 1919, would serve to promote peace. Further, if peace were the dominant motive of several states, they could combine, probably under the aegis of the League, and guarantee peace. The experiences of the interwar years, in particular the rise of Nazi Germany, did not favour this more optimistic doctrine. The Second World War put realism back as the dominant way of looking at the international system.

The realist's concern with the state comes from the concern with security and issues of power. For the most part, states are the only organizations that can direct military power on any significant scale. States raise armed forces and can impose order internally. Externally these forces can be used to threaten and defend the state in a way no other organization can do on a systematic basis, making the state a central actor.

The emphasis on security and potential violence in its turn derives from a pessimistic but plausible argument. Suppose we have a collection of peaceful states without foreign ambitions and wishing only to organize the government of the lands in their jurisdiction. However, one state has mobilized for war and seeks advantages from other states. As it has the means of violence available it can impose its will and make other states suffer. The other states have to defend themselves by organizing the means of violence – armies, air forces and so on. Thus, just one potential initiator of violence pushes us into the realist world where the survival of states, and the societies they embody, depends on putting security as the dominant goal. Given that this is always a possibility, and that the history of the world shows it has often happened, security has to be the dominant goal of states, even peaceful states.

The situation is aggravated when states acquire armaments in anticipation of threats. No matter how genuinely peaceful their intentions, suspicious neighbours might mistake their behaviour as preparations for offensive rather than defensive war. Unfortunately there is no clear distinction between offensive and defensive weapons so this suspicion is hard to allay and the neighbour may itself increase its weapons thus creating further suspicions in the system. This pattern of interactions is known as the *security dilemma*.

The picture according to the realists is not quite as bleak as it might appear at first sight. The world is not necessarily going to plunge into perpetual war. There are ways, even within realist principles, which permit at least some degree of stability and peace. The most important of these is the *balance of power*. Though power is central in the realist view, it can be manipulated and by appropriate juggling we can get some form of international stability. The balance of power is such a form of juggling.

There are two forms of the balance of power. The *simple balance of power*, often known as a *bipolar system*, applies when there are just two states involved. The *complex balance of power*, often known as a *multipolar system*, is when there are more than two states involved. In the simple balance of power, it is argued that, if two states have approximately the same amount of military power, they will not fight. A war is likely to produce a stalemate with enormous cost and nothing much gained. Both parties will realize this. Hence there will be peace – or at least an absence of war. In some ways this can be regarded as the seesaw model of the balance of power. Blocs of power are put on the two ends of a seesaw and, as long as they are equal, they will stay in balance. However, if one gets heavier, then that end goes down and gains a dominant position. It will then attack the weaker side. Failing that, it can, at least, threaten to do so if it does not get some benefits, perhaps in terms of trade or land, as a reward for its restraint. Superficially this looks a rather precarious model particularly if the seesaw analogy is taken too seriously. A slight shift in relative power would seem to make the seesaw move away from its point of balance. This is too pessimistic, however. A successful military attack normally requires the attacker to have larger forces than the defender. How much larger depends on the technology of the time. It also depends on the particular characteristics of the situation. Thus Switzerland, which is very mountainous, is harder to attack than Belgium, which is very flat. Nevertheless the proposition holds in general. A range of relative forces are consistent with a peaceful balance.

The situation is complicated when there are more states involved because of the possibility of alliances. States want power for themselves but, as a corollary of this, they are anxious to avoid being dominated by other states. Suppose we have five states which we shall call abstractly A, B, C, D and E. They need not be identical in power though we can suppose for the sake of argument that they are of the same order of magnitude. Each state would like to dominate the system, but all states are likewise very hostile to the idea that any other state will be dominant. Suppose A sees that B is rather less powerful than itself and is tempted by the rich pickings which would be available if it were to attack it successfully. C gets uneasy about A with its greater power and makes common cause with B in an alliance. This deters A's ambitions. However, the alliance of B and C now looks threatening to D and to A even though its power started the spiral of concern. Thus, A and D join together in an alliance to deter the alliance of B and C. If there is a balance of power between the two alliances, this situation can persist. However, if one alliance looks more powerful than the other, then the weaker bloc will try and entice E into their alliance. E will be ready to accept the invitation as it has no desire for a dominant coalition in the system either. An actual alliance may not be necessary. A threat to form one may be sufficient to deter the would-be aggressors. Arguably Britain played this role in the nineteenth century in Europe. Thus, by various shifts of alliance, a balance of power in the system is maintained. As the different powers in the system alter their relative powers, due to economic growth and the like, there will need to be constant shifts in the alliances needed to maintain a balance. The balance of power is not likely to be static over long periods so we should expect a constantly shifting pattern of alliances.

The balance-of-power system produces a relatively peaceful system, at least in theory. However, balance-of-power theorists do not argue that war never happens. Small wars may occur from time to time to redress an imbalance but they will not get out of hand. The overall pattern of behaviour means that a stable system will be preserved and one in which there is not too much war. In order for this system to work, one condition is very important. States should join alliances, or leave alliances, purely on the basis of the power structure of the system. This means that any state must be ready to ally with any other state however distasteful they may find its domestic policies. It must be an exercise in power alone or it will cease to work.

Realists argue that nineteenth-century Europe illustrates this. There were five major powers, Britain, France, Germany (earlier Prussia), Austria-Hungary and Russia. They operated a complex balance-of-power system. There were various wars, such as the Crimean War (1854–56) between Britain, France and Turkey, on the one side, and Russia, on the other. There were also various wars fought by Prussia, such as the Franco-Prussian War (1870). These were, however, limited wars and did not threaten the overall stability of the system. As a theory, it gives a plausible account of this. Unfortunately it all broke down in 1914.

Let us summarize the basic tenets of realism:

- First, states are the dominant actors in the international system.
- Second, states pursue power. They do this both in the sense of trying to get more powerful positions at the expense of rivals and by defending themselves against the encroachments of these rivals.

- Third, as the relationships of states with each other are dependent entirely on their power relationships with each other, they have nothing to do with the internal structure of the state or the type of regime. Internal politics and external politics are therefore separate. This is known as the 'billiard-ball model' of international relations. The movement of billiard balls, like the movement of states, can be explained completely in terms of the movements of the other billiard balls.

It follows that, for the realist, international relations is the analysis of states pursuing power. The achievement of comparative peace is the result of the manipulation of power. All other issues are subordinate to this.

Some objections to the realist view come from the picture it paints of a world perpetually on the edge of war. It presupposes a particular view of self-interest involving a ready use of violence which, understandably, many people find unappealing. The enthusiasm of some of the more strategically inclined for military matters, with their pose of a macho toughness in debates on international issues, combined with a self-consciously disparaging attitude to moral issues, raises suspicions that some realists rather enjoy their moral vacuum. This is far from a necessary position. Some realists deplore the picture of the world they feel obliged to paint and wish it were different. However, they argue that this is what people are like. One must work with the world as it is and not how one would like it to be. To deplore power politics is like deploring the fact that lions kill their prey in cruel ways. It may be regrettable but this is the nature of lions. If one comes into contact with them, one should take prudent precautions. Likewise this is the nature of human beings. Realists need not like the world as they see it, or justify it morally. However, they argue that it would be dishonest and self-defeating to pretend it is otherwise.

Variants of Realism

Neorealism (or New Realism)

Some realists recognize that economic actors are significant in the international systems and are not just details on the edge of the serious matter of power politics. They are reluctant to dethrone states whose power politics they still feel are central to the international system. Nevertheless, they promote multinational corporations and other economic actors from the purely peripheral fringe they occupy within classical realism, to a central, though still fundamentally subordinate, role in the international system. There is a debate also about the nature of state interactions even within a power framework. Power is a relational concept; a state is not powerful in the abstract but only in relation to other states. Thus, for a true, hardline realist wanting power necessarily means wanting more power than some other state. Therefore there is no scope for cooperation between states except when an alliance is called for between some states who are all in conflict with some other states. Other theorists, often called the *neoliberals* view international cooperation of self-interested states as possible and promoting stability. Cooperation, even in an anarchic system, is much more obviously self-interested than has sometimes been realized. The neoliberals are called realists only on a wide definition of the term.

Structural Realism

Some neorealists (particularly Kenneth Waltz in his influential book, *Theory of International Politics*, written in 1979) stress that to understand the behaviour of the international system, we have to start with the system and move down to the individual actors rather than the other way round as traditional realists have done. Waltz based his argument explicitly on the economists' analysis of individual markets, in which the individual buyer of, say, bread has to accept the price of bread in the market, although buyers as a whole are an important determinant of this price. We can only study price and the behaviour of individual actors in the market through analyzing the system as a whole. Structural realists argue that, in effect, states are in a similar situation. They have to react to the system as it is given, although it is the cumulation of their reactions that determines the system.

  Structural realists argue that states, power and security are central as with classical realism, although they also recognise the importance of economic actors. However, these are ultimately subordinate to states, even though all play their role in a much more tightly defined system. Because all states are pursuing power the situation in which any given state is placed broadly determines the sort of policy it must follow. It has very little freedom of choice and this applies to big, powerful states

as well as small ones. Thus, given the situation in 1945, the Cold War
or something like it was probable. The USA was big and powerful and,
though much more battered, so was the Soviet Union. In such
circumstances hostility was more or less inevitable. Given the state of
technology and the development of nuclear weapons this also meant
that the mutual tension between the powers inevitably produced
mutual deterrence. If the Russian Revolution had gone differently in
1917, resulting in a constitutional monarchy with a liberal capitalist
system (which was not too far-fetched a possibility: the early years of
the Russian Revolution were marked by a civil war that the Bolsheviks
– or Communists – only just won), there would still, according to this
version of events, have been a Cold War or something like it. What
determines the behaviour of states is the system as a whole, which in
effect imposes behaviour on the individual states, giving them only
freedom of choice.

Pluralism

Discontent with the realist version of affairs came not so much because
people found it morally offensive but because they found it either
empirically incorrect or inadequate. There seemed to be too much
which was clearly important in the international system that realist
theory ignored. This certainly seems true of the world today and
perhaps for the world as it ever was. In particular, the economic
aspects of international relations were largely ignored or, if noticed,
were relegated to a subordinate position. The fields of international
relations and international economics proceeded in apparent mutual
ignorance of each other's work. Their different textbooks dealt with
different worlds. Obviously some dialogue was desirable.

   If realists assume that states exist as independent, self-interested
entities, pluralists rely on a notion of complex interdependence. Complex interdependence, which is captured by a cobweb metaphor, is
characterized by multiple links between different types of actors and an
absence of hierarchy between issues. To say that states or other actors
are interdependent is to say that they cannot entirely separate their own
interests from those with whom they closely interact. Actors may be
sensitive to the acts of others to the extent that they feel the effects of
those acts. For instance, a decision made by a group of Middle Eastern
states to increase the cost of oil may be felt to differing degrees by

actors across the world. These actors will also be vulnerable to the extent that they are able or unable to adjust policies to minimize the adverse effects of the increased cost of oil. Thus, the state that can produce more oil at home or that has an alternative supplier will be less vulnerable than one that does not.

Pluralists argue that international activity is not just a matter of the behaviour of states but of other actors too. Further, but logically separate, they argue that states are not quite as security and power conscious as the realists make out. For example, economic issues are issues in their own right. Economic actors, such as multinational corporations, are organizations that, in a straightforward sense, make decisions. Sometimes these decisions conflict with what any state would want in what the state decision-makers would see as an ideal world. Thus, if we want to analyze the ever-important oil market, we cannot do so solely by reference to economic actors, such as the firms who produce and sell oil. Oil is central to modern economies, both directly and because of its relation to military capability. This means the state is also involved when there is a threat to oil supplies. To interpret the oil market either purely in terms of economic actors or in terms of state actors seems inadequate, certainly to the pluralist. They argue that both aspects are important.

While most forms of pluralism emphasize international economic behaviour, they do not neglect other international actors. Religious movements, national movements and so on are regarded as actors in their own right and not just the tools of states. Thus, a realist would argue that a religious movement, such as the relatively recent upsurge of militant Islamic movements, was merely tool of some state or another. It might be convenient for the leaders of a religious state such as Iran to claim, and indeed many members of its élites to believe, that its policy was based on Islamic principles aimed at promoting Islam throughout the world. According to the realist, this would be successful only if it coincided with a reasonable interpretation of state interests. If the Iranian government were to neglect state interests in the pursuit of Islam then they would come to grief. However, the pluralist argues that Islam is a factor that should also be considered independently of the state. While not denying that governments manipulate religious movements in the interest of power politics, there is much more to the story than this. Islamic movements cannot simply be subsumed under state behaviour. An account of the international system that tried to do so would be seriously deficient.

The same applies to other forms of religion, and in particular to fundamentalist religions. Fundamentalist Christianity in the United States is clearly a movement that tries to influence policy. Inasmuch as this influence is successful, governments' policies may deviate from a realist norm. The export of fundamentalist Protestant beliefs to the strongly Roman Catholic Latin America is definitely an international phenomenon but not too obviously related to state behaviour (though it is alleged that some intelligence groups in the US are sympathetic to it, believing that the Protestant fundamentalists will be solidly right-wing). Fundamentalist Zionists, particularly within Israel, also have an important effect on international politics, influencing policy in Israel in a more nationalistic direction.

Finally, we can consider the international organizations set up by states. Conspicuous amongst these is the United Nations. Obviously there is a realist potential here as the organizations are set up by states and the membership consists of states. The realist argues that they are not truly independent actors but merely devices to facilitate interaction between states, at times behaving together in much the same way as they might do in an alliance. They point out, for example, that the UN has never seriously embarrassed the United States. Similarly, the World Court (also known as the International Court of Justice) is ignored if it makes a judgement that offends a powerful state. The international organizations might expand the range of fruitful cooperation between states but they are not themselves major international actors. Their significance is that they can help states, though this is very debatable. Clearly the realists here seem to be on stronger ground than they are in dealing with economic actors (see also Chapter 3, p. 34) By contrast, regime theorists point out that institutions composed of states develop an identity of their own. As they interact over a period of time, expectations begin to converge on a shared set of norms, customs and practices.

Structuralism

Accounts of the international system have emphasized the actors involved. They disagree over the significance of states and their behaviour. The critics add to the range of actors who are involved but they are not disputing the significance of the actors. However, another approach is to look at the structure of the system rather than the actors and see to what extent this provides a better explanation of some significant aspects of the international scene. Structuralism is more an approach to theory than a theory in itself. Under its heading are clustered many different theories. I concentrate on the underlying features, rather than a specific theory as such.

It is easiest to explain this with an example. We can refer back to the case of the independence of the Indian subcontintent which, in 1947, became independent of British rule to form India, Pakistan and Ceylon (later Sri Lanka) (see also Chapter 5, p. 68). One way of looking at the history of independence would be to follow the independence movement, which existed almost throughout the period of British rule. It would lay great stress also on the activities of Mahatma Gandhi and, in the immediate period before and after independence, on people like Pandit Nehru and Lord Mountbatten as the last British Viceroy. To understand what it was like at the time, it would be necessary to have an account such as this.

However, a look at the underlying structure of events at the time provides a different picture. The willingness of most Indians to put up with British rule was diminishing and probably would have been extinguished completely had the British remained. On the British side, Britain was economically emaciated and could not afford the major military presence, which seemed increasingly necessary in order to remain in India. In any case, by 1945, British confidence in the rectitude of empire had faded. Many members of the governing Labour party favoured independence because they saw it as morally right and not just because it was forced on them. These background forces made the independence of India, roughly at the time it happened, almost inevitable. Perhaps the precise dates and the actual pattern of events, were determined, or at least influenced, by the individuals around at the time. However, the independence of India was determined by the structure of the international system, the structure of India, the structure of Britain and the events that had taken place in the previous years. The most any decision-makers could do was flow with the tide. To pose the question another way – which perhaps makes the point clearer – is it conceivable that India today still would have been a British dependency? The structure of the overall system was such that this would have been impossible. The same point could be made about the United States. Do we really believe that, if George Washington had been a little more foolish and George III had been a little more wise, the United States would still be a British colony?

Structuralists hold that this is the most effective form of explanation. Instead of looking at actors such as states we look at structures such as relative wealth, population, trade patterns and so on. Within such a structural framework the actors, whether states or not, have very little freedom of manoeuvre. The emphasis on decisions, which the pluralists make, restricts us to looking at what the structuralists would consider rather minor issues.

Structuralists are sceptical of the influence of organizations making much impact outside the structural constraints. They are even more sceptical of the influence of individuals. However, this conflicts with other interpretations. In my account of Indian independence above, individuals influenced only the details. Was this also true in 1930s Germany? Accounts of the period often assert that 'Hitler invaded the Saar Land' or 'Hitler attacked Poland' as if, without Hitler, these things would not have happened. This raises the whole question of how much an individual can influence social processes. A structuralist would argue that Hitler was merely the product of the social and political environment within Germany at the time. An authoritarian, expansionary regime, with extreme anti-Semitic and racist attitudes, inevitably came out of the structure left by the First World War. In such circumstances, an authoritarian leader would arise. It happened to be Hitler, but someone else would have carried out in essence the same policies. Only the details would have been different. As with India, the structure brought the leader, not the leader the structure. However, in the German case, we primarily concentrate on the internal structures within Germany to explain Hitler, not the international structures. These are brought in to explain how Germany could behave externally in the way it did in the 1930s. The German case is less compelling than the case of Indian independence. It is hard to imagine a set of events resulting in India still being a dependency of Britain. It is easier to imagine a set of events in which Germany might have been less aggressive. Intuitively, at least, it is more plausible that Hitler and a few associates exploited the structure to turn it in one direction, whereas another group of people might have turned it in another.

A similar point arises with women in major decision-making roles. While there are still relatively few, there are a number of states that have had women heads of government. While neither of the two Cold War superpowers have had a woman leader so far, several states which are significant actors in the international system have or have had, such as India, Pakistan, Britain and Israel. Some people have thought that if women occupied such positions, they would be more inclined to peaceful policies. This does not seem to be borne out by an examination of the policies of any of the above or any other woman leader. The structuralist of any sort would not be surprised. If the leader is constrained by the structure, then it does not matter very much who they are and their sex is irrelevant. Another form of structuralism concentrates not on the international system but on the domestic political system. On this view, a woman could attain a leadership position only if she conforms to the norms and procedures of the society she is in. Thus she must behave like a man and only women with male attitudes are likely to get to the top. A further brand of structural theory, which has been prominent in international relations, today originates in Marxism. As a form of critical theory, this will be discussed in the next chapter.

Structural analyses differ according to the groupings that the analyst regards as crucial. The structural realists are structuralists who regard states as central. Marxists regard class and social structures determined by the economic system as central. Feminists argue that gender is central. These are not necessarily inconsistent. Class and gender can be intertwined as significant variables. There are several overlapping views of the role of gender in international relations. A stronger assertion is that gender is a central feature which defines a social structure. This does not mean that women as a distinct social group are necessarily actors, though on occasion they may be. It is an assertion that gender groupings are major and relevant in determining what goes on in the international system along with another assertion that people are influenced by the international system along gender lines (see Chapter 7, pp. 120–2).

A Comparison between the Different Viewpoints

The different views of the international system can be represented in diagrammatic form. Let us represent states by circles (in deference to the frequent characterisation of the realist view as the 'billiard-ball model') and multinational firms by clear squares. In this simple world represented by Figures 6.1 to 6.4, there are just four states and three firms. The interactions are represented by arrows. We illustrate the contrasting views of the different theories about the nature of these interactions.

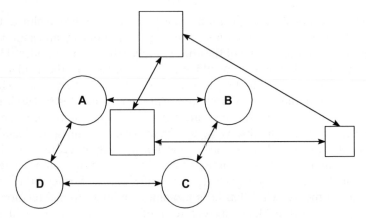

Figure 6.1   Classical realism

Note: In all diagrams, circles represent states; squares represent multinational companies; triangles represent intergovernmental organisations; and small shaded squares represent sub-state organizations (e.g. cities, regions).
For clarity, only a selection of the interactions are shown in each case.

Classical realists analyze the behaviour of states entirely in terms of each other (Figure 6.1). Thus the behaviour of state A is done purely in terms of its links with the other states B, C and D. The squares (that is the firms and other organisations) are ignored and do not affect the behaviour of the balls (or states). The international economic system is a separate system, whose elements interact amongst themselves and which can be ignored as far as the relationships between states are concerned. Obviously the international economy exists, but as far as international relations is concerned, it is something separate.

The neorealists have a broader view and they acknowledge the existence of the international economic system as impinging on the state system. The dashed lines in Figure 6.2 represent these interactions. However, the lines go only one way from the states to the firms. The states are still dominant. While they influence the behaviour of firms, the reverse is not true unless, improbably, the firms may alter power relationships. The states and their interactions are dominant though the international economy is recognised as significant and a factor which must be taken into account. However, in any conflict between the two, the political and military system will always dominate. The states, we notice, remain as billiard balls, though more permeable ones than in the strict realist theory. The fact that we

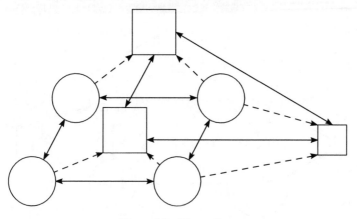

Figure 6.2　Neorealism

consider MNCs as actors in their own right implies we look at economies. This involves looking inside the state for some purposes at least. The firms, likewise, are solid, but this is a convention to make the diagram clear. There is nothing in neorealism as such which precludes investigating the inside of firms.

The pluralists go further. In Figure 6.3, the broken lines have arrows going both ways. Firms can now challenge states and the state system and can do things even if they do not fit into the power model of the

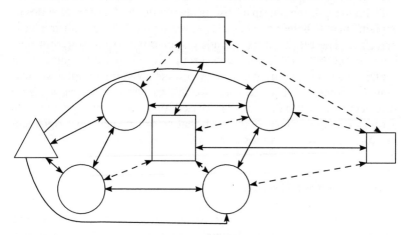

Figure 6.3　Pluralism

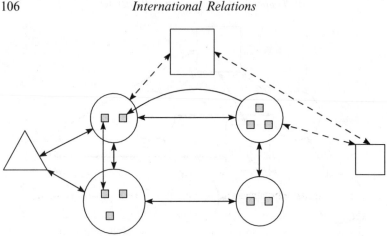

Figure 6.4   Complex interdependence

realists. Similarly, the intergovernmental organizations such as the UN and the IMF, represented here by the triangle, influence states and are influenced by the states. They are autonomous actors and not just the tool of the states. They can interrupt the power relationships in a way that neither realists nor neorealists allow. Thus, the behaviour of one state cannot be explained purely in terms of the other states. International organizations, multinational corporations and other aspects of the international political economy intrude and need to be included.

In Figure 6.4, the pluralists also bring in internal features of states to explain their behaviour. The solid cover of the billiard ball model is breached. The other actors are not just external to the state but also internal actors, such as religious groups, need to be brought in to explain state behaviour. We have an altogether more complex system. Going further on this spectrum we get to *complex interdependence* where the billiard-ball state has ceased to be so solid and substate actors gain significance as international actors in their own right and not just as pressures on governments.

Why Do We Need Theories?

Why do we need to be realists, structuralists or whatever? I gave some brief answers at the beginning of the chapter but these need elaborating.

Let us consider the alternative. We could give a list of international events, one after the other in the 'first this happened, then that happened, and then the other happened' mode. Thus, we can list the dates when various countries exploded their first nuclear weapons (USA 1945, Britain 1949, Soviet Union 1949, France 1960, China 1964, India in 1974 and Pakistan in 2000, following a second detonation by India). On its own this list is of limited interest. Why was the list not extended when many expected it would be? Why did Britain and France develop nuclear weapons but not Canada and Italy? To answer these questions we need a combination of theory and a knowledge of the particular circumstances of the case. Neither is sufficient on its own.

Facts, on their own, do not get us very far. We need to collect together things that appear to us to be similar and argue that similar sets of circumstances will lead to similar sorts of results. We want to look at the general conditions when wars start so that we can give some general account of this. A list of wars tells us what happened but not why it happened. A theory tries to pose, and hopefully answer, the 'why' questions which link different cases to each other and not just the 'what' questions. Thus scholars try to find patterns in the international system. If all events are *sui generis* (that is, things on their own which cannot be categorized together with any other events) then we just get into a muddle. If there is no pattern to behaviour, then truly the outlook is grim. Only by exploiting the patterns we detect can we seek to alter them.

In developing the theories we need to make sense of the world, we formulate concepts such as 'state', or 'power' or 'globalization'. We categorize things with the aim of making the world comprehensible. We go further than merely categorizing. We say what will happen in various circumstances. We assume that there is some consistency to behaviour so we can go a little further than talking of patterns and talk also of causes and consequences. Thus, those who believe in the realist principles of states and power are able to put the events in the world into a comprehensible framework. One thing they would argue would be that war is more likely when there is no balance of power and one state dominates the others (they would normally say 'more likely' rather than 'inevitable'). They identify the cause of a war as being the imbalance of power.

As there are different theories, we need to find out which picture of the world is the most useful. This means that we must formulate a theory carefully such that in the end it can be tested against the facts.

The fact that there are still disagreements shows that this goal is far from being achieved. A lot of effort has gone into collecting data and in testing particular hypotheses but there are still serious splits in the profession. This is only partly a matter of the facts. It is that the theories we have are sometimes very difficult to pose in testable form, such that a straightforward set of uncontentious facts would discriminate between one theory and another. Testing has been more successful as far as partial theories are concerned. One such partial theory connects democracy with peaceful relationships; this is examined in Chapter 8 (pp. 142–5). The grander theories discussed in this chapter are still issues of controversy.

If scholars quarrel over the very basis of their argument, what hope is there for anyone else? However, these disagreements, though significant, are not as damaging as may appear at first sight.

There are two broad sources of difference. First, people find different topics interesting. One person might be concerned with the behaviour of states while another might find it rather dreary. This difference usually goes back to deeper problems, which are commonly morally based, such as a concern about interstate war. Second, there may be differences about the theory itself. Thus, the realist argues that the behaviour of states can be explained purely in terms of other states. The pluralist denies this and argues that state behaviour cannot be analyzed in terms of states alone but other actors must be brought in. The problem is not solved yet (otherwise everyone would be a realist or no-one would) but it is solvable by further analysis and one day, we hope, it will be. Proponents of different theories are asking and answering different questions or asking the questions over a different time scale. Thus, realism does rather well in helping to understand interstate war in Europe in the nineteenth century. It does less well in explaining colonial and imperial wars. It is wholly inadequate as an explanation of the American Civil War. Similarly, if our aim is to understand trading patterns between rich and poor states or the role of gender relations in world poverty, realism and realist concepts will be practically no use whatever. This does not matter very much providing we realize what the limits of a theory are. The mistake is to assume we can have general theories that will explain everything. If we consider theories as being more limited in scope, the disagreements may turn out to be less significant, in that they result from asking different questions about different actors. There are still disagreements, but they are of a more moderate order.

Let us consider the three categories of realism, pluralism and structuralism again. It has been argued that these are three totally different ways of looking at the world which are incompatible with each other. With sufficient ingenuity, realists can always interpret everything in terms of power. Part of the popularity of realism is due to the intriguing exercises one can carry out to overcome apparent anomalies in the theory, while simultaneously giving the illusion of clear-headed toughness.

The self-contained capacity to explain everything is also true of structuralism. We can interpret the whole world in terms of structure. This has led some scholars to argue that the different ways of looking at things should be regarded as *paradigms*. Paradigms are complete worldviews in themselves, which can incorporate anything and everything. One cannot decide between them as they are simply different ways of looking at the world. This is a fatalistic view. If we accepted it, our interpretations of the international system would be matters of taste and temperament rather than matters of fact. It is a view I reject. I argue that, not merely can we compare theories with each other and test them against the facts but we can have mixed theories also. Thus, we could argue that pluralism and realism merge into one another. Both are based on the idea that we are concentrating on the actions of organizations. For the realists, states alone count. For the pluralists, not only states but many other organizations count as well. To some extent our problem comes in deciding what the questions are we wish to understand. If it is the imminent approach of war, then perhaps it is the state and power on which we need to concentrate. If it is the development of trade between two countries, it is firms and other similar actors. In the last, in particular, there may be disagreements about the significance of states but these can be settled in principle by an analysis of the facts.

Let us reconsider structuralism in relation to the decision- and actor-based theories of realism and pluralism. It is hard to see how anyone could deny that structure is relevant to the analysis of any social behaviour. Decision-makers act in some sort of context and their behaviour must vary according to that context. Thus, decisions are different in a world of sailing ships and no radio or telephone from those taken in a world of fast jet aircraft and instantaneous communication around the globe. These structural factors circumscribe decision.

However, it is also extreme to suppose that decisions are totally irrelevant and structure determines everything. War between the

United States and Japan may have been inevitable around 1941, but there was a decision by the Japanese to attack Pearl Harbor and initiate this war. The decision itself cannot have been inevitable. Saddam Hussein's Iraq invaded Kuwait in 1990. It was not inevitable that this should happen. Nor was it inevitable that a coalition led by the United States should oppose it. Or so it would seem. One could argue a contrary case, but the immediate supposition is that sets of decisions were taken which could have been taken otherwise.

The question of whether behaviour is best explained by structure or the consequences of decisions is fundamental in all social sciences, including international relations. However, it is better to pose the question differently. How much does structure matter? Alternatively, how much freedom of decision do policy-makers have and how much are they constrained by the structure of the situation? It is a matter of degree rather than a question of alternatives. Thus, in practice people disagree on the amount of constraint that actors operate under, rather than whether their behaviour is totally determined by the situation they find themselves in, or whether they have total freedom of manoeuvre (whatever that might mean).

Can Theories 'Tell the Truth'?

I argued above that if the concept of paradigm was used strictly to categorize theories in international relations, then, providing they have some internal plausibility, we would be left with taste and temperament as the prime arbiters of what is true and false in international relations and not the facts. I presupposed that there are 'facts' in international relations that can be found. There are some, notably many post-modernists – of whom more below – who dispute this.

First, let us discuss the view of those who think there are 'social facts'. A large body of work in international relations does not regard it as particularly problematic to give an account of such things as the Gulf War in terms of military activity, diplomatic activity, media activity in the war, the social consequences of the war within Iraq and so on. Indeed, this is a fairly conventional approach. Many go further and try to derive theories of the causes of war or any other sort of social event and the ways in which such events develop when they do. Thus, Vasquez (1993), in a detailed statistical study, argues that boundary disputes have been a potent cause of war. An early scholar in this area, Lewis Fry Richardson (1960, though relevant work was published as early as 1938), formulated theories of arms races between states. In a field bordering on international relations, Amartya Sen (1981) investigated famines and argued that the primary cause of famine was a shift in the distribution of income and not, as was conventionally thought, a failure in crops (though this might be a subsidiary cause). These scholars all endeavoured to develop theories of the processes they were involved in and test them against the 'facts'. 'Facts' were such things as the occurrence of interstate war, the level of armaments, or deaths from malnutrition. No one would dispute that the statistics used often raise major problems but they would not see the concepts of 'war', 'armaments' and so on as inherently problematic. Further, many aspects of these things are in some sense measurable. Their view of theory is that it comprises a set of generalizations that can be tested against the facts and that such facts are in principle available. A great deal of effort has gone into making collections of facts, or *databases*, to examine the nature of the international system. People who follow this broad approach to international relations are often known as *behaviouralists*, particularly if they use statistics and statistical methods. In the social sciences in general they are often referred to as *positivists* and occasionally, though more accurately, as *empiricists*. Centrally, they argue that we can test theories about events in the social world against the facts. A successful theory coordinates the facts and enables us to explain such things as the cause of a war or the causes of wars. This is the sense in which a theory can be said to 'tell the truth'.

Further Reading and Sources

On theory in general, Chris Brown, *Understanding International Relations* (Basingstoke: Palgrave, 2001, 2nd edn) is an excellent recent introduction. Rather more old-fashioned, and not considering many of the topics such as feminism that are widely discussed today, is Philip Reynolds, *An Introduction to International Relations* (London: Longman, 1994, 3rd edn), which still has a good rigorous attitude to theory. Various essays on international relations and its philosophical underpinnings are edited by Steve Smith, Ken Booth and Marysia Zalewski, *International Theory: Positivism and Beyond* (Cambridge: Cambridge University Press, 1996). More directly on the philosophical underpinnings is the excellent book by Martin Hollis and Steve Smith, *Explaining and Understanding in International Relations* (Oxford: Clarendon Press, 1991).

My own views on these problems are presented in Michael Nicholson, *Causes and Consequences in International Relations: A Conceptual Study* (London: Pinter, 1996). A.J.R. Groom and Margot Light (eds), *Contemporary International Relations: A Guide to Theory* (London: Pinter 1994) is a collection of bibliographical essays by various experts on aspects of international relations theory. It is invaluable as a source of further reading. The title of the book is descriptive of the contents of James E. Dougherty and Robert L. Pfaltzgraff Jr, *Contending Theories of International Relations* (New York: HarperCollins, 1990). Another broad survey is Scott Burchill *et al.*, *Theories of International Relations* (Basingstoke: Palgrave, 2001, 2nd edn).

There are only a very small handful of books on international relations which one might recommend to one's friends to read for fun. Most are from the realist stable (but see Irving Janis, *Groupthink: Psychological Studies of Policy Decisionmaking and Fiascoes* (Boston: Houghton Mifflin, 1992, 2nd edn) and Michael Walzer, *Just and Unjust Wars* (New York: Basic Books, 1992, 2nd edn)). One would have to be unbelievably pure not to be charmed by the cynicism of Machiavelli's *The Prince* (first published in 1532 and available in numerous editions) which has the additional quality of being short. Another realist masterpiece, though the purity of his realism is doubted by some recent scholars, is by E.H. Carr, *The Twenty Years' Crisis* (Basingstoke: Palgrave, 2001, 3rd edn).

On realism we can go back almost indefinitely. Thucydides' *The Peloponnesian War* is often quoted as the first classic of realism dating from the fifth century BC. There are many translations and editions. Hobbes, *The Leviathan* (in many editions, but try that of J. Plamenatz (London: Collins, 1962) should be read at some point by the serious international relations scholar even though he is concerned with domestic rather than international anarchy. It is anarchy nonetheless. More recently, Hans Morgenthau wrote the classic *Politics Among Nations* (New York: Knopf, 1948, 6th edn, rev. by K.W. Thompson, 1985), which I would recommend although it is a bit heavy going. A powerful critique of realism is given by John Vasquez in *The Power of Power Politics: A Critique* (Cambridge: Cambridge University Press, 1999). Kenneth Waltz, *Theory of International Politics* (Reading, Mass: Addison-Wesley, 1979) is the classic on structural realism. Robert

Keohane (ed.), *Neorealism and Its Critics* (New York: Columbia University Press, 1986) is a collection of articles on the state of the debate which is still important. That rational self-interest can nevertheless result in higher degrees of cooperation than one might expect intuitively is argued in Robert Axelrod, *The Evolution of Cooperation* (New York: Basic Books, 1984).

I cite three important studies in international relations and related topics in the text. The first is by Amartya Sen, *Poverty and Famines: An Essay on Entitlement and Deprivation* (Oxford: The Cavendish Press, 1981). Sen's work has been fundamental in altering our understanding of the causes and processes of famines. The second is by Lewis Fry Richardson, *Arms and Insecurity* (Pittsburgh: Boxwood Press, 1960), published posthumously. Richardson was the pioneer, in the 1930s of the social scientific approach to international relations and is regarded by many as the founder of peace research. Many scholars in this tradition (including myself, though many of my friends regard me as eccentric in this matter) regard Richardson as one of the finest minds to have applied themselves to international relations. This is a minority view in Britain though many hold it in the United States. Equally important is Richardson's *Statistics of Deadly Quarrels* (Pittsburgh: Boxwood Press) also published in 1960. John Vasquez, *The War Puzzle* (Cambridge: Cambridge University Press, 2001, 2nd edn) is an important, more recent study of the causes of war. A lot of hard research has gone into investigating the causes of war. I refer to more at the end of Chapter 8 (pp. 151–2).

7

Post-Positivist Theories and Change

The Role of Theory

Those who study international relations often do so in the hope of improving the working of the international system which all too often features wars, threats of wars, poverty and other causes of suffering for many people. The search for patterns and theory in international relations is rarely inspired by curiosity alone, though curiosity is a perfectly proper motive for a scholar. Many scholars of international relations want to go beyond this. They hope the harmful features of the system are not inevitable and try to find out what can be done to improve things. This is, of course, true in all the social sciences.

In all areas of life there are those who are temperamentally conservative and those who are temperamentally radical. International relations is no exception. Some are essentially content with the status quo, adding the occasional improvement here and there, but seeing the present system as either desirable or at least the best we can get. It is not so much a view that denies change, which appears inevitable. It is rather a view that sees change occurring in the present structure, proceeding, as it were, naturally. Others are dissatisfied and argue that the present structure will not produce the benevolent change they desire. Even here there are divisions between those who favour incremental change and those who want to attack the bases of the international system more radically.

In the last section of the previous chapter, I put the case for a broadly empiricist view of how we should analyse the international system. Some critics argue that this is too passive. By studying what is the case, rather than what could be the case, it becomes a defence of the

114

status quo and leads to mere tinkering at the edge with marginal reforms. It leads to *problem-solving theory* instead of *critical theory* directed at more fundamental change in the international system (or indeed any other social system). *Critical theorists* are sometimes linked with postmodernists (of which more below) and, indeed, with any sort of view other than the empiricist view. This is misleading, and strongly resisted by the many critical theorists who abhor postmodernism. Here a distinction between types of critical theory is useful. While postmodernism has a critical intent, it has a completely different philosophical basis from forms of critical theory that belong to the Marxist tradition.

Marxism and Critical Theory

Building on the discussion in the last chapter, there are structural theories indebted to the German philosopher Karl Marx, which can be considered critical insofar as they seek a major change in the structure of the international system. One of these is *dependency theory*, which was worked out with particular reference to Latin America but applies to all less-developed countries. Basically, dependency theorists argue that if we have powerful economic actors, whether state firms or private firms, which can profit by using their monopoly or near-monopoly power to enrich themselves, then they will do so, even if it means keeping the poorer countries poor. This is not just the consequence of a small group of a firm's directors taking decisions. It follows from the structure of the international political economy, which determines the patterns of such decisions if not their detail. The political and economic structure of the system determines the general pattern of its behaviour. Only the details may vary according to the particular decisions made.

World systems theory shifts attention to the emergence of a hierarchical structure in the capitalist world economy over several centuries. This structure has a core, made up of manufacturing states, primarily in the northern hemisphere, whose increasing wealth has historically been a function of its relationship to peripheral areas. The periphery exists in a position of structural dependence, given its inability to move beyond the production of raw materials. States in the semi-periphery, which produce luxury goods, are the linchpin in the system, as they provide a buffer against polarization between the wealthy and the poor and thus revolution. While particular states might move out of one position in the structure to another, this layer-cake structure in and of itself would be sustained. In recent times, states that were previously in the dependent periphery, such as the Celtic and Asian tigers, have managed to move into the semi-periphery as their economies have roared ahead.

In contrast to structural theories that are critical, the genre most often referred to as *critical theory* has its origins in the work of the Frankfurt School in the first half of the twentieth century. Critical theory originated with a critique of Marx. Followers of Antonio Gramsci, an Italian Marxist, also fit within this category. Critical theorists argue that theories aspire not just to 'tell the truth' in a detached and dispassionate sort of way, but also that they necessarily serve some purpose or interest, whether intentionally or not. These interests are normally those of people in power. Thus, much economic theory does not just describe and explain the processes of a capitalist economy but also, implicitly, justifies it. One can detect implied claims that capitalism is inevitable (though these two positions are not necessarily the same – one can dislike and disapprove of something that one believes to be inevitable). It is argued that the same is true of international relations theory, and was particularly true in the realist era. Structural realism in particular has an aura of inevitability about it. Many embraced the theory as much to justify the status quo as to explain it. Others accepted the status quo as inevitable – though more regretfully – which is one interpretation of Morgenthau, whose work was mentioned at the end of the last chapter.

Critical theories in the Marxist tradition seek some form of emancipation from hierarchical power relations. A structuralist approach such as dependency or world systems theory, in making a critique of international hierarchies, seeks to subvert more conventional explanations that ignore inequality and point the way to *emancipation* for people or states without power. A critical international relations theorist does the same, as would a Marxist economist, while neither would accept any clear demarcation of the boundaries of their discipline as 'economic' or 'international relations'.

Some adherents of critical theory in the Marxist tradition, and particularly the structuralists, would argue that, of course, theory should also 'tell the truth' and will not be effective unless it does. They would be allies with postmodernism in criticizing a passive attitude to truth but would not deny that there is a form of truth that is not arbitrary and to which facts are relevant. Critical theory of this kind would be distinguished from conventional theory, or so it is claimed, by asking more critical questions. However, the answers should be accepted as true by a broader set of people than would actually share the full political agenda of the critical theorist. Critical theory is done very much in the spirit of Marx's famous remark, which is so characteristic of his work that it appears on his gravestone in Highgate Cemetery in London, 'The philosophers have only *interpreted* the world, in various ways; the point, however, is to *change* it'. The change must not just be seen as immediate and superficial but must go to the centre of the analysis of the international system and other social systems.

There is some ambiguity about the nature of critical theory; an ambiguity partly caused by disagreements amongst critical theorists. Do critical theorists ask a different set of questions from those asked by more conservative theorists, and questions the conservatives do not care to ask? On this view the critical theorists regard conventional theory as inadequate, though possibly correct as far as the limited range of questions asked is concerned. Alternatively, do they disagree about the nature of the international system? In this case, critical theorists regard more conservative theorists as offering the wrong answers even to the questions they purport to answer. Finally, do critical theorists regard theory as a different sort of enterprise from others? Critical theorists differ on this. The first question would gain general agreement. The second would gain widespread but not universal agreement, while on the third there would be substantial disagreement. As amongst all groups in international relations, there are disagreements amongst critical theorists too.

Postmodernism

Some scholars, called the *postmodernists*, argue that facts and *objective truth*, which the empiricists assume, and which have been implicit in a lot of my earlier argument, are a delusion. Postmodernism is a widespread set of ideas extending from literary criticism (where it started) to architecture and geography. It is a general intellectual movement represented by philosophers such as Foucault, Derrida or Baudrillard. I shall focus on its manifestation within international relations. Postmodernists are unwilling to define themselves in any precise way and there are many different strands of thought. However, they all regard the notion of objective truth as, at best, ambiguous. I describe one or two prominent aspects of postmodern thought relevant to international relations, without making any claim to being comprehensive.

The postmodernists are critical of what they call 'modernity' – hence their name. Modernity is used to describe the rise of notions of objective science, initially about the natural world and subsequently about the social world that emerged as Europe moved out of the medieval world into the eighteenth and nineteenth century. This led to the rise of technology, the industrial revolution and so on. Post-modernists argue that modernity has made rationality an end in itself and, far from being a progressive force, this has resulted in outcomes such as the Holocaust and nuclear weapons. This is in part because the drive to find technical solutions to problems has largely sidelined moral and political questions. Thus, in modernity, deterrence is seen as a technological problem rather than a moral problem. This is true of physical military technology for which one designs weapons such as missiles and nuclear submarines (or in earlier days, battleships and machine guns). This is also true of social science in which people analyse the conditions for effective deterrence, deterrence failures and so on. In the effort to perfect deterrence, as a rational solution to the nuclear arms race, moral questions about the consequences of a nuclear war or responsibility for seeking more political solutions to conflict are ignored. The postmodernists see the vice of modernity as trying to make issues, which should really be left in the political and moral realm, into technical problems. For example, conflict resolution 'tech-niques' try to make conflict into a technical problem that is separated from morality rather than a moral problem with a central question of choice. Making problems into technical problems, they argue, can lead to moral amnesia and often does.

Many postmodernists also doubt the possibility of generalization, which is central to the constitution of a social science. Generalizations form the bases of the laws for which the social scientists search. However, for the postmodernist, historical contingency and, indeed, the contingency of the moment is central. The search for generalization is not only misguided, but serves to reinforce the legitimacy of existing power structures as expressions of an 'objective' reality. The applica-tion of a generalization to a particular case obscures its particularity and disguises the need for moral and political judgement. In the postmodern view, the deconstruction or critique of dominant representations, which are implicated in the production of power, should replace the search for generalization.

For postmodernists, scientific claims that the world is essentially one way or another are bound up with regimes of power. Rather than one necessary truth, there are always multiple stories to be told. Consider the Gulf War which, in 1991, followed on the invasion of Kuwait by Iraq a few months earlier. The postmodernist might raise questions about the necessity of this event. Even as we start, there is an ambiguity. The position of the Iraqi government was that it was merely reoccupying territory which was its by right. Postmodernists probe more deeply and look at multiple possible interpretations of what happened. From the point of view of an Iraqi conscript it was probably a frightening experience which was yet another manifestation of a life of powerlessness. (I say 'probably' as I have never met an Iraqi conscript and nor, I suspect, have most of my readers.) From the point of view of a member of an élite Iraqi corps, such as the Revolutionary Guards, it might have been an opportunity for honourable warfare. For a general in the army it was an opportunity for promotion, but for an impoverished woman bombed in Baghdad and worried about her family it was another instance of powerless suffering. She might attribute it to fate, the Americans, or see it as punishment from Allah for some sin. For a British corporal it would be one thing, and for an Egyptian corporal something else, as the latter was involved in a battle with his coreligionist. For President George Bush the Gulf War was a necessary response to the emergence of a 'Hitler' in the Middle East who had to be stopped.

Multiple stories can be told about any event. One particular story, that of the powerful actor, in this case the US regime of the time, provided the justification for action. In the process, a range of other stories that may have shaped an alternative response, were silenced. The critical intent of the postmodernist is to deconstruct the conventional wisdom in order to create a space for silenced voices to speak.

The media were also implicated in this fabrication by turning the Gulf War into a television spectacle and form of entertainment. Today, for academics and journalists, it is still something to write about and use, as I am doing, as an illustration for a theory! The postmodernists argue that there is not a single event but a multiplicity of interpretations such that the objective reality is not clear. We tend to think of the Gulf War as an unproblematic event because the people who define the agendas of what is proper to talk about, and whom we listen to, are in broad agreement and had much the same perception. But why the editors of newspapers and directors of television stations should have any more privileged insight than the Iraqi victim of bombing is not clear. Indeed, the victim, being a participant, however inadvertent, might be accorded a more, not less, privileged position.

There is obviously a lot to this argument, though it is not beyond human ingenuity to devise some formulation of something like the Gulf War such that we can agree to talk about it even though people's interpretations are different. However, the postmodernist goes further. All social events are filtered through our narratives about them. A social 'event' such as the Gulf War is just a collection of these. On this analysis, social 'facts', which are central to most analyses of international relations, become insubstantial and may fade away altogether. There can be no shared knowledge of these facts. The postmodernist doubts the existence of facts or at least their usefulness.

Feminist Theories of International Relations

Many feminists argue that the point of feminist theory is to generate an awareness of gender with a view to emancipation, particularly of women, as a general project. Further, this is not just a question of altering a few superficial aspects of society. It requires a fundamental reorientation towards the issue of gender.

There are many forms of feminist theory. As with other forms of critical theory there is some dispute whether feminist approaches, on the one hand, draw attention to sets of issues that were earlier neglected but whose incorporation alters or expands existing theory, or, on the other hand, whether it constitutes a different sort of theory.

Both critical theory, in the Marxist tradition, and postmodernism have expressions in the feminist literature. Standpoint feminists, like critical theorists, have emphasised emancipation, in this case of real flesh-and-blood women. Postmodern feminists, on the other hand, have focused more on gender, or how classifications of masculine and feminine form a hierarchy of power by which the former is more highly valued than the latter. They look to the way in which these oppositions provide the foundations of power.

Standpoint feminists – emphasising the standpoint of women – might share some of the empirical concerns of the more orthodox camp, looking at the ways in which women have not been properly considered and gender neglected. Thus, although wars have largely been fought by men, women usually form the overwhelming majority of civilian casualties. According to one estimate, 80–90% of casualties due to war since the Second World War have been women. The relationship between gender and violence is discussed on pp. 148–50. Similarly, issues of gender can hardly be neglected in talking of economic development, which is now accepted as being intimately intertwined with international relations. In general, the more international relations expands beyond the narrow confines of an analysis of interstate relations into such areas as global political economy, the more gender issues become important for their analysis.

Many feminists, however, argue that the very topics that have traditionally concerned international relations have been determined by the masculine orientation of an overwhelmingly male profession. The concerns of realists with power and war are aspects of a set of interests that are primarily male. Thus there was a bias from the beginning about what was to be considered as international relations. A realist world of international relations, in which distrust and violence is endemic, is the sort of world one would expect to find in a profession consisting largely of men. One question here is whether this male profession was distracted by its male obsessions into producing a theory that was wrong. Are the relationships between states really red in tooth and claw or, at least, always ready to become so? Cooperation does take place in the international system, not as an occasional anomaly but as a consistent and frequent pattern of interaction between states and other actors. By concentrating on power and violence, traditional international relations obscured some of the crucial aspects of the international system. This is not to argue that only women can consider issues of cooperation. However, an over-whelmingly male intellectual culture, as international relations has been until comparatively recently, is likely to neglect them. Standpoint feminists would be concerned with formulating a more specifically feminine version of international relations theory, incorporating as-pects traditionally associated with women, such as communication and dialogue. A postmodern feminist might explore the masculine and feminine hierarchies constituted in the categories of international relations theory or in the world of international relations. In this case, the finding is often that the feminine is largely invisible. For instance, women who serve as prostitutes at military bases or secretarial staff provide an invisible underpinning of global military structures.

These feminist theorists raise new issues but, arguably, their view of theory and its role is similar to the notion of theory expressed in most of this book. Many feminists have been drawn to postmodernism with its different and much more sceptical attitude to theory.

Constructivism

In recent years there has grown up an emphasis on the meanings we attribute to things in the social world and how we construct the world from, so to speak, the raw material of things. To give an example. At any given time, two, sometimes three, French submarines sail around the world with enough nuclear missiles in them to wholly destroy the United Kingdom and many other countries besides. However, they are not construed by the British as a threat, nor have they ever been. Few people in Britain go to bed fearful of what the night might bring in terms of a French nuclear assault. However, in say 1980, physically very similar submarines, armed with very similar missiles but manned by Soviet sailors, were seen as a threat which was only kept at bay by the nuclear deterrents of the Western powers. Today these same submarines are not seen as a threat, or not as much of one. They are, admittedly, older and many are decrepit, though that might lead to greater fears of accidental war than when they were more diligently cared for. However, that is not the principal reason. We have changed our minds about them or, more particularly, about the people who control them. They are no longer the enemy.

Friends, allies, enemies, interests and all the other material of international relations involve not just physical things, but the meaning we give to these physical things. They are, in some sense of the word, socially constructed by human beings within a context of social interaction. For instance, imagine two space aliens who met for the first time. They would have no reason to see the other as an enemy or a friend until, through a process of back and forth gesturing, they established a pattern of actions belonging to the category of either friend of enemy. The emphasis on this aspect of social relations, both in general and in international relations, is known as *constructivism*.

At some level this is not new. If we take another social institution, money, it is all too clear that something becomes money because we have attributed it with value as money. We are only able to engage in exchange or interact with it as money because everyone else agrees that it is money as well. Without this valuation it would be merely pieces of paper or metal objects. In this respect, then, money is a social construction. Likewise, we construct much of the material of international relations (if material is quite the word) in terms of promises, agreements, threats and so on which involve not only things but speech, acts and other forms of interaction. The things, even when they are such substantial things as nuclear submarines and missiles which have potentially disastrous consequences, are only transformed into threats or reassurances of safety when they are interpreted in terms of a social context of ideas.

Theory, Policy and Change

Theorists in the various critical traditions seek change of one sort or another. Implied in their critique of more mainstream theories is a claim that empiricism is caught up in the trappings of power and a desire to prevent change. I have argued that many scholars of international relations are attracted to the field by the thought that an increase in our knowledge is the way to improve the workings of the international system. Critical theorists make it clear that this is what they are doing, but many, who would not want to be identified as such, also see themselves as working to improve things.

To make things better, whether in general terms or in rather specific ways of carrying out foreign policy more effectively, we need to have some theory of how things work and how people behave in certain circumstances. For example, in Chapter 2, pp. 29–31 we discussed crisis decision-making. We are concerned that crises should not get out of hand and explode into war accidentally, as may have been the case in 1914. To suggest better ways of arranging decision-making structures to achieve desirable outcomes in crises, we need to have a theory of crisis behaviour. We need some notion of what will bring one consequence rather than another. At one level this might be regarded as problem-solving theory. A crisis occurs when things have gone badly wrong anyway. The more fundamental issues of peace concern the more basic structures of the international system. However, it is surely important to solve such problems. The problems are significant. It is not inconsistent with also attacking the problems of more fundamental change.

There are many other instances where theories are required if we want to intervene successfully and usefully in the world. If we are engaged in negotiations, we want to know the conditions under which a conciliatory approach is likely to bring about results and those when a tough, uncompromising approach will. It is widely believed that Germany in the 1930s was encouraged to be more demanding and expansionary by the appeasement policy of Britain and France. In the postwar era this led to many suggestions that concessions by the Western powers would be doomed to failure, particularly if they involved the Soviet Union. The German case has inhibited the analysis of concessions in international relations ever since. However, concessions are part of the negotiating process. When will they be effective and when not? This requires a theory.

Similarly, we need to know just what range of choices decision-makers realistically have. What sorts of things are possible and what not? What are the conditions under which an armed intervention in a humanitarian cause, such as an intervention in a racial war like Rwanda's can be effective? This requires a theory of intervention based on facts and analysis. What range of action does a single state have in an environmental problem? When is a state likely to be able to build up a coalition to take effective environmental action and what groups are likely to try and impede such action? These are all theoretical questions which, when answered, may make action more effective.

Implicitly decision-makers must have such theories otherwise it is hard to see how they could make any decisions at all. Sometimes these theories are not articulated clearly. Often they are not tested and challenged against the facts – not just against one instance of the facts, but against a number of instances. Sometimes one prominent case is quoted as if it were definitive, for instance, the appeasement of Germany in the 1930s, noted above. One of the jobs of the international relations theorist is to make these implicit theories explicit. This is where theory is not just an optional extra to studying the 'facts of the case' but is a requirement for more effective behaviour .

However, there are some very different notions of the relationship of theory to practice. The basic position of many empiricists or positivists is that, in order to change the world, we need to understand the world as it is. This does not imply an endorsement of current structures. Only by analysing what exists can we fully understand its capacities for change. Thus, to cure or ameliorate heart disease we need to under-standfully fully the workings of both the healthy and the damaged heart. From this we can improve the functioning of a damaged heart. The empiricists, for the most part, argue that this is also true of the social world. While there are plenty of conservative empiricists, seeking to justify the status quo, there have also been plenty of radical empiricists who were profoundly dissatisfied with the prevailing international order. In fact the big upsurge in behavioural or social scientific international relations which came about in the 1950s and 1960s was powerfully driven by many authors who were profoundly disturbed by the state of the world as it was. They sought to alter it by understanding how it worked. Many in the *peace-research* tradition in international relations, which actively posed the problems it sought to examine as those likely to promote the cause of peace, worked within the empiricist mode and still do. The peace-research tradition, though, is a very mixed one incorporating many different traditions besides the empiricist one.

Some critical theorists regard as naive or misconceived an approach to change that looks initially at existing structures. One becomes a 'problem solver', tinkering with problems within the existing structure and not fully getting to grips with the serious problem of change. Conversely, the empiricist thinks the critical theorist is often likely to blunder off into unexplored and sometimes disastrous directions while agreeing that questions about how to bring about change might lead on to fruitful analyses both of what is and what can be. Nor does the empiricist necessarily endorse only superficial change that fails to get at the heart of the problem. On the contrary, many see themselves as working to produce profound change. It is necessary to understand the observable exterior and construct theories that explain it in order to have some understanding of the deeper structures that can be altered to produce, say, a more peaceful world. However, any theorist, whether critical or otherwise, would be optimistic to the point of delusion to suppose that our present knowledge of 'deep structures' was anything more than extremely speculative.

It is hard to see how change can come about in the postmodern picture of the world. If knowledge is always implicated in power, and power silences alternatives, then it is hard to see how one could have a very coherent picture of where it could go. Indeed why should we be bothered to change anything if it is impossible to tell whether the new position is better or worse than the old? This argument is at the base of the common accusation that postmodernism ends up by being conservative despite the radical origins of many of its proponents.

Further Reading and Sources

On critical theory Andrew Linklater's, *Beyond Realism and Marxism: Critical Theory and International Relations* (London: Macmillan – now Palgrave Macmillan, 1990) is very readable. For a good overview, see Mark Hoffman, 'Critical Theory and the Inter-Paradigm Debate', *Millennium*, Vol. 16, No. 2 (1987). The journal *Millennium* contains many articles on critical theory, postmodernism and feminism as they apply to international relations and often carries articles which mark the state of the debate. For an overview of the issues related to various post-positivist theories, see also Steve Smith, Ken Booth and Marysia Zalewski, *International Theory: Positivism and Beyond* (Cambridge: Cambridge University Press, 1996).

In a more general book Chris Brown, *International Relations Theory: New Normative Approaches* (Hemel Hempstead: Harvester Wheatsheaf, 1992) makes postmodernism comprehensible, as does Richard Devetak in his chapter in Scott Burchill *et al.*, *Theories of International Relations* (Basingstoke: Palgrave, 2001, 2nd edn). A general introduction is by Richard Appignanesi and Chris Garratt, *Postmodernism for Beginners* (Cambridge: Icon Books, 1995) though its relationship to international relations is not at all direct. One of the central texts for an understanding of post modernism in international relations is the *International Studies Quarterly* (Vol. 34, No. 3, Sept. 1990). This journal normally publishes hardheaded behavioural analysis of international relations but produced a special issue on postmodernism called 'Speaking the Language of Exile: Dissidence in International Studies'. See in particular the first essay by Richard K. Ashley and R.B.J. Walker. For a postmodern analysis of the Iraq case, see David Campbell, *Politics before Principle: Sovereignty, Ethics and Narratives of the Gulf War* (Boulder: Lynne Rienner, 1993). A critical approach to postmodernism in social science in general is Pauline Rosenau, *Postmodernism and the Social Sciences; Insights, Inroads and Intrusions* (Princeton: Princeton University Press, 1992).

For a good overview of feminist approaches, see Jill Steans, *Gender and International Relations: An Introduction* (London: Polity, 1998). Cynthia Enloe is a major scholar who has done a lot to develop feminist international relations. See anything by her, but I mention particularly her *Bananas, Beaches and Bases: Making Feminist Sense of International Relations* (Berkeley: University of California Press, 2001, updated edition) and *Maneuvers: The International Politics of*

Militarizing Women's Lives (Berkeley: University of California Press, 2000). Spike Peterson and Anne Sisson Runyan, *Global Gender Issues* (Boulder: Westview, 1999, 2nd edn) has also been influential. For an example of standpoint feminism, see J. Ann Tickner's work, including *Gender in International Relations: New Directions in World Politics* (New York: Columbia University Press, 1992) or *Gendering World Politics: Issues and Approaches in the Post-Cold War Era* (New York: Columbia University Press, 2001). For an exploration of some of the issues related to postmodern feminism, see Christine Sylvester, *Feminist Theory and International Relations in a Post-Modern Era* (Cambridge: Cambridge University Press, 1994). For an analysis of gender and war, see Carol Cohen, 'Wars, Wimps and Women: Talking Gender and Thinking War', in M. Cooke and A. Wollacott (eds), *Gendering War Talk* (Princeton: Princeton University Press, 1993). Sandra Harding's classic, *The Science Question in Feminism* (Ithaca: Cornell University Press, 1986) is a more general discussion of science and feminism, which has had significant impact in international relations.

For an analysis of the meaning of constructivism within international relations, see K.M. Fierke and Knud Erik Jorgensen, *Constructing International Relations: The Next Generation* (Armonk: M.E. Sharpe, 2001). The most frequently cited text on constructivism in international relations is Alexander Wendt's, 'Anarchy is What State's Make of It', *International Organization*, Vol. 46, No. 2 (1992), although the word was first applied to the field by Nicholas Onuf in *World of Our Making: Rules and Rule In Social Theory and International Relations* (Columbia, SC: University of South Carolina Press, 1989). There has been a range of studies constrasting constructivism with approaches, including E. Adler, 'Seizing the Middle Ground: Constructivism in World Politics', *European Journal of International Relations*, Vol. 3, No. 2 (1997) and my article with K.M. Fierke, 'Divided by a Common Language: Formal and Constructivist Approaches to Games', *Global Society*, Vol. 15, No. 1 (2001). For a sympathetic critique of constructivism, see R. Palan, 'A World of Our Making: An Evaluation of the Constructivist Critique in International Relations', *Review of International Studies*, Vol. 26, No. 4 (2000).

8

Security, Violence and the Military

The Study of Security

Physical security is at the heart of social life. Life is hard to endure if there is a constant fear of death, pain or destruction. Hence the preservation or creation of security is at the heart of what many social scientists in all branches study. Human beings invented tools at an early stage and tools have enabled us to live the life we do. Unfortunately the military tool is the weapon. Thus human beings find it comparatively easy to kill each other, and they have done so with gusto throughout recorded history. This does not seem to be diminishing and violent conflict is widespread in the world today.

Security studies is the study of the security of people against violence. Sometimes it is more broadly construed to mean defence against all forms of insecurity including economic insecurity, environmental insecurity and so on. Some scholars have regarded violence as any situation in which security is violated because of the actions of other people. Violence is divided into *somatic violence* and *structural violence*. Somatic violence is violence as normally understood; that is, it is the deliberate attempt to hurt or kill someone, whether at the individual level of murder or the group level of war. Structural violence happens when people die because of the activities of other human beings even though they did not intend to kill them as such. Thus, death or debility because of unnecessary poverty is regarded as structural violence. Violence on these two counts constitutes the negative aspect of international relations. There are doubts about whether it is appropriate to call those things described as structural violence as 'violence'. In this chapter, we shall narrow the discussion to the problems of security against the deliberate violence of others at the group level.

We shall concentrate on interstate violence but not to the exclusion of other sorts of mass violence or war. Though wars are an important class of 'deadly quarrel' (see p. 3), and interstate wars are an important subclass of all wars, revolutions, civil wars and so on are also significant. Between 1900 and 1987 these together resulted directly in the death of about 43 million people, though many more indirectly. Estimates, unsurprisingly, vary widely. Nor can we feel it is something that is passing away. Around five-and-a-half million people died of political violence in the first five years of the 1990s. This is dwarfed by the number of people killed by governments or their neighbours which, as we pointed out in Chapter 1, may have resulted in the deaths of 170 million people – about four times as many as have been killed in wars. This is a central security issue but raises different issues from the questions of more orthodox war.

In this chapter, we shall discuss the nature of the military world, and the ideas of those who think about these things, and discuss the world of large-scale violence and threatened violence, particularly nuclear violence. This study is called *strategy* (or *strategic studies*) which deals with military matters, how the military system works, how to achieve advantages in military situations, and how to achieve military stability. *Peace research* is the approach that makes the achievement of peace the dominant goal.

Traditionally war has been thought to be inevitable and many people still think so. There certainly seems to be no diminution in its frequency though some people optimistically hope that, like slavery, someday it will become a defunct human institution. However, this is unlikely to happen if we avoid the responsibility of understanding why and how it happens.

Nuclear Weapons and Deterrence

Since 1945, the whole military scene has been dominated by the existence of *weapons of mass destruction*. These are forms of weapons, such as nuclear weapons, that can cause unparalleled destruction and wholly eliminate societies in a way which has not been possible before. Nuclear weapons are the ones we usually think of and they are perhaps the most important. However, both biological and chemical weapons can be used on a large scale and wreak similar sorts of destruction. We should not forget their existence, though we shall concentrate the discussion on nuclear weapons.

Fortunately, nuclear weapons have not been used since the end of the Second World War. Armed conflict has been carried out with so-called *conventional weapons*, which in practice means weapons which are not nuclear. These can nevertheless be extremely destructive. However, with nuclear weapons, it has become possible to destroy the planet. Thus, the problem has become correspondingly more serious. It dominated the discussion of international relations during the period of the Cold War when many people were anxious for the survival of the world. Discussion of these issues is more muted today, as the threat seems less acute. However, there are still many nuclear weapons in the world, and many states look at other states with undisguised hostility. It is premature to assume that the world is safe from nuclear destruction. We need to understand the problem in order to tame it.

In 1945 an atomic bomb was dropped on the Japanese city of Hiroshima. A few days later another was dropped on Nagasaki. These are the only nuclear weapons that have ever been used in anger, though, in many ways, they were only the beginning of the security drama which has dominated the world ever since. The size of nuclear detonations is now without effective limit and whole societies can be destroyed. This has led to a revolution about how we think about war, or at least certain sorts of war. Strategists have traditionally considered how to win wars or, at least, how not to lose them. Now strategists ponder how to prevent wars, or at least nuclear wars, without sacrificing the national interest unduly. This has led to the development of the doctrine of *nuclear deterrence*. This doctrine was developed in the context of the Cold War but it applies to any context where there are nuclear weapons.

The threat of nuclear extermination profoundly affected many people during the era of the Cold War and was a dominant political factor for forty years. With the big reduction in the fear that the USA and Russia would go to war, interest has waned and political energies are focused on such equally important things as the environment and world poverty. However, the threat still exists. There are many tensions in the world between nuclear powers such as India, Pakistan and China, where at least a latent nuclear deterrence is present. Between

India and Pakistan, the nuclear threat is open. There is the fear that more states will acquire nuclear weapons. It would be quite possible for a small and erratic state to get hold of one and threaten others – this, indeed, is still the rationale the British government uses for retaining and updating its nuclear forces.

The Theory of Nuclear Deterrence

Briefly, the argument is as follows. Suppose we have two states, A and B, which both have nuclear weapons in sufficient quantities to destroy the other country as a functioning society. If there is tension between them there is some pressure for one side, say A, to release its nuclear weapons and destroy B. Further, if such an attack by A could destroy B's nuclear weapons, B would not be able to respond. Thus A would be strongly tempted to initiate an attack on B if only to stop B from initiating an attack itself, as clearly this logic applies to both parties. In this situation, a nuclear war could break out easily, even if neither side really wanted it, simply because each distrusted the other. This problem was recognized early on and the doctrine of the *second strike* was formulated. If both sides could effectively defend their nuclear weapons against a nuclear attack, no matter how large, then they would be in a position to counter-attack even if the aggressor had destroyed the country as a whole. The military machine would still exist and be effective. This would mean a counter-attack would be possible even though practically everything else in the society was destroyed. This became know as mutually assured destruction, which had the appropriate acronym of MAD. This may seem a very unpleasant way of reasoning but it permitted the following policy to be asserted. 'We, the government of A, will not initiate a nuclear attack on country B. However, if country B should attack us, then we will respond with a nuclear attack.' Thus, any attack on A by B would be self-defeating. Though B can destroy A, it will only be at the cost of being itself destroyed. Thus, a military system was built up whose whole point was that it should not be used. In other words, if the weapons are used, deterrence has failed. However, to succeed it must look effective, for it is crucial to the argument that a putative opponent should believe that an overwhelming counter-attack will be the consequence of initiating an attack.

The Technicalities of Nuclear Deterrence

The heyday of nuclear deterrence was the period of the Cold War between the so-called Western states, led by the United States, and the so-called communist bloc, led by the Soviet Union. Though the Cold War has passed in its original form, the principles remain the same.

Nuclear bombs can have enormous destructive power. However, the bomb has to be conveyed to the enemy country where it is to go off and the problem of delivery is as crucial as the design of the bomb itself. Though bombs can be carried by aeroplanes, these are very vulnerable. The more usual plan is for them to be carried by rockets. Rockets and their capabilities are an integral part of the whole argument, an important class of these are the inter-continental ballistic missiles (ICBMs) which go up into the stratosphere. They are virtually impossible to shoot down once launched, at least in the current state of technology, though this could change. Thus, a would-be victim of such an attack tries to destroy the ICBMs before they are launched while, of course, their owners want to protect them even against a nuclear attack. Broadly, there are two ways of doing this. First is to put the missiles underground in holes with very strongly built sides that will not readily collapse even if there is a nuclear detonation near by. These are known as *hardened silos* and will survive anything other than a direct hit. Although rockets are remarkably accurate, providing there are enough missiles in hardened silos, they will not all be destroyed. Because of the extraordinary destructive power of modern nuclear weapons, only a few need to survive to inflict appalling damage on an opponent. The other technique is favoured by countries with a smaller land mass than either the USA or the former Soviet Union. Missiles are put in submarines. Submarines are vulnerable if an opponent knows where they are, but they are very difficult to find. Surface ships can easily be spotted with radar (as can aircraft) but there is no equivalent of radar that works under the water. Because there is a lot of water in the world, submarines can hide and fire their missiles with impunity should the time come. A few might be found and destroyed but it is unlikely that they all will. In these ways, the nuclear powers try to make their weapons invulnerable to attack and keep the opponents from attacking from fear of a whole-scale attack against them.

Conditions for the Success of Nuclear Deterrence

For nuclear deterrence to be a successful strategy there are three requirements. Success, of course, means that war does not break out. First, it has to be technically possible to protect sufficient missiles against a rival's attack so as to maintain an ability to respond in a devastating manner. Second, there has to be an organizational structure that can survive an attack in order to arrange for the counter-attack. That is, there has to be someone to give the order or some procedure to ensure that missiles are fired. Third, the putative victim has to be willing actually to carry out the counter-attack. More strictly, both rivals have to *think* their opponent will be willing and able to counter-attack. It is this *belief* which is central to the argument.

The first question was considered above. There seems to be general agreement amongst strategic experts that second strike nuclear capacity is possible and that the various nuclear powers have in fact achieved it. The problems arise with the other two.

The second question is more problematic. It is known as the problem of *Command and Control* (or, in a more extended form, Command, Control, Communication and Intelligence or C^3I). Whether a state can organize a nuclear response to a nuclear attack is partly a technical question and partly an organizational question. There have to be procedures such that, even after a devastating nuclear attack, there is someone available who can give the order to respond and, further, has the means to convey the order. The people receiving the order have to know that it is genuine – perhaps not a problem in stable times, but in a time of total destruction a serious problem. It is difficult to convey orders to submarines at the best of times (radio does not work very well under water). The procedure may have to be that if they do *not* get a message after a number of occasions when they could do so, they will interpret this as permission to fire their missiles.

The point to emphasize is that this is all a question of belief. The opponent has to *believe* that its rival has effective C^3I procedures as the aim is that they should never be activated which, the theory goes, will be the case if people believe with confidence that they could be activated.

Belief is the crux of the final question. Do each of the rivals believe that the victim of a nuclear attack would have the determination to counter-attack? There is, after all, very little direct advantage in doing so. Revenge, or possibly some bizarre sense of justice, would be the only motive. Even then, one might feel that some human beings should live rather than none, even if the survivors are the less worthy. However evil one feels the other regime to be, most of the people killed are as likely to be victims themselves as perpetrators of the crimes.

Conveying one's willingness to carry out something that, if the situation were to arise, would be only dubiously rational is another problem. However, it is a necessary part of the argument. To repeat: what is central to a deterrence policy is that the opponent should *believe* that the deterrer will carry out the policy if necessary. Fundamentally, deterrence is a state of mind induced by the deterrer in the deterree. The whole concept of deterrence is based on the ability of opponents to convince each other that, if the crunch came, they would be willing to carry out some act which, on all reasonable criteria, would be totally against their own self-interest and, indeed, manifestly self-destructive.

Did Nuclear Deterrence Prevent a Superpower War?

The two superpowers of the USA and the Soviet Union stayed hostile to each other for over forty years without actually fighting. A cold war of this length is unprecedented historically. Admittedly there were the so-called 'proxy wars' such as Korea and Vietnam, where the USA fought communist regimes as some sort of surrogate for the Soviet Union, but the two central parties never fought. It is possible that, on rare occasions, Soviet and American troops exchanged fire. If so, they took care to dress in someone else's uniforms.

That the USA and Soviet Union did not fight each other directly while in a state of mutual suspicion and enmity is clear and undisputed. The normal explanation for this is that it was because of nuclear deterrence. Neither side dared offend the other too much for fear that a nuclear war would break out, and peace was therefore preserved by the mechanism explained above. Clearly this is a possibility and perhaps the most likely explanation. However, there are alternatives that we should briefly consider.

In Western countries, the conventional view is that the United States did not have any malicious designs on the Soviet Union. However, the Soviet Union was a likely aggressor or would have been if it could have got away with it. This is often disputed. It is argued that the United States extended its influence in all parts of the world when it felt it could, but was unwilling to intervene in Eastern Europe because of nuclear deterrence. Thus, its behaviour can also be regarded as an instance of deterrence working.

An alternative view denies the significance of deterrence. Once the Soviet Union had control over Eastern Europe it did not particularly want to go any further. Russian history (for Russia is both the predecessor and successor of the Soviet Union) suggested that invaders, of whom there had been many, came from the West. Russia could be safe only if it controlled a sufficiently large group of *buffer states* on its Western borders. Once it had achieved this, it had no further territorial ambitions. Its initial eagerness for these buffer states after 1945 was misinterpreted as a general imperialist desire for as much territory as possible, which was frustrated only by the nuclear threat from the West.

A totally different alternative to the conventional picture is that the Soviet government was deterred not by nuclear weapons but by the trouble it would be put to if it imposed unpopular governments on yet further tracts of territory. Their domination of Eastern Europe was always uneasy. The Poles, Czechoslovaks, Hungarians and others were restive and caused much trouble, making the balance sheet of gain and loss to the Soviet Union always suspect. To have added yet further territories and their possibly rebellious populations to their empire would have been too much. Thus, prudence was induced by fear of the rebels rather than fear of nuclear weapons.

I am not arguing that nuclear deterrence did not apply. The different factors could have reinforced each other. Perhaps nuclear deterrence was central but in our present state of knowledge we cannot be sure. We should not assume it just because many other people assume it. Almost any form of behaviour can be explained in a number of different ways. As responsible analysts of the social world we should explore alternatives and work out what evidence would support or refute the different points of view.

Proliferation of Nuclear Weapons

I explained deterrence in terms of the relationship between the United States and Soviet Union until the end of the Cold War. They were not the only nuclear powers at that stage but the tension between them dominated the world scene. The fear was that deterrence at some stage might break down, though thankfully it never did. Three other countries openly had nuclear weapons during that period – Britain from 1952, France from 1960 and China from 1964. Some others also probably had them. Israel almost certainly is a nuclear power though it still does not admit to it. Countries such as India and Pakistan have effectively had nuclear weapons from about the late 1980s in the sense that the knowledge and materials were there and the weapons could have been assembled quickly. It is generally thought that many states could get nuclear weapons with relative ease, but their governments would rather hold back, believing that the fewer countries who have them the better.

The spread of nuclear weapons to more states is called *nuclear proliferation*. A common view is that, as the number of states with nuclear weapons increases, the more likely is nuclear war. There are thus two problems. First, is significant nuclear proliferation likely? Second, how dangerous is nuclear proliferation if it happens?

One of the surprising things about nuclear weapons is how slow proliferation has been. In 1963 President Kennedy expressed the fear that in twelve years (that is, by 1975) there would be 15 or 20 nuclear powers. This view was widely held at the time but the prediction turned out to be wrong. There is no general agreement as to why this was so. Some argue that the standard realist hypothesis of an obsession with security is simply false. States did not really believe they would be threatened by nuclear attack and saw no reason to make extravagant preparations to counter-attack in the face of what appeared to be an improbable threat. Others argue that many states felt protected by the existing nuclear powers. A country such as Italy, for example, might feel protected by the American nuclear umbrella (though there is no adequate explanation for why Italy should feel protected while Britain did not).

Optimists have suggested that non-proliferation is the consequence of the Nuclear Non-Proliferation Treaty signed by many states in 1970 and which, by 1989, had 119 signatories. This prohibited the purchase of nuclear weapons by hitherto non-nuclear states and, to be on the safe side, also prohibited the export of nuclear weapons to states who already had them. Thus it sought to stabilize the number of states with nuclear weapons at the existing level. Unfortunately it was conspicuous that those states, such as India, who were most likely to want to acquire nuclear weapons were not signatories to the Treaty. Nevertheless the Treaty might be thought to have established a tentative norm that would act as some sort of inhibition on proliferation.

Others argue that, though states such as Sweden and Canada are not nuclear in the sense of having acquired nuclear weapons, they have the expertise and knowledge to build them at very short notice if they should need to. If they were to introduce nuclear weapons, this might break the taboo many states seem to feel on getting them. This probably would be followed by widespread nuclear proliferation. Keeping an option to build nuclear weapons quickly, without actually doing so, means such countries can have the benefits of a comparatively low level of proliferation in the world without sacrificing very much if non-proliferation breaks down. Further, domestic opposition to nuclear weapons, which is vociferous in countries like Sweden, is avoided.

The last of these hypotheses seems very plausible, though none of the possibilities stands out as obviously true or obviously false. The fact remains, however, that nuclear proliferation to date has been much slower than was earlier expected. For many, it is one of the rare cheerful things about international relations today.

The governments of some states, however, remain discontented with being in the non-nuclear category. Iran, Iraq and Libya, for example, regard the small number of rich or big states with nuclear weapons as demonstrating the arrogant domination of the West. Even if, rather reluctantly, they would allow the USA and Soviet Union, or now Russia, to have nuclear weapons, it is not clear that they would extend this tolerance to Britain and France. Both Britain and France, whose security concerns do not seem to be particularly acute, are reluctant to dispense with nuclear weapons. This suggests to some non-nuclear but vulnerable states that they have a legitimate interest in becoming nuclear. Thus they, and probably a number of other states, are interested in the nuclear option.

The break-up of the Soviet Union has added two problems to the equation. First, there are many former Soviet citizens with the considerable engineering and technical expertise required to build nuclear weapons and their near-necessary accompaniment of powerful rockets. Further, the poverty of these experts makes them swallow what doubts they might feel about helping other countries build nuclear weapons. Likewise, material can be provided clandestinely from the former Soviet Union, while the eagerness of many other powers to sell related materials can fill most deficiencies. Thus, the practical problems for even poor countries building nuclear weapons are less severe than they were and some nuclear proliferation can be expected. Secondly, there are a total of five former Soviet republics which have nuclear weapons stationed on their soil, though only Russia is in full control of them. None of the regimes, including that of Russia itself, is very stable and the possibility of virulent nationalist regimes with nuclear weapons cannot be ruled out. The greater the number of states with nuclear weapons, the more uneasy the still non-nuclear states become and the situation could get out of hand. The errors of prediction regarding proliferation make one cautious in making predictions now. Nevertheless, it does seem likely that further proliferation will take place. Further, the politically unstable nature of some of the states that might acquire nuclear weapons at some point causes justifiable unease.

How serious is further proliferation? Conventional wisdom is that the more nuclear states there are, the more likely it is that a nuclear war will break out either deliberately or by accident. A few scholars, notably Kenneth Waltz (1981), have argued to the contrary. Waltz argues that states in a nuclear situation begin to act much more cautiously. Would Iraq have attacked Iran if Iran had had a nuclear weapon? Perhaps the relationship between India and Pakistan is more stable rather than less because of general fears of the nuclear capabilities of the other. Indeed if we believe in the theory of nuclear deterrence for the USA and former Soviet Union, then, by extension, it should have more general application. If we believe that nuclear weapons preserved the peace in the Cold War, then, to be consistent, we should applaud rather than deplore the proliferation of nuclear weapons. If nuclear weapons kept the peace between the USA and Soviet Union, why should it not do the same between all hostile states from North Korea and South Korea to Israel and its Arab neighbours?

There are a number of powerful arguments on the other side. First, though the probability of accidental nuclear war may be very small, it is not totally negligible. The more sources of nuclear war there are, the greater is this probability, so the fewer states with weapons, the better. Second, it is widely believed that the probability of accidental war is much lower now than it was. The older nuclear powers have strengthened Command and Control procedures, having been frightened by the danger that they ran earlier. It is possible to argue that the world was lucky to get away without an accidental nuclear war in the 1950s and 1960s. New nuclear powers, however, are likely to want to get their nuclear systems in place first and worry about the problems of Command and Control afterwards. An eager military dictator might well not worry too much about problems of Command and Control anyway. This makes the probability of accidental nuclear war greater. Third, even if a fully developed situation of nuclear deterrence, instituted between two hostile powers were stable, the dynamic of the weapons build-up would be one of great instability. The relevant states are unlikely to be at an equal stage throughout the build-up. The leader might well initiate an attack on its rival early on while it still had a first-strike capacity. This attack might be conventional, but it might be nuclear. Fourth, although some leaders of the existing nuclear powers have caused moments of unease among friends and enemies alike, the governments have been relatively cautious. Above all, they understood the general principles of nuclear deterrence and were very anxious to preserve their own societies. Enthusiasts for nuclear deterrence argue that this is because of the nuclear situation and it is not fortuitous. However, many argue it was because of luck. A leader absorbed in some extreme religious, nationalist or racial ideology might not place much store on the preservation of the home society unless it was 'pure' in some form. It is surely quite credible that someone such as Hitler, at least towards the end of the Nazi regime, would have been prepared to unleash a nuclear attack, even if it would have resulted in the destruction of his own society as well as others. Thus, even if the argument is correct in most circumstances, the 'Mad Ruler' problem (which is often referred to as the 'Crazy State' problem) makes the spread of nuclear weapons disturbing. Finally, the argument rests on the assumption that nuclear deterrence has worked. While this is the traditional view, as I argued above, it is not as conclusively established as is sometimes implied.

The point remains that, if nuclear deterrence works, it is unclear why it should not be encouraged rather than discouraged. There are good reasons for caution but we should think about them explicitly.

There remain, of course, moral questions that are particular to nuclear war and, by extension, to nuclear deterrence. It can be argued that war, though regrettable, is morally permissible when technology is such that societies and the world in general can survive it, albeit in a damaged form. Nuclear war is something different. With nuclear war we run the risk of destroying everything and even ending human life. Its destructiveness raises new moral problems, which we discuss in the chapter on morality.

Alternatives to Nuclear Deterrence

After the Cuban Missile Crisis in the early sixties, there were significant moves toward arms control. Having approached the brink of nuclear war, the two superpowers stepped back and recognized the need for improved communication in future crises. From this emerged an arms-control regime that included limits on the proliferation of nuclear weapons, attempts to keep the arms of the two sides in rough balance and efforts to halt the development of defensive or anti-ballistic missile (ABM) systems. The latter were understood to be particularly desta-bilizing. If one side developed a protective shield, which would allow it to neutralize incoming nuclear weapons prior to detonation, it would then be less inhibited about launching its own weapons against a rival. At the same time, a rival which lacked a protective shield of its own would have an incentive to launch its weapons early in a crisis situation. This phenomenon is often referred to as 'use 'em or lose 'em'. Throughout the 1970s and 1980s, the conventional wisdom was that anti-ballistic missile defences should be avoided.

In the 1980s, sentiments in regard to both arms control and ABMs changed dramatically. A new generation of nuclear weapons was developed, characterized by a reduced warning time, because of their increased speed and first strike capability. While many leaders, and particularly US President Reagan saw this development as enhancing nuclear deterrence, other groups in the USA and Europe, frightened by the prospect of nuclear war, began to call for an end to the nuclear arms race and disarmament. Against this background, President Reagan introduced his intention to develop a Strategic Defence Initiative (SDI), popularly referred to as 'Star Wars', as a protective shield against Soviet nuclear missiles. Many scientists believed the system to be technologically impossible since it presupposed the potential to shoot down incoming nuclear missiles over the entire air space of the USA. Many strategists feared this development would be destabilizing politically insofar as it would abrogate the ABM Treaty. The Soviet Union, which saw this treaty as a foundation of peace and global stability, was particularly concerned about the prospect of SDI. A new leader, Mikhail Gorbachev, who came to office in 1985, shifted the international momentum towards actual disarmament. Riding on the wave of anti-nuclear sentiment, he made unilateral gestures, for instance by stopping nuclear tests for a time, as a way of increasing pressure on the USA to respond in kind. In 1986, Reagan and

Gorbachev met in Reykjavik and agreed in principle to total nuclear disarmament, although Reagan would not give up on SDI. A year later the Intermediate Nuclear Forces Treaty, which was the first disarmament provision of the Cold War, was signed.

As the Cold War ended, serious disarmament negotiations involving the range of nuclear systems were underway. However, in a recent review of the Non-Proliferation Treaty in 2000, many states expressed concern that the nuclear powers had not taken their disarmament obligations seriously enough and that progress had stalled since the end of the Cold War. The parties to the treaty identified several important steps to be pursued over the following five years, in addition to the bilateral strategic arms reductions that were already under way. These included further unilateral efforts to reduce nuclear arsenals, more information on nuclear capabilities and the implementation of disarmament agreements, and the involvement of all five nuclear powers in nuclear reduction and disarmament negotiations. In May 2001, the UN Secretary-General Kofi Annan described the Final Review document as an 'historic consensus' extending the reach of the Treaty to 'new efforts aimed at the total elimination of nuclear weapons'.

In the USA moves toward disarmament continue to be combined with an interest in defensive systems. With the end of the Cold War, as nuclear weapons were depoliticized, SDI for a time receded into the background. It has re-emerged, however, particularly since the election of US President George Bush Jr, in the form of 'Son of Star Wars'. One of the justifications for the system, at the turn of the millennium, was the fear that rogue states, such as Iraq, would launch a nuclear missile against the United States. Questions about this need were raised by the simplicity of the attacks on the World Trade Center and Pentagon on 11 September 2001. If terrorists could cause this degree of devastation with passenger airplanes, many argued, the real threat did not necessarily come from nuclear missiles.

Renewed fears of terrorism have also highlighted concerns about more accessible forms of non-nuclear weapons of mass destruction. Chemical weapons rely on super-toxic liquid and gaseous substances that can be dispersed in bombs, rockets, missiles, artillery, mines, grenades, or spray tanks. Chlorine and mustard gas were widely used in the First World War, causing over one million injuries. Chemical weapons were used in North Africa and China by Italian and Japanese forces, respectively, during the Second World War, although not in Europe. These weapons were used more recently in the Iran–Iraq War during the 1980s. Biological weapons, such as the anthrax found in a series of American postboxes in the months following the attack of 11 September 2001, are also a source of concern. At the core of biological weapons are bacteria or viruses, which rapidly reproduce, or toxic poisonous substances. While some of these can be treated with antibiotics, germ weapons are ideal for terrorists since they can be readily acquired, easily concealed, kill a very large number of people with small quantities and do not require an advanced delivery system. The Geneva Protocol of 1925, signed by 140 states, banned the use of chemical and bacteriological weapons. There have been numerous attempts since to control the proliferation of both of these deadly forms of warfare. The Chemical Weapons Convention, which as of 2001 has 174 signatories, goes beyond banning chemical weapons, to stipulate that those states possessing them must dismantle their stocks over a ten-year period. This is seen as the most significant agreement to stem the proliferation of weapons of mass destruction since the 1968 Nuclear Non-Proliferation Treaty. While a Biological Weapons Convention has been in effect since 1973, the process was thrown into disarray at the Fifth Review Conference over issues of verification.

Who Fights Whom and Why?

Which states fight which and why they fight each other is a central problem in international relations. We could of course make a list of wars and the reasons they were fought, treating every case individually. As we argued in the chapter on theories, this would involve abandoning theory and thus, to a large extent, the hope of at least reducing the incidence of war. Some believe that this is all we can do. Perhaps it is, but some, at least, are more optimistic and search for some general causes.

We are a long way from being able to assert a set of general causes for war. Few things in social life have single causes and war is not one of them. We would expect multiple causes that reinforce each other . Our lack of anything like a definitive solution is not for want of effort on the part of many scholars. Much of the work has been done on interstate war – the normal meaning of war until towards the end of the twentieth century. It is broadly true we know more about interstate war than we do about other forms of large-scale violent conflict. Even if we lack a compelling overall theory, scholars have produced many interesting and relevant findings. Some of these factors predispose states towards war, and some predispose them towards peace. The work of Vasquez (1993) has brought to the fore the significance of territorial disputes. Territorial disputes are frequently involved in rivalries between states. States with such disputes more often go to war than those without them. Not surprisingly, territorial disputes are more likely to occur between contiguous states rather than those that are distant from each other, though this is not always the case. Britain and Argentina were not contiguous states but managed a war in 1982 over the Falklands/Malvinas. Nevertheless, contiguous states are more likely to go to war than distant states. That territorial disputes lead to war is not too surprising. Often the relevant piece of territory bestows wealth on the owner. In recent times, Kuwait's oil provided a powerful incentive for war, as did the oil around the Falklands/Malvinas. It is perhaps more surprising that territorial disputes stand out as such an important cause of war, but this seems clear from the evidence. This leads to the further unsurprising result that crises relating to territorial issues are more likely to escalate to war than other crises.

States are more likely to go to war if they have been in conflict over a long time – the so-called 'enduring rivalries'. A crisis is more likely to escalate to war if it is one of a sequence of such crises than if it emerged between two hitherto relatively amicable states. This overlaps with the previous factor. Territorial disputes by their nature tend to be long-lasting.

The issue of power and its relation to war is one that is still not clearly settled despite its long history of discussion in international relations. Classically people thought that if power were in balance there would not be war. Indeed, it seems rather commonsensical that it should be so. However, it is much more complex than that, and sometimes counterintuitive. It is important to distinguish between 'satisfied states' who are broadly content with their current position in the international system and 'dissatisfied states' who are not and want some significant change in their favour. If there is a dispute between a satisfied power and a dissatisfied power, it is more likely to escalate to war if there is a balance of power than if there is not. Despite what one might think, imbalances of power do not provide a particularly strong predisposition towards war.

Table 8.1   Dispute behaviour ('relevant dyad years' 1946–86)

Dispute level	Both states democratic	One or both non-democratic	Total
(a) No dispute	3864	24 503	28 367
(b) Threat or display of force	6	155	161
(c) Use of force and war	8	545	553
(c) as % of (a)	0.2%	2.2%	

Source: Russett (1993).

We also know of some factors that predispose states towards peace. The most significant of these is the so-called 'democratic peace' factor, one of the strongest findings in all the statistical literature in international relations. It seems clear that, while democratic states fight in general as much as non-democratic states, they rarely fight other democratic states. I give a few illustrative statistics in Table 8.1, which summarises relations between pairs of states, or dyads.

From these figures, it appears that, when wars occur, overwhelmingly they involve at least one non-democratic actor. The pie chart in Figure 8.1 illustrates this.

This is just one study, but there are many more which consistently support this finding. Thus, analyzing the longer period of 1816–1967, Stuart Bremer (1992) estimated the conditional probability of two

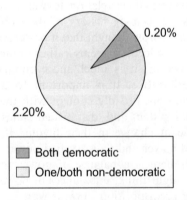

Figure 8.1   Percentage of dyad-years when force was used

democracies going to war as one-fourteenth the probability when a non-democracy is involved.

Obviously there are queries about arguments based on statistics. Two of the most important are the problems of definition and the possibilities of alternative explanations.

Democracy can be defined in many different ways and different definitions provide us with different sets of cases. As with all statistical problems, we must ask how sensitive the result is to different definitions of democracy. In fact, the results seem insensitive to the precise definition. No reasonable definition of democracy, lax or tight, has, so far, failed to give a clear demonstration of this relationship.

However, there may be alternative explanations. There are many causes of peace and war and it may be that one of the others subsumes the so-called democratic factor. One possibility is that many of the cases of democracy come after the Second World War and this may be a feature in some way or another of the Cold War. Of course, the results may come about from chance alone. It could be a coincidence but, given that there are 545 non-democratic cases and only 8 democratic cases (none of which, in fact, went to full-scale war), this is rather unlikely. Both statistically and definitionally, the result has so far survived assault. It is surprisingly robust and, despite picking at the edges, has so far withstood attempts to overturn it. The finding is inconsistent with the realist position, at least, if interpreted strictly in the billiard-ball form. Unless, improbably, this is a gigantic coincidence, the type of regime does affect its foreign policy. This is an anomaly in the realist position rather than a refutation but it is an anomaly to which realists must attend.

Though the most spectacular and the most talked-about factor in promoting peace, it is by no means the only one. Another study by Russett and Oneal shows that economic interdependence and common membership of international organizations also predispose towards peaceful relationships, particularly when in conjunction with each other. This again supports the view that explanations of peace and war are multiple and reinforcing. The democratic peace factor is unusual in standing out on its own as a single factor.

One final factor of significance is the importance of the development of norms between states. While the cynic might be sceptical, the development of codes of conduct between states, either generally or over particular sets of issues, decreases the likelihood that a dispute will be settled by violence.

Economic Sanctions

There are different types of weapons and different types of war, but there have also been other methods suggested for states to impose their will on others that do not involve military violence. Conspicuous amongst these are *economic sanctions*. Briefly, suppose that one state wishes to influence another's policy, such as many states did with South Africa when it was under the apartheid regime. Another instance is the desire to persuade Iraq to relinquish its search for nuclear weapons. States may be reluctant actually to use military force. In this case they might use economic sanctions. These involve the refusal to import or export goods and services to or from the target state and thus impose strains on the victim's economy. The sanctions may involve a total boycott of all goods and services or a partial one involving, say, military weapons only. Alternatively it could be a general boycott except for medical supplies.

Superficially sanctions seem very appealing. They seem to be a method of putting significant pressure on a state without the horrors of war. In the 1930s there were some who optimistically thought that they would replace war. However, a closer examination suggests that, while sanctions have been useful, they have been less effective as coercive tools than one might think. Further, they sometimes impose a lot of suffering on the wrong people.

As far as effectiveness of sanctions is concerned, even a very optimistic study (by Hufbauer *et al.*) suggests that they are only effective in about a third of the cases. This study was criticised for its claims that the successes were not in fact successes at all, or alternatively were due to other causes. Thus, there were hardly any successes at all. The issue is still controversial, though no-one would argue that their success rate was particularly good, at least as far as the ostensible goals of the sanctions were concerned.

There are three main reasons why this is so. First, to be effective all significant trading states must agree to the sanctions. If one state refuses to apply sanctions, not only does this undermine the sanctions policy (though it still may make things a little uncomfortable for the targeted state, as it will have to buy some of the commodities rather more expensively), but it provides lucrative openings for the defector state. This tempts states that are not too concerned over the issues that inspired the sanctions policy not to join in. One defector makes other states have second thoughts. The thought of a lucrative market disappearing elsewhere reduces the enthusiasm for sanctions quite remarkably. A government faced with intensive lobbying from export firms can usually find some good reasons to follow another policy.

Second, economies are often much more flexible than is sometimes supposed. They can start to produce at home what was previously imported, with some loss but not necessarily a crippling one. Clearly it depends on the nature of the economy and what products are at issue. A big economy is likely to be able to readjust less painfully than a small one. It also depends on how well the economy is managed and how flexible people within the society are. An economy is more vulnerable if it depends on one single export or alternatively depends on one or a small group of imports for which it is hard to find a domestic substitute. Thus, the Cuban economy had great difficulty when the United States refused to buy sugar from it, as sugar was the dominant export. Sanctions also provide lucrative markets for smugglers. Illegal sales of arms, for example, sustained both Iran and Iraq in the war of the 1980s. Though nominally these arms were destined for some other state, it was comparatively easy to divert them to the warring states, quite possibly with the covert blessing of the governments concerned. Zimbabwe, in its former incarnation as the white-dominated state of Rhodesia, managed to do very well under sanctions. The one commodity it really needed from abroad was oil but illegal shipments, much of which came through the friendly state of South Africa, were ample to satisfy requirements. Coupled with a well-managed and flexible economy, sanctions were little more than an inconvenience. The hoped-for collapse of the white supremacist government was much delayed and, when it came, had little to do with the sanctions.

The third reason is that, when sanctions are effective in seriously damaging an economy, they normally do not affect the élites who are making the decisions. Even in a devastated economy, or for that matter a society which is very poor for whatever reason, it is possible for a small number of people to live well, or even extravagantly. If the government of a target state is concerned about the suffering of its citizens, then sanctions can be effective. If they are unconcerned, and many governments seem concerned about the welfare of their citizens only in rhetoric, then the sanctions will have little effect on those whom they are primarily intending to influence. This was a major factor in the ineffectiveness of sanctions against Iraq during and after the Gulf War. It also raises the issue of whether sanctions do not impose as much, or even more, suffering than acts of war. Thus, 3.5 million children in Iraq have been put at risk since 1990 because of economic sanctions. It is hard to judge how many children have died because of this amidst the clamour of competing propagandists, but it is foolish to suppose that sanctions do not have serious humanitarian consequences which may, at times, exceed those of war.

This does not mean that sanctions are always of no value. It means that they have to be considered carefully from the point of view of their likely success and their humanitarian consequences. Even though they might have limited direct economic effect, or through the economic effect the appropriate political effect, they can sometimes be of symbolic use. Thus, it is unlikely that the various sanctions and boycotts that were imposed on South Africa during apartheid had any very direct effect in finally overthrowing that regime. However, the symbolism was potent and gave an encouraging message to the internal opponents of apartheid that there was much support for them in the outside world.

Women, Violence and the Military

Until very recently, military violence has been an exclusively male phenomenon. Soldiers are largely young men under the age of about 26. The victims were often women, but the practitioners were men. Women's role in fighting has been as a support, as often as not as a sexual support, either as the loyal wife at home or as camp followers and prostitutes. Until revolutionized by Florence Nightingale and her disciples, nursing was a crude activity, often closely associated with prostitution. Until the latter part of the nineteenth century, the role of women was primarily as camp-followers. They were drawn from the same desperately poor parts of society as the private soldiers. Even these women, viewed with contempt by the rest of society, kept clear of the actual fighting.

By the time of the First World War, the role of women was institutionalized, with women in uniform and military ranks. Their role, however, was strictly a support role and they carried out the administration, cooking and so on. The idea that they might be combatants would probably have been regarded as comic by practically everyone, including the women. Nursing became more acceptable and, particularly in the war, 'respectable women' were nurses. Though not combatants, nurses often worked near the front line in conditions of great discomfort and danger. The participation of women in the military in non-combatant roles developed in the Second World War in all countries, and is now firmly established. With the widening view that women should be able to take all roles in public society on the same basis as men, there are moves in many countries for women to be combatants. There were women combatant soldiers in the American Army in the Gulf War.

The predominantly male nature of military conflict has led to the speculation that this represents some inherent gender differences in approaches to military violence. As military violence is an important aspect of international relations in all schools of thought and central in some, this leads to the view that international relations is centrally a gender-dominated issue. It went unnoticed because it was so automatically accepted. This view is reinforced by a number of issues. The dominant role of men in fighting is common to virtually all societies and is not specific to European societies. The interest in war films, books about war and so on is widespread among males but less so among females. On a smaller scale, crimes of violence are largely committed by men. This all seems to confirm, what many believed in any case, that women were less prone to violence in general and military violence in particular. This can be extended to conflict in general. There is both experimental and anecdotal evidence suggesting that women are more apt to look for consensual methods of solving problems whereas men tend to follow conflictual, combative methods.

Terrorism is a significant anomaly to this. Women are more frequently found to be amongst terrorist groups than in any other form of violent group. The one exception to the widespread rule that women were not sent into combat in the Second World War were the women who were occasionally sent to fight with resistance movements.

What are the implications of this? If women are genuinely less prone to violence than men, then the greater roles that women play in society might make for a peaceful society. This does not seem to happen. We have already noted that women in governmental positions seem to be as conflictual as men, though this is what one might have expected from a structuralist perspective, at least in the short run. Further, as women participate more in public society, they seem to be attracted to such professions as law and finance where conflictual norms predominate as well as professions such as medicine where conflictual norms are less obvious. The avoidance of direct military conflict by women

until recently might be more an aspect of the general difficulties of
women playing a role in public society than anything specific to
military conflict. Military conflict has been an activity of men when
young and much less so as they grew older. Young women, the most
likely groups of women to be attracted, were often pregnant or had
young children which social norms dictated they, not the fathers,
should look after. This made widespread participation in conflict
difficult. The greater control over reproductive life, and the ease with
which child-bearing can be postponed, might be another partial
explanation of the recent change. The situation is obscure. It is hard
to dismiss the long-run fascination of males, particularly young males,
with violence as just an accident of society, which will now alter as
societies change. However, recent changes in the attitudes of some
women towards military violence as potential participants and not
supporters (and many have been avid supporters in the past) cannot be
ignored. It is not what the earlier feminists had expected.

The different attitude of women to violence and their tendency to
favour more consensual methods in conflict resolution might have
significant implications for peace-keeping. Peace-keeping under the
United Nations and other groups such as NATO is increasing rapidly
(see Chapter 3, p. 39). Armed forces are central to this but it is a very
untraditional role for the military. Peace-keepers are in the business of
conflict resolution, humanitarian aid and so on. They are not there to
fight and release their aggressive impulses. They are often subject to
considerable provocations which the traditional military 'red-blooded
male' needs great self-control to withstand. It is possible that women
would do this better than men. There are certain aspects of peace-
keeping that they certainly would. It has become clear that in the
former Yugoslavia, mass rape was used as a deliberate tactic to
subjugate and humiliate a population. It may have been used historically more often than we realize – certainly military rape has been a
commonplace aspect of military activities. Women here would be
clearly better at dealing with the immediate consequences of violence.
But the superiority of women in peace-keeping might well go beyond
directly gender-relevant issues such as rape. If the supposed differences
between the sexes are real differences then this would be the case.
Peace-keeping is likely to be a significant part of future military
operations. It is clearly an important and expanding aspect of military
activity, which might have profound implications on the constitution of
military forces.

Further Reading and Sources

Detailed material on military issues is contained in the *Military Balance* (mentioned also in Chapter 1). This is published annually by the International Institute for Strategic Studies (IISS) in London, along with the annual *The Strategic Survey*. These and the regular *Yearbook of the Swedish International Peace Research Institute (SIPRI)* (published by Oxford University Press) are invaluable sources of military-related data. The IISS also publishes a regular series of short monographs called the *Adelphi Papers*.

For the general issues in nuclear deterrence and security see Barry Buzan, *An Introduction to Strategic Studies* (London: Macmillan – now Palgrave Macmillan, 1987). For his more profound attempt to develop the notion of 'security', which is a part of a continuing debate, see his *People, States and Fear: an Agenda for International Security Studies in the Post-Cold War Era* (New York: Longman, 1991, 2nd edn). On attempts to rethink the notion of security in the post-Cold-War world from a variety of perspectives, see Michael Clarke *New Perspectives on Security* (London: Brassey's, 1993).

The view that proliferation may not be bad is put clearly by Kenneth Waltz, *The Spread of Nuclear Weapons: More May be Better* (London: Adelphi Papers, no. 185, International Institute for Strategic Studies, 1981). An optimistic view of the future (and long-run lack of a future) of war is in John Mueller, *Quiet Cataclysm: Reflections on the Recent Transformation in World Politics* (New York: HarperCollins, 1995).

A very useful book which summarises and assesses our present state of knowledge with regard to the statistical study of war is edited by John A. Vasquez, *What do we know about War?* (New York and Oxford: Rowman & Littlefield, 2000). Vasquez's own summarising chapter is masterful and clear even for those who have a horror of statistics. The sources used for the 'democratic peace' come from Bruce M. Russett, *Grasping the Democratic Peace* (Princeton: Princeton University Press, 1993). A recent book which extends this is Bruce Russett and John Oneal, *Triangulating Peace: Democracy, Interdependence, and International Organizations* (New York and London: W.W. Norton & Co, 2001). I also cite Stuart Bremer, 'Dangerous Dyads: Interstate War 1916–65,' *Journal of Conflict Resolution* , Vol. 36, No. 2 (1992), pp. 309–41.

For an optimistic account of sanctions, see Gary Hufbauer, Jeffrey Schott and Kimberly Elliot, *Economic Sanctions Reconsidered: History and Current Policy* (Washington, DC: IIE, 1990). The pessimists include Robert Pape, 'Why Economic Sanctions do not Work' in *International Security*, Vol. 22 (1997), pp. 90–136, which was followed in the same journal by some exchanges with the optimists. See also Geoff Simons, *Imposing Economic Sanctions* (London: Pluto Press, 1999). For a look at both sides of the issue see Richard N. Haass and Meghan L. O'Sullivan (eds), *Honey and Vinegar: Incentives, Sanctions and Foreign Policy* (Washington, DC: Brookings Institution Press, 2001). The figures of war deaths in the 1990s and the number of vulnerable Iraqi children were taken from Dan Smith, *The State of War and Peace Atlas* (London and New York: Penguin Reference, 1997, rev. edn).

9

The Global Political Economy

The Significance of Economic Factors

Throughout this book, I have suggested that an exclusive focus on states and their power and security was inadequate for a comprehensive theory of international relations. To define the subject as concerned with just these is to be unduly restrictive. Clearly international interactions involve far more than this. Further, even if the centre of our interest is the state and military security, they cannot be understood purely in their own terms without bringing in other factors. Of course, it has always been understood that the underlying power of a state depended on its economy and that relative power could change as different countries' economies developed at different rates. However, this was regarded as a background factor to be analyzed in other terms, namely those of the economic system, and fed in to the international system from the outside. This narrow view is now open to doubt. Many now believe that the economic system is much more intertwined with the political and international system than was earlier thought. The systems are not separate but are more appropriately treated as a single system. The international economic system is not just something that is added on to the state system as a sort of optional extra. This chapter considers the global political economy as a feature of international relations in its own right, as an important feature of global interactions without which other more political interactions cannot be understood properly.

There have always been those who deplored the subordination of the economic to the political in the analysis of international relations, particularly, though by no means exclusively, the Marxists. However, only since the 1970s has there been a significant growth in international

153

political economy. The name itself emphasizes the interdependence of politics and economics stressed by its practitioners. Political economists argue that in real life, as opposed to abstract theory, economics and politics are inextricably intertwined. This is true whether one is discussing the domestic political economy or the international political economy. Economics takes place in a political context and politics takes place in an economic context. It is useful to separate them for analytical simplicity from time to time but the analysis of the real world requires that the two must be brought together.

Two terms are frequently used in this context, *international political economy*, usually abbreviated to *IPE*, and *global political economy*, usually abbreviated to *GPE*. These reveal a different emphasis, though both involve the same general issues. 'International' still involves the state even though the state might be thought to be dwindling. Indeed IPE specialists often concern themselves with the declining significance of the state in international trade and international monetary affairs. 'Global' involves looking at the global political economy as a whole and stressing the global features of the system such as the division between rich and poor which cuts across state cleavages. It is often argued that we are moving from the international to the global. Certainly the environmental issues discussed in Chapter 11 are more directly issues in GPE.

There are three separate reasons why there has been a growth in the development of IPE and GPE. The first is the recognition that economic factors are important in the global system. An exclusive concentration on security is unnecessarily restrictive. The second is that there have been some changes in the world that have made economic issues more intrusive now than they were earlier. For example, multinational corporations (MNCs) are much more important now than they were fifty years ago. Likewise, environmental problems, with their intimate connection to the economy, have become more significant. Third, there has been a development in theory that brings economics and politics closer together. This last reason is perhaps the most controversial of the three.

These three reasons are different from, and independent of, each other. The first is a change in what interests people. The second is a change in the nature of the world we are analyzing. The final reason is a development of intellectual understanding. Factors that were earlier thought to be separate or, at least, fairly independent of each other, are now thought to be closely connected and interdependent.

Traditionally economies and states have been thought of as closely coinciding. In particular, a state had its own currency system of dollars, marks, rupees or whatever, which fairly clearly defined the economy. Sometimes these currency systems were closely tied together as under the *gold standard*. Under the gold standard any currency could be exchanged for gold at a fixed rate, which meant that currencies stood in a fixed relationship with each other. This system prevailed in the latter part of the nineteenth century and meant, in effect, that gold was a form of common currency or, at least, operated as a common standard by which to evaluate currencies. At other times, the relationship between currencies has been more variable. The rate of exchange between them would depend on the supply and demand for the currencies. This is known as a system of *flexible exchange rates*. The virtues of these different systems have been widely debated. Whatever the system, the concept of the British economy, the Australian economy, the Argentinean economy and so on was clear cut, as was the concept of a British bicycle, a French aeroplane or a Japanese car. It led to a *theory of international trade,* which was thought of as trade between states or, if one were being particularly careful, trade between economies using different currency units. Theorists of the classical theory of trade were anxious to point out that there was nothing particularly special about international trade as such except that labour could move less freely between states than within them. Trade between two regions of the same country followed the same general principles. However, for financial reasons as well as the political importance of states, international trade had a particular importance. A theory of international financial transactions was something that existed only if there were different currency systems. The classical theory of trade pointed to the minimum interference in trade in order to get the maximum benefit for all countries including poor countries. The more international trade became like internal trade the better. In this respect the classical trade theorists became rather early exponents of the globalization thesis.

It is now argued that the distinction between economies is getting weaker and we are getting closer to the global economy that the classical trade theorists admired. Clearly in some respect this is true. Complex commodities such as aeroplanes are becoming more and more transnational with parts of them made in a whole variety of places. The multinational corporations, discussed in Chapter 3, which were comparatively minor organizations in the 1930s, have become

major actors in the international economy over the last few decades.
There is nothing like an international currency, but the international
currency markets have become more and more internationalized and
extraordinarily complex. Stock markets, trading in the stocks and
shares of corporations (and the debts of governments known as
government bonds), are very international. The Tokyo market is closely
interrelated to the London market and to the New York market so they
rarely deviate too far from each other. The money markets (as these
markets are collectively known) owe their internationalization to the
speed of communications, which has reached new heights with the
widespread use of computers, meaning that information moves instantaneously between all the financial centres.

There are three broad approaches to international political economy:
the *liberal approach*, the *nationalist approach* and the *dependency
approach*. There is often confusion as to whether these approaches
are descriptions of the international political-economic system, as it
actually is today (or at some point in the past) or, alternatively, that
which ought to be the case. First, I shall describe these approaches in
the second sense (known as the *normative* sense) and then ask how far
any of the approaches, or some mixture of the approaches, can be reinterpreted to act as a theory of how the world behaves today.

The Liberal Approach

The liberal approach is based on the notion of free markets. It is
usually assumed that productive capital is primarily, if not exclusively,
privately owned, though this is not the rigid requirement that is
sometimes assumed for the theory to work. In its normative form,
liberals argue that, by letting free markets dictate what should be
produced and by what techniques, we maximize production and
produce more wealth than by any other means. Internationally this
implies that barriers to trade should be reduced to a minimum so that
markets can operate as freely as possible. Thus, economic liberals argue
that tariffs, which are taxes levied on goods imported from abroad,
almost always harm trade and hence economic development. In effect,
the argument comes down to saying that trade between states is in
principle no different from trade between regions or any other geographical unit. The closer international trade approximates to inter-
regional trade, the better.

In its positive or descriptive form, the liberal argument is that, since the end of the Cold War, this has become the predominant form of economic organization in the world. Hence an understanding of international political economy involves an understanding of free markets. In this model, the state should play a minimalist role. Even interventions in the free market can best be understood by reference to the norm of the free market's allocation of resources.

I shall give a brief exposition of the concept of free markets as understood by economic liberals. Let us consider it in terms of shoes, which are comparatively simple products. Shoes are produced by a firm, which buys raw materials, hires labour and gets them together in the productive process. It does so in order to make a profit, so the costs have to be less than the revenues earned from selling shoes. If the firm can make a bigger profit by selling strawberries then it will shift its resources into growing strawberries. Similarly, if shoes can be produced more cheaply in another country then producers there will make them and sell them in the first country at a lower price. In this way, production will always be carried out in the country in which it is the cheapest.

The tale of more complex commodities, such as automobiles, is appropriately more complicated. Automobiles have rarely been made in a single factory. Many components have always been bought from outside and the automobile assembled at a central factory where some, but by no means all, the components were manufactured. The seats, doors, different parts of the engine and so on are made in a many different factories and the final manufacture is the assembly of the numerous component parts. However, in 1960, the concept of a British car was fairly clear-cut. Most of the components were manufactured in Britain. The concept of a British (or a French or a Japanese) automobile is now less clear and has been for some time. Its components come from around the world. For example, in 1984, the General Motors Cavalier II, which was assembled in Britain, had an Australian engine, an automatic gearbox from the USA (though the manual versions were made in Japan), a French carburettor and the pressing from Germany. This is a fairly typical story. It is part of the process of globalization discussed in Chapter 10. The same phenomenon is found in aircraft manufacture, for aircraft are even more complex. Wings are made in one country, engines in another and so on. The components themselves are made from many subcomponents, which are likewise made in many countries.

The internationalization of production in general makes for cheaper products in that each individual part is made where it is cheapest. The worldwide market in which plane makers can shop for aircraft seats, for example, ensures a high degree of competition in the industry. In principle such a productive regime could be operated without a market. In major products such as aircraft there is often a substantial political element in the choice of country in which to make the various parts. This is particularly true of high technology items. Despite protestations to the contrary, these choices are not always market guided. However, decisions in the institutional context of a market are generally sensitive to cost factors and, importantly, changes in cost factors.

The liberal regime is not just confined to trade in commodities and services. Capital, in the normative version of the argument, should move between countries in search of the best return. Again we have to be careful about what we mean. 'Capital' is used to mean many related things. Here I am using it to mean the provision of funds to enable the creation of equipment that will be used in the production of further goods. Thus, funds can be used directly for the purchase of machinery or indirectly to build a dam or a road. In the latter case, the immediate expenditure may be on the wages of the workers to build the dam but the purpose of the expenditure on wages is to get the dam built. The provider of the capital gets it repaid over a period of years and makes money by getting a rate of return, either profit or interest, in addition to this. The capital may come from abroad so the lender may have little to do with the actual operation involved. Alternatively, the providers of capital may set up the enterprise in the recipient country and run the whole operation themselves. Multinational corporations do this more and more. They invest their capital in whichever country is the most profitable.

The liberal economist thinks in terms of a global economy. According to this view, where and how things are produced should be determined by economic cost considerations. The country of production is of minor importance. There should be one big global economy and this will produce the best consequences for all of us.

The Nationalist Approach

The nationalist approach is the parallel of the realist approach in security affairs and can be seen as its economic corollary. On this view, a state's economic policy should be to maximize the benefit to the citizens of the state. According to the liberal theory of the economy, described above, this can best be done by a liberal trading regime. In this way, the wealth of the state will be maximized, as will the wealth of other states. Here we have to be careful. In the realist framework, the underlying goal is security. Wealth is desirable in its own right and the realist would rather be rich than poor. However, it is the relationship of wealth to military strength and hence to power which most concerns the realist. Power, of course, is a relative concept. State A is not powerful in the abstract. It is powerful only in relation to other states. The realist or nationalist member of A wants it to be more powerful than another state, B. There is a rough relationship between wealth and the means of power, though not a precise one. Thus, what state A wants is to be wealthier than state B, so what matters is not *absolute* wealth but *relative* wealth. In this case, the liberal policy, which makes both countries rich, is not a very useful one. State A wants wealth but it also wants to stop state B having wealth. When looked at from a security point of view, wealth is not a homogeneous blob but consists of different commodities which have very different and complex implications from a security point of view. Shirts and strawberries have few military implications and a nationalist state may still be quite happy for a perceived rival to buy them, particularly if a profit is made in the process. However, computers and jet engines are a different matter. Selling them may be profitable and increase a country's wealth; however, they will also increase the rival's military strength which runs counter to the goal of maximizing relative strength.

In the past, most governments did not doubt that they had a role in economic policy designed in the interests of the state. Thus, the German government in the late nineteenth century maintained strong heavy industries such as steel and coal which, with the technologies of the day, were central to military strength and thus the pursuit of power politics. A strong agricultural industry was needed to feed the population in time of war. These countries actively pursued an economic policy designed to maximize their military power and their economic power relative to other countries. This involved restricting imports in the interests of building up a domestic industry, and the widespread use of subsidies to encourage the strategically significant areas of the economy. Forgoing the short-term benefits of cheap imports was seen as a minor cost in building up a powerful state. Economic policy was the tool of security policy. It followed that states were major actors in the international political economy of the day. Britain was something of an exception to this in the later part of the nineteenth century. The British government supported the liberal view of trade with passion, preaching the merits of free trade to everyone, with apparent indifference to the security aspects. It has been more cynically suggested that, in the late nineteenth century, Britain profited particularly from free trade. Its lead in industrialization made it the relative gainer from a liberal market system. Britain's economic lead began to wane in the 1890s and with it the enthusiasm of its élites for liberal policies. By the 1920s it was as keen on protectionism as the rest of the industrialized Western world.

There are still elements of nationalist economic policies today, even in countries which in general espouse liberal doctrines. Understandably, this particularly applies to arms sales. Most countries have some restrictions on arms sales as these are very directly related to military security. In principle, many countries refuse to sell arms to countries with bad human-rights records, particularly if these arms can be used for internal repression. However, this is an issue where principle and practice do not always coincide. Sometimes more general embargoes are put on trade in pursuit of political objectives. The United States' embargo on trade with Cuba since the beginnings of the communist regime is a classic case of this. Liberal economics gave way to political interests.

Any form of high technology can have military implications and broad restrictions on their trade have been in force, particularly by the United States in the days of the communist Soviet Union. These embargoes were not imposed with the intention of bringing down the government of the Soviet Union but of impeding its military capability. One problem is that almost anything can be interpreted as having some military use. Thus, soldiers wear shirts. If shirts can be bought more cheaply from a rival than they can be made at home then this helps the military effort if only slightly. A more significant case is agriculture. Agricultural produce is a necessity for feeding a population in wartime. In order to keep a viable wartime productive capacity it is necessary to keep it going in peacetime as well, even if the produce could have been bought more cheaply abroad. Hence, most countries have supported their agriculture with subsidies and restrictions on foreign imports. However, nowadays, while long wars like the Iran–Iraq war have taken place between less-developed countries, they are unlikely to take place between industrialized states. This rationalization for the artificial support of agriculture is no longer valid, certainly in the developed world. This does not stop many countries from giving governmental support to agriculture. The European Union is notorious for supporting agriculture in its member states at what many people believe to be an absurd level. The security implications of this policy are now almost totally non-existent. Whatever its present justification may be, the origins lie in the significance of agriculture in wartime, which has created a social habit of regarding it as a privileged mode of economic activity.

According to the nationalists, the primary aim of a national economic policy is to preserve and, if possible, increase military security. However, there are other goals too. Certainly in the short term states try and protect industries in the hope of protecting employment and so on. During the 1930s, most governments imposed tariffs in the hope of defending themselves against the serious fall in demand caused by the worldwide economic depression. This was a desperate attempt to protect employment in the face of low-priced imports. Unfortunately everybody did it, so each country's exports decreased and the net effect was to reduce overall employment.

Dependency Approaches

Adherents of the *dependency theory* school (though, like the other approaches, it is a collection of related schools) concentrate on the relationship between élites in rich and poor states and in particular their economic relationships. They argue that the activity of the *developed countries* (DCs) in the *less-developed countries* (LDCs), spearheaded by the MNCs, has a different effect from that claimed by the liberal school. Far from a poorer economy developing under the impact of foreign capital and business methods, as the liberal claims, it will remain in a subordinate position purely in the service of the richer economy. It will not grow and develop into some sort of equal with the developed economies, partly for economic reasons. Profits are repatriated to the developed country that provided the capital. They will remain and be reinvested only if the less-developed country provides the highest profits. The large business firms can keep wages low in places where there are poorly organized trade unions. The labour market is not in reality a free market. The employers can be well organized and the workers poorly organized. There is little pressure or incentive to adopt techniques that are appropriate to higher wage economies which, of course, LDCs aspire to be at some stage. The situation is often a near monopoly, which the producers are happy with. A developing economy might become an unwelcome competitor. There are also political factors. Economic activities are most profitable in places where there is political stability. Poor countries are stable when there is an authoritarian government. Those that attract foreign capital are usually sympathetic to the political right. Hence major capital-exporting countries such as the USA have frequently backed the authoritarian governments of the right, notably in Latin America.

Thus, many low-income countries do not develop because their position in the world economy is very convenient for many interest groups. Their continuing poverty is not due to deficiencies in the countries themselves, or, at least, not primarily so, but to their position in an unsympathetic world economy. The relationship between élites in North and South makes it possible for élites in the poorer state to benefit at the expense of their own population. The dependency approach can explain the experience of parts of the Third World quite convincingly but there are some difficulties with other parts. The rapid growth of the so-called NICs (newly industrialized countries) such as South Korea and Taiwan does not fit in with the theory. Perhaps these cases can be explained by special factors but the theory has some explaining away to do at this point. As noted in Chapter 6, the emergence of the NICs is more adequately explained by a theory, such as world systems theory, which takes into account a semi-periphery composed of states whose economies are improving. Dependency theory seems to be true for some countries but not others, though we would really like a satisfactory explanation of why this should be.

The dependency view is close to a Marxist analysis of the international political economy and Marxist analyses of international relations normally incorporate a dependency analysis within them. Basically it is argued that the capitalist nature of the international economic system is fundamentally to blame for continued poverty. It is basically a structuralist argument which downplays the decision-making aspects of behaviour.

The Relationship between the Approaches

The liberal view and the dependency view both give accounts of the economic activity occurring under market systems in poorer economies that are penetrated by rich countries. Both agree that the capitalists are pursuing their self-interest in terms of maximizing profits. However, their accounts of the consequences of this differ dramatically. The liberal believes that the capitalists from the advanced countries are, in effect, inadvertent mentors of the poorer states. In due course the operations of the market, involving self-seeking individuals, will produce growth and wealth in the underdeveloped economy. The governments will more or less keep out of this apart from providing internal security and stability. It is important, of course, that the LDCs should have access to the world market and be able to sell their produce to the world as a whole. Some argue that the failure of the DCs to open up their markets freely to LDCs is a major reason that development in many places has been so disappointingly poor.

Dependency theorists hold that this is not how markets work. Even if the free market did exist, it is doubtful if it would work in the benevolent way that the liberal describes. However, it is naive to suppose that the free market will be allowed to work unimpeded when both political and economic power lie so strongly on the side of the capitalist. Monopolies will grow and be allowed to maintain themselves. Governments will intervene to make sure that this occurs and that the workers can be exploited as far as possible. A genuine development in the economy is not in the interests of the large capitalists, at least in the short run, and therefore will not take place.

The nationalist view is a normative view. The nationalists might agree that the pursuit of riches would be better carried out in a market economy with the minimum of constraints. They argue, however, that this is not the central goal of policy. The real aim is national power which is best gained by improving a state's relative situation, and stimulating those industries which give national independence, even if their products could be bought more readily abroad. The liberal and the dependency theorists differ significantly in how they believe the world *in fact* works. They may often have disagreements also in how they think the world *ought* to work but it is not logically implied that they do. The nationalist might agree with either (though obviously not both) on how the world in fact works but disagree about what the goals ought to be.

The three approaches can thus be distinguished by the role of the state in the economy. In the liberal view, the state only intervenes to adjust for the most negative effects of the free market, maintaining a 'hands-off' policy in regard to the economy. In the dependency view, intervention will be a function of the power and interest of northern élites. In the nationalist model, states are the key players and intervene in the economy for the explicit purpose of increasing national wealth and improving the state's relative position in the global economy.

The Direction of the Global Political Economy

The overwhelming sentiment within governments and 'official' opinion is in favour of the liberal approach to the global political economy. This is sometimes known as the 'Washington Consensus'. The arguments for the liberal approach, laid out on pp. 156–8, are broadly accepted. Further, actual policies are moving more and more in that direction. This has been the trend amongst the basically capitalist economies more or less since the Second World War. The basic argument for the efficiency of free trade was more or less accepted, though with many reservations, particularly in the earlier days. The poor experiences of the interwar years and the repudiation of free trade by most governments reinforced this trend, even amongst those who lacked enthusiasm for a full free-market regime. The move towards free international markets in trade and in capital movement was accelerated with the collapse of the Soviet Union and its economy which was functioning badly under the opposing set of principles. This enthusiasm for free-market systems continues and is supported now by many who might earlier have been sceptical.

The liberal economic regime is given institutional form in the *World Trade Organization* (WTO). This started in 1995 and was the successor body of the *General Agreement on Tariffs and Trade* (GATT) which was founded in 1948 to promote ideas of free trade by mutually-agreed tariff reductions. The journey to free trade had, at times, been a slow process, as its near five decades of existence would indicate. The WTO is a much more ambitious body. Its central theme, common to many tariff agreements, is the so-called 'most favoured nation' rule, which indicates that if a concession is made to one country, it must be made to all. However, as a major development, the conditions of the WTO are actually part of international law. A state, or a corporation, which feels another has broken one of the principles of the WTO, can take its complaint to the WTO. If it is upheld, and the state still persists, then the WTO can impose sanctions. Private corporations can initiate such action. Further, private corporations can sue states. The members of the WTO are states but it is not just an interstate organisation. The WTO has proved very controversial. It defenders argue that by putting things as a question of law, small and powerless states can challenge powerful states. There is in some sense, in a metaphor favoured by politicians, a 'level playing field'. The fewer impediments there are to trade, the more will take place, the richer everyone will be, and this will include the poorer states as well as the richer ones. Further, poorer states desperately need capital and this will be greatly assisted by a regime regulated by law.

The opponents fall into numerous camps. Two strands can be picked out. First, there are those who are sceptical of all the virtues of free trade and, second, those who, while possibly accepting the theoretical virtues of free trade, argue that the whole agreement is naive about the issue of the power of corporations.

Those who are sceptical of the virtues of free trade themselves are sceptical for a number of reasons. Most industrialized countries, and this includes the United States as well as most European economies, went through the early stages of their industrial development well-defended by tariff barriers. It is not always clear that an immediate exposure to world markets is the best start to an economy in the earlier stages of industrialization. This is controversial, and there are counter-examples. However, it is clear that there are plenty of cases of economies going through an early and successful stage of industrialization with tariff barriers. Free trade is definitely not a necessary condition. However, another reason for scepticism has nothing to do with growth. Environmentalists have been concerned that the dominant imperative of the world economy is commercial production. A country's environmental laws may be found to be discriminatory and a state to be effectively unable to carry out important aspects of an environmental policy. A similar issue arises over cultural issues. The French have been particularly concerned that a fully open market for films will destroy the French film industry, which is something of a cultural icon. With the increasing privatization in many states of functions formerly carried out by the state such as education, these activities are open to the public – which now means international – bidding. There may be solid reasons why one wants schools to be under the control of local bodies rather than of some totally different culture. However, there are dangers that the use of a cultural argument will violate the provisions of the WTO. It is, nonetheless, as reasonable for the inhabitants of a London borough to be concerned that the ownership and management of their schools is the responsibility of a Texas corporation as a small town in Arkansas would be at the thought of a London corporation running their schools. Cultural issues can be significant. Some of these complaints could be met if the WTO had a less fundamentalist view of free trade and were willing to entertain more exceptions to what could still be a general rule. There is still some uncertainty about how the WTO regime will settle down. Some of its earlier unpopularity, which manifested itself most vociferously in the Seattle demonstrations during the WTO meeting there in 1999, was due to the rather extreme and tactless way it initially presented itself. It looked very much like a charter for big business and, in particular, US big business. A readiness to concede that, whatever the general merits of free trade, a more open-minded attitude to other values, which would provide the grounds for significant exemptions, would increase its popularity.

However, this would still not meet all the objections of those who argue that the WTO is naive about power. They argue that it will become the tool of the big corporations and act primarily in their interests. Further, the rules of the WTO, which supposedly defend small states and producers, will not do so as the large producers will always have the advantage. If the rules of the game cease to favour the rich and powerful, they argue, then the rules will alter. Corporations will always go to their governments and expect a hearing. The following is such an illustration. The Dole Food Corporation felt it had been put at a disadvantage, with respect to Chiquita Brands International over the sale of bananas to the EU, by an agreement between the USA and EU, which was conducted under the aegis of the WTO. The *New York Times*, chillingly and without obvious irony, remarked, 'Dole officials met with American trade officials and contributed money to political campaigns, but trade experts said Chiquita *contributed more and lobbied harder to get the situations resolved*' (*New York Times*, 14 April 2001, 'Business Day', emphasis added). This seems a long way from free trade.

Of the three ways of looking at the global political economy, clearly the liberal one is dominant and seems to be progressing the fastest politically, despite some intellectual and political reservations. The creation of the WTO is very much in its image. This does not stop the dependency theorists from mounting their criticisms, but they are not politically in any position of power. It is also not always clear just what policies are being advocated, even if we know a number of them are critical. The nationalist view, once very powerful, is now very much in decline, looking even sorrier for itself than the political realist theory of international relations, of which it is a close ally. It has its residual presence in some overtly political moves such as sanctions and, in particular, the control of the arms trade where, indeed, many economic liberals would wish it well.

Further Reading and Sources

Susan Strange, who died on 25 October 1998, was a leading writer in this field and her work is to be strongly recommended. *Casino Capitalism* (Oxford: Basil Blackwell, 1986), though now slightly dated, describes the international financial system from a rather caustic point of view. *States and Markets* (London: Pinter Publishers, 1994, 2nd edn) is a broader but still provocative account of the international political economy.

Other books that are well worth consulting include Robert Gilpin, *Global Political Economy* (Princeton: Princeton University Press, 2001); Richard Stubbs and Geoffrey Underhill (eds), *Political Economy and the Changing Global Order* (Oxford: Oxford University Press, 1999, 2nd edn); Ronen Palan (ed.), *Global Political Economy* (London: Routledge, 2000); and a recently revised book by A. Hoogvelt, *Globalization and the Postcolonial World* (Basingstoke: Palgrave, 2001, 2nd edn).

For background on the World Trade Organization, see Rorden Wilkinson, *Multilateralism and the World Trade Organisation: The Architecture and Extension of International Trade Regulation* (London: Routledge, 2000); Bernard Koekman and Michael Kostecki, *The Political Economy of the World Trading System: From GATT to WTO* (Oxford: Oxford University Press, 2001, 2nd edn) or *The Political Economy of the World Trading System: The WTO and Beyond* (Oxford: Oxford University Press, 2001, 2nd edn); Anne O. Krueger, *The WTO as an International Organization* (Chicago: Chicago University Press, 2000).

Details of the wide range of countries producing car parts are taken from R. Church, *The Rise and Decline of the British Motor Industry* (London: Macmillan – now Palgrave Macmillan, 1994).

10

Globalization

Introduction

The world at the beginning of the twenty-first century is a much more interconnected place than it was at the start of the twentieth century. Messages and information can be sent to any part of the world at a small cost. Similarly people can move very quickly and comparatively inexpensively. Thus, to go from London to New York in 1900 took ten days or seven on the fastest liners. In 1890, the cheapest rate from Liverpool to New York was £5, which was around five per cent of the average male's annual wage in Britain at the time. This is surprisingly low. Today a similar journey takes about twelve hours even allowing for the difficulties of getting to airports and so on. The cheapest return fare costs only about two per cent of an average male worker's salary. The reduction in time is dramatic though that in expense is rather less so. Nevertheless, few working class people went to New York for a holiday at the turn of the century.

We can quote many more examples as is done in various books and articles. The overall phenomenon is undeniable. It has led people to talk of *globalization,* meaning that geography is becoming less and less relevant to how people live and in particular how they interact. If one's main means of communication with someone is by telephone, it does not matter very much whether that person is in the next street or 10 000 miles away. It is of course, easier and cheaper to meet people if they are in the next street but it is possible, at least for wealthier human beings, to travel to meet together even if they live a long way apart.

Does this degree of interconnectedness, which undoubtedly exists, mean that the globalization of the world has introduced something genuinely unique, forming what Scholte calls a new paradigm? Alternatively, is it just more of the same or has it moved from being a process of incremental change to something qualitatively different? There are also some sceptics who look at trade patterns and argue that the whole business has been exaggerated.

Perhaps the most spectacular aspect of this interconnectedness is the ease with which information can flow. We can talk on the telephone between Buenos Aires and London, write emails between New York and New Delhi or see vast amounts of information on the Frankfurt Stock Exchange while in Adelaide, all at the time it occurs. There are no delays. Further, we can do so easily and, often more to the point, cheaply. These sorts of exchanges are not just restricted to the affluent participants in money markets. The starving people of Africa cannot participate in this but a modestly-paid immigrant worker in Bradford can telephone his aunt, who is the custodian of the family telephone, in Islamabad without being too concerned about the cost.

There are other aspects of this also. We can travel both quickly and relatively cheaply around the world. Thus travel for both business, family connectedness and tourism has escalated dramatically. Further, goods can be transported more cheaply, partly due to the improved techniques of transport; partly, also, due to the lowering of the weight and bulk of commodities so the value–weight ratio has increased markedly in many cases. Thus, the interconnectedness is not just those things that are directly electronic but also physical things (like people) are much more mobile, though much of this depends indirectly on electronics too.

Clearly then, geographical distance is not as significant as it used to be, though, as I reason below, this process has been going on for a long time. Scholte argues that for some purposes this is more than interconnectedness between different geographical locations. The *deterritorialisation* of various activities has taken place. In a sense, the geography is irrelevant. Stock markets could be anywhere. All the financial traders in the world could move from their various locations and operate from one South Sea island. Alternatively they could all work from home (and may do so in the not-too-distant future). It does not matter very much. It is not just that it could happen anywhere, but it is not clear that the question 'where is it?' has any meaning. The prices on the stock market do not exist in any particular point in space but can be seen at any point in the world where appropriately connected computers are available. When it does have meaning, in the sense the participants in the market must be somewhere, it is not a question of any substantive interest. Scholte argues that this detachment from the physical place where the activities take place is different from interconnectedness as such. He calls interconnectedness *internationalization* and readily admits it has increased. He regards globalization as the growing deterritorialization, or super-territorialization, of various activities. This is something different from internationalization – though we should point out that, whatever the merits of this distinction, many people use 'globalization' to mean both.

Global Interrelations

We can probably agree that relationships over distance have increased radically over the last few decades. Distance is not as important as it was. We shall now examine the different forms of this interconnectedness and how they have changed.

We all have to be somewhere. The vast majority of us spend most of our time on the earth's surface. Except for a few astronauts, we are never more than a few miles away. Thus, our experiences take place somewhere and it does seem to matter to us as individuals where we are for a lot of purposes. For other purposes it may be irrelevant. If we can experience something, such as a satellite broadcast anywhere, then location is irrelevant for those purposes. 'Where did you see that movie?' is a request for biographical information, not information about the movie as such (and someone who is well-travelled, but has a bad memory, may well not know, though he is still not debarred from talking about the movie). The crucial question is, 'When is geographical location relevant?'.

There seem to be four possibilities, though they are points on a spectrum rather than self-contained categories. First, there are still some activities that need to take place in a particular location. For instance, to drill oil, we have to go to where it happens to be. Second, many economic activities have to be in a particular spot, and its location is relevant. However, such activities can be moved fairly readily if there are a number of alternatives. Car manufacture is this sort of activity. Even more marked are the various component parts of cars, such as, say, the speedometer, which can be made in many places far removed from where the car is assembled. For many commodities, the place of its manufacture can move with disconcerting ease. Third, there are activities, such as meetings between people, that can take place anywhere but nevertheless have to take place somewhere. The fact that people can move quickly and cheaply is relevant here. Mobility is central. Fourth, there are those activities that are truly globalized and deterritorialized.

The first two categories have clearly changed radically over the last hundred years. In the late nineteenth century, manufacture was much more dependent on heavy materials like coal and steel. Like oil, coal exists in certain locations and, because of expensive transport costs, alternative locations for production were limited. In developed economies, reliance on heavy materials has gone down, though, of course, in many parts of the world heavy materials like coal and iron are still significant. Likewise, the flexibility of manufacture is something that has developed very rapidly in recent decades. Part of this again is due to the increase in the value–weight ratio, though part is simply due to the breadth of information about alternative sources that is an aspect of the electronic revolution. Part is also political. The much more liberal trade regimes of the world have broadened out the range of alternative sources radically. However, though these aspects of the international economy have clearly developed, it is not clear that they are different in kind from what has been going on since industrialization began to take off in the late eighteenth century. Location and geography does matter. Indeed, trade takes place precisely because location matters.

For the third group of activities, it matters that things, or more often people, are physically gathered together, though it does not matter very much where. Suppose some conflict has reached a point where the participants and perhaps some neutral observers need to meet. They have to get together, but they can get together more or less anywhere. In the days of rapid air transport they do so quickly and without difficulty. Thus, two conferences held over the conflicts in Yugoslavia were held outside Yugoslavia. One was held in Dayton, Ohio, in the USA and the other at Rambouillet in France. Neither of these had much to do with the former Yugoslavia previously. That, indeed, was the point. There was no symbolism attached. However, they could have been almost anywhere outside Yugoslavia and the choice of location was determined by little more than convenience. My point is twofold. There was a wide choice of venues and everyone could get there quickly. The second factor in particular has had a huge effect on interactions between governments as well as corporations. The foreign ministers of Europe, and many other ministers besides, are in constant communication with each other. State leaders meet each other frequently and often know each other well on a personal basis. This is a long way from the nineteenth or early part of the twentieth century when state leaders met only rarely, usually at state funerals and royal weddings and the very occasional grand conference.

Though geography is important it can be easily circumvented. It seems only a short move to the point where it can be superterritorialized, to use Scholte's terminology. Presumably foreign ministers meet because they need something more than a telephone call, though exactly the same thing can be said over the telephone as can be said face-to-face. As the techniques of videoconferencing advance and become more reliable, the illusion of being physically present will become more powerful.

To consider this more carefully, we need to digress and look more carefully at what we do when we transfer information electronically. Of the five senses with which we experience the external world – sight, hearing, smell, taste and touch – only sight and hearing are relevant to the material that can be communicated instantaneously by electronic means and in good quality. We can see things on television screens, computer screens and the like and we can hear people on the same media or on the telephone. The speed is instantaneous and the quality is usually excellent. (Though not directly relevant to globalization, these images can also be stored cheaply.) However, nothing can be communicated that can be experienced with the other three senses, except as evoked by pictures or language. Nor does there seem any immediate prospect of doing so. The huge, at times almost incredible, developments in communications have entirely taken the form of improving the communication of sounds and things we can see with our eyes, like writing. Though these developments have had, and will continue to have, enormous implications, it still means that location matters – as any lover separated from a beloved will confirm.

Statespeople, however, are only rarely lovers of each other and the need for tactile contact is less acute. However, we simply do not know how much the physical proximity of people matters. There are probably a host of messages we pick up in personal interactions, which may not just be detected by eyes and ears. The very sense of occasion probably makes a difference, even to conference-hardened ministers. As the techniques of videoconferencing improve, there may always be something missing. No doubt psychologists are investigating how much physical contact matters. It may not be important but, then again, it may be.

This does not deny that some things are supraterritorial. Items such as stock market prices are in some sense both everywhere and nowhere. This is a trend that is increasing. Whether we want to call this, and only this, globalization or bring in all forms of interconnectedness is to some degree a matter of taste. However, even this is not novel. We can say, for example, that Harry Potter is supraterritorial in that the question 'Where is Harry Potter?' is meaningless. But if it is true for Harry Potter, it is also true for *Alice in Wonderland* and she preceded the electronic age by a century. Thus, I would argue, supraterritoriality is increasing in our globalized age but it is not a novelty. As I said earlier, international relations is an argument in which all can join and globalization is a particularly important topic to argue about.

The Growth of Globalization

The process of globalization has been a long one and there is no reason to suppose that it is over yet. However, it is not a characteristic of just the last few decades but something that has developed, sometimes erratically, over the centuries.

One of the major globalizing developments was the steam engine. Prior to that energy came from animals such as horses, the wind, occasionally water and human beings themselves (sometimes provided by slaves). The steam engine was the first big development that liberated human beings from this rather narrow and limited range of sources of energy. This quickly led to the steam train, which enabled people to travel quickly and cheaply over long distances once the track was laid. By the last third of the nineteenth century this led to a big expansion of fast travel within Europe. It made it possible for large countries like the United States and Canada to operate as single states because people could get from one end to the other more quickly than had hitherto been possible. Similarly the railway made India, with its huge distances, possible to rule as a single entity. Steam also revolutionized shipping, making it faster and more reliable. By 1900, it took half the time to get from London to Calcutta that it had taken in the middle of the nineteenth century when passengers had travelled on leisurely and erratic sailing vessels. Before the age of steam, only the very rich travelled far from home on a temporary basis unless they were seamen or soldiers. However, many people had journeyed on a permanent basis. The nineteenth century had seen big population movements, particularly from Europe to North America. Between 1820 and 1920, 38 million Europeans emigrated to the United States. In all, 62 million people moved from the old world to the new worlds of the Americas (including Canada and Argentina) and Australasia. In the eighteenth century and before there had been big involuntary movements of slaves from Africa to both North and South America. Until the end of the slave trade (officially the last state to ban it was Portugal in 1830 but slaves were smuggled after that), at least eight million slaves were transported and probably more. Prior to 1770, more African slaves went to America than Europeans. Trade, of course, was widespread in the eighteenth and nineteenth century and while the fall in transport costs with the development of steamships meant that it expanded more than proportionately, nevertheless this was all part of a trend. The modern degree of globalization is just the continuation of a long historical process.

The big development since 1900 has been in air travel. Passenger travel by air grew in the interwar period though it was largely restricted to the wealthy. In countries which covered a large geographical area like the United States and Canada, air travel was important internally in drawing the country closer together, rather as the railways had done earlier. By the 1960s, the development of quick and cheap jet transportation made the aeroplane a mass carrier. It has had a big impact on both pleasure and business travel and some impact on emigration. Tourism has become a major industry with people travelling vast distances for a week's holiday. As we remarked above, emigration on a large scale took place in the nineteenth century and, indeed, has always done so. However, the style of immigration has altered. In the nineteenth century, European immigrants to the United States would not expect to go home again unless they were unusually successful. For their children, their parents' homeland would be the material of stories, not something to visit or have any realistic links with. A European immigrant to the USA today would expect to come home for a Christmas holiday. Thus, there is a greater tendency for an immigrant to straddle two cultures and for their children to know their extended family as people to visit at least occasionally. This can be both enriching and stressful, leaving people awkwardly caught between two cultures, but itself is an aspect of globalization.

Trade has expanded steadily for centuries increasing as the means of transport became cheaper, more reliable and less dangerous. In the twentieth century steamships and, later, vessels driven by other fuels have continued this process. World trade has had its ups and downs in this century as economies have gone up and down but the actual mechanics of trade have become cheaper.

Trade has also varied according to attitudes to trade. *Free trade*, the view that there should be the minimum of legal impediments to trade for all to benefit, was discussed in Chapter 8. It was enthusiastically supported by many in Britain before the First World War but rather less well supported by most other countries, for nationalistic reasons. Between the wars, and particularly in the 1930s, the fearful slump in economic activity meant that most countries tried to defend their own economies, bringing an additional reduction in trade beyond that which followed from the reduction in economic activity in general. However, in the postwar world the goal amongst the capitalist economies has always been free or relatively free trade. Along with improved techniques for carrying cargo, this has led to a big increase in trade.

These technical developments resulting in cheaper and fast transport are of considerable significance as a factor in the expansion of trade. Containerization in shipping has brought down transport costs markedly. Large ships can sail with small crews. The business of loading and unloading, and transferring to other forms of transport such as trains and lorries, is vastly cheaper. Air freight has developed with jet aircraft. Obviously this is more useful for commodities which have high value relative to volume, but it is surprisingly widespread. It is not just computer parts which travel by air. Fresh strawberries can be flown from Latin America to Britain in the British winter and sold at modest prices.

This has an impact on the style of production. Commodities of any complexity are often manufactured in several countries. Computers are just one example. Cars, CD players and televisions all contain components manufactured in a large number of countries, such that the ostensible country of origin of the total product is often little more than the place where it is finally assembled. The internationalization of manufacture has greatly increased during the last few decades.

Various technical developments have led to the globalization of entertainment. Tourism is one aspect of this that resulted from cheap travel. Entertainment is perhaps more pervasive. Films became major sources of entertainment after the First World War. Films could be produced as a large number of copies and a film could be watched by millions of people. Videos have extended this. Though many countries have made films, the American film industry has dominated, resulting in the Americanization of a lot of entertainment. It is one of the factors which has led to the increasing use of English, particularly American English, as a world language. Though many countries produce films – indeed India produces the largest number of films made by any single country – the main exporters are the Americans.

Television since the Second World War has increased this tendency. Television is now widespread throughout the world both directly, through broadcasting, or through videos. Even in poor parts of the world, there will be a television set in a village or neighbourhood which will be watched by many people. Unlike newspapers, television and films do not require literacy.

The globalization of culture, which is essentially Americanization, is not universally welcomed. In both rich Western countries, particularly France, and poorer countries it is felt to dominate other cultures to the general loss. The picture of the United States is in any case often misleading. Fewer citizens of the United States live in mansions than might be thought from a cursory look at American television. It is also closely linked up with the provision of news. CNN is an active news channel which straddles the world but it inevitably provides news which, often unconsciously, comes with an American slant.

The flow of information is a further characteristic of globalization. In the nineteenth century, information was carried by letter, which travelled as fast as a human being could. From India it took several weeks to Britain and from Germany a few days. This improved along with other forms of travel. Visual signalling by means of a series of signal stations, each passing on the signal to its successors, was used in the Napoleonic wars over distances of a hundred or so miles. In principle visual signals could have been used over much longer distances but never were. They were used primarily for military information though, again in principle, they could have been used for commercial or private purposes. The big increase in the speed of information transmission on a widespread basis came with the development of the use of electrical currents to transmit messages. The electric telegraph became widely used around the middle of the nineteenth century. A transatlantic cable was laid in 1866. Telephones came into use in the early twentieth century though nationally rather than internationally. An international line between Britain and France was set up just before the First World War. The discovery that radio waves could be transmitted over long distances heralded the future. A transatlantic radio signal was broadcast from England to Canada in 1901. Radio became a mass form of entertainment in the interwar period. Though international telephone calls were not everyday events at that time, they were feasible. Transatlantic telephone links began in 1926, relying on short-wave radio. Using satellites, a European can now contact New York, Buenos Aires or Tokyo almost effortlessly. For people operating in financial markets where information is vital, they became more commonplace. News of events began to be spread around the world shortly after they happened.

This developed further in the postwar period. Telephones became cheaper and more convenient. Now, by means of interlinking computers, vast quantities of information can be transferred around the world cheaply and instantaneously. This means it is not just something which is done for very important issues but is widely done by many people on a routine basis. At least from the point of view of the information received and transmitted, geographical location has ceased to be of much significance. This has a big impact on such things as markets. What is happening in Tokyo is known immediately in London.

A problem with the globalization of information is that it accentuates the plight of those who are excluded. Glowing accounts of globalization (though I have stressed it is, in fact, a process of evolution, possibly accelerating these days) often overlook the fact that, while people are excluded from little because of geography, they can be excluded because of poverty. Globalization has done little to remedy the big discrepancies in wealth in the world and may well have done some things to make it worse. Computers are still expensive for those on a Third-World income. The hope and expectation is that computers will continue to follow the normal historical trend that complex equipment comes down radically in price – as indeed they are constantly doing. Fifty years ago, an international telephone call was effectively restricted to a small élite. Now it is much more widespread, though still we should remember that it is an unlikely luxury for perhaps at least half of the world's population. This is likely to continue for the other features of globalization but the problem of exclusion is still there. The rich are globalized; the poor are less so.

Globalization and Economic Sovereignty

One of the paradoxes of the classical realists and their theories of international relations is that, while they were very concerned over issues of sovereignty, they neglected economic factors which, arguably, most effectively undermine the sovereignty of a state. Once any sort of trade takes place there is some diminution in sovereignty in that the variations in trade are out of the control of a government while affecting its economy. The more a country becomes a trading economy, the more the economy is influenced by what goes on outside it. As the economic world has become more global, the less governments have had control over their economies. This seems to be more and more the case, such that many people are becoming worried that there is very little control over the economy of a state and none over the world economy. This is not necessarily good for the welfare of the people who are, after all, the world's producers and consumers.

There are a number of ways in which this reduced control is especially serious. First, there is the general control of the economy. Some pessimists argue that such domestic matters as full employment are beyond the reach of domestic government because of globalization. When the new French socialist government in the early 1980s tried to cure unemployment by what had earlier proved to be successful expansionary economic policies, they were forced into a humiliating retreat by world markets. From 1945 until the Oil Crisis of 1973 it seemed that the problem of unemployment in advanced capitalist states had been conquered. This is clearly no longer the case. Unemployment in rich capitalist states is higher than it was and security of employment is less. While some of this is due to a change in political attitudes which in many states has put high employment as a social goal rather lower than formerly, it is at least possible that some of the higher unemployment can be attributed to globalization.

Secondly, states need to raise taxes in order to provide all the services such as education, defence, health and so on. There is great disagreement as to how far the state should be involved in such activities and how active it should be in providing *collective goods*. Collective goods are those that cannot be provided very well by individuals or the market, such as fire-fighting services. They are often extended to include those that are more effectively provided by state action than by individuals, such as education. However, even people who would like to see as many things as possible provided by private individuals accept that some things should be provided by the state. Adam Smith, the hero of the market writing in a different age, thought that defence should be provided by the state and, indeed, could not visualize any other way of ensuring that it was provided. Almost everyone agrees that the state must do some things and this requires taxation; the disagreements regard the extent of this activity. The globalization of finance impedes the abilities of many states to do this. It is now possible to evade taxes in all sorts of legal ways that were not possible before.

A major way of doing this is by *offshore* activities. One form is widely familiar, namely, duty-free sales at airports and on ships. An aeroplane or a ship in international waters is outside the taxation jurisdiction of any state and, therefore, does not have to pay the various taxes which most states levy on sales, particularly such things as alcoholic drinks and tobacco. Thus we can all drink alcohol when on or over international waters without paying taxes. There is no reason why such goods sold over international waters should not be taxed if they are brought into a state, but most states have decided to let travellers bring in a certain amount for their own use without paying taxes. Governments have gone further and most designate an area in the airport as being the equivalent of international territory as far as tax is concerned. Travellers rush to the 'duty free' and buy drinks and cigarettes and the like, saving some money, and providing the airport operators with some handsome profits. However, the lack of taxation means that governments get less revenue. The duty-free practice has been going on for a long time but it is now much more significant than it was because of the vast increase in foreign travel.

It is not just taxes that firms can avoid by exploiting the ambiguities of territory. Shipping companies register ships under *flags of convenience*. Thus, a British-owned ship can register under the flag of a small state such as Panama, which has lenient tax laws, no trade unions and undemanding safety regulations. Seamen hired from poor Third-World countries are grateful for any work even if it is dangerous and for low wages. This cuts the running costs considerably. This practice is widespread and has been for a long time; it is not a novelty.

The financial system is also tailored in some ways to tax avoidance. In particular, a number of small states have set up banking systems involving very light taxation, if any at all, with the express purpose of attracting foreign funds whose owners are interested in avoiding taxes. It is not uncommon to have agreements for the salaries of the very rich to be paid in the Cayman Islands, one of the many small states which has a banking system designed expressly to accommodate such trans-actions. The laws and taxes in these 'offshore islands' are lenient except for those on confidentiality. It is rarely possible to trace who has deposits with these banks, which makes them ideal repositories for money acquired from criminal activities including the vastly profitable drugs trade. It can then be 'laundered', that is, reinvested in some perfectly proper economic activity so that its criminal origins are impossible to detect. Strict confidentiality was not an invention of these small states, but started, and still is centred, in the Swiss banks, making them havens for the proceeds of crime. By the mid-1990s, this had come under a lot of criticism as it became clear that the Nazis of the 1930s put a lot of money, which was unaccounted for, into Swiss banks.

The multinational corporations do not need to take advantage of the financial facilities provided by these very small states. They operate in a variety of states. Costing of the various stages of an industrial opera-tion is frequently very difficult and, indeed, often arbitrary. It is a comparatively easy operation to attribute a disproportionate amount of the costs to high-tax states and the benefits to low-tax states and minimize the amount of taxation that is paid. A good accountant can be worth a fortune.

The financial system as a whole is detrimental to the economic sovereignty of states. Most of the financial moves that are made in the buying and selling of currency are made for speculative reasons. Only about 5 per cent of financial transactions are to finance trade; the rest are for speculation, where speculators hope to make a profit on the movements of the money markets and so on. Monetary policy, and thence all of economic policy, is very dependent on what happens in the financial markets and it is a major constraint on governments' activ-ities. Economic sovereignty is thus severely restricted. The concern is that this is becoming even more the case, and that state control over economic activity is decreasing in ways that are often detrimental to the population.

Globalization does not necessarily imply that governments are at the mercy of other actors who have a clear idea of what is to be done in the relevant aspects of behaviour. No group of wicked capitalists meets secretly to decide on the fate of the world, its governments and its peoples. Even if they tried, the globalization argument suggests they could make only minor differences. Rather all, including the MNCs, are at the mercy of a collection of decisions, particularly in the case of markets. People do not decide to have a recession. It is merely that the collectivity of their acts produces a recession though none of the individual actors desired this consequence. It is claimed that, in the globalized economy, there is not very much we can do about it, though the rich and powerful can usually protect themselves personally against the worst consequences of these collective actions.

While conspiracy is lacking, there are some actors who exert considerable power over governments, such as the IMF and World Bank. The IMF helps countries out of balance-of-payments problems, that is, situations where they want to buy more from abroad than they can pay for with imports. However, the IMF imposes a variety of conditions including *structural adjustment programmes,* which means that, in order to get the economic system they often desperately need, the countries must restructure their economies. Restructuring is usually in the direction of cutting government expenditure and, in general, making the control of inflation a priority. Effectively this means taking some major aspects of economic policy away from governments, which is clearly a severe reduction in sovereignty. Third World governments have suffered particularly from the edicts of the IMF but rich governments too have found themselves needing help from the IMF and have been obliged to conform to its requirements. Theoretically they could decline to do so but this would impose vast costs in trying to go it alone. However, unlike the general process of globalization, this reduction of sovereignty was designed. The IMF is an institution created explicitly with the control of balance of payments as its primary task. It is intended to reduce sovereignty and it is inappropriate to criticize it for doing so. People have criticized the types of recommendation that the IMF have made, which, in many people's eyes, have been too conservative and unimaginative, lacking concern for the poorer members of society who have, for the most part, born the brunt of the costs of these programmes. The IMF is itself operating within the context of views that are widely accepted in financial and banking circles. Thus, though there is not a conspiracy of bankers intent on fashioning the world in a conservative image, they form an *epistemic community* of people who think more or less alike on these sorts of questions. In the 1930s, John Maynard Keynes, the great British economist, brushed aside the beliefs of the epistemic community of his day, but we lack a Keynes for the globalized era.

While it is clear that governments have less control in the globalized economy than they had, some of this is because governments voluntarily abdicated their sovereignty to gain economic benefits. It may be the case that governments could retrieve this sovereignty if they so wished. Part of the process of globalization followed from the liberalization of international capital markets in the mid-1980s. Perhaps this could be reversed and governments given more say in the control of their economies. If they wished, they could take a less liberal attitude to free trade. The question is how much this would cost – and there is little agreement.

We must still be careful not to see the state as completely helpless even in these globalized days. Taxes are still raised. Fears that the tax base would evaporate have not so far materialized, though the danger for the future obviously exists. The constraints on raising money for governments is as much to do with the supposed reluctance of middle-class tax-payers to pay taxes at the same level as they did in the much poorer decades after the Second World War, as it is to do with the ability to avoid taxes in a globalized world (though the evidence for this supposed reluctance is ambiguous). Balance-of-payments problems have often plagued governments and it is not clear that this is any worse today than it often has been in the past. The extent of globalization itself can be exaggerated. In the case of Britain, trade and capital flows as a proportion of Gross National Product were larger in the Gold Standard period in the early years of the twentieth century than they were in the 1980s (Hirst and Thompson, 1996).

The state has a necessary role in some important issues that are aspects of globalization. Consider environmental degradation. Take a specific case such as the emission of carbon as a result of using fossil fuels. The policy goal has to be the reduction of the amount of carbon released. Now carbon has to be released on the territory of some state. But that state can impose rules on the polluters by making them reduce the use of coal or insisting on anti-pollution devices and so on. Indeed, if there are to be worldwide controls over fossil-fuel emissions, states are the likely controllers of emissions. It is theoretically possible that polluting firms might get together and agree, though rather unlikely. Some globalization theorists argue against the state as the primary controlling body by saying that it will be sidestepped. Economic activities will simply shift from the jurisdiction of the state with strict environmental controls to another state with a more relaxed attitude to the environment. This is possible because one characteristic of the modern economy is the ease with which economic activities can be moved. Suppose the Indian government put strict controls on carbon emissions, the producers could go abroad. The more likely possibility is that if China did not put restrictions on carbon emissions, it would have an advantage over India in those areas where energy is important. There are many other forms of economic activity that are easier to move than coal and could be carried out in many different circumstances. Thus computers can be assembled wherever there is a dextrous labour force, though the compensation here is that computer manufacture is a benign activity from the point of view of the environment. In general, economic activities that have adverse environmental effects can be combated only by international agreement, by which I mean interstate agreement. If all the countries that could host some form of economic activity agree to impose the same sort of environmental rules, there is nowhere for the producers to go to get cheap but environmentally unfriendly facilities. This principle lies behind most environmental agreements, as we discuss in more detail in Chapter 11. However, states are the bodies that carry out agreements and have the power to impose rules on the firms within their jurisdictions. States, or more properly governments, are central in this activity. However, in claiming they are significant actors, we fall a long way short of affirming that they are the lone, anarchic actors of traditional international relations theory.

Further Reading and Sources

The literature on globalization is vast and growing rapidly. One of the most popular textbooks on the subject is John Baylis and Steve Smith, *The Globalization of World Politics: An Introduction to International Relations* (Oxford: Oxford University Press, 2001, 2nd edn). A useful collection of essays is edited by Martin Shaw, *Politics and Globalisation: Knowledge, Ethics and Agency* (London and New York: Routledge, 1999). A sophisticated 'globalist' view is to be found in Jan Aart Scholte, *Globalization: A Critical Introduction* (Basingstoke: Palgrave, 2000). A somewhat more sceptical view of globalization is given in Paul Hirst and Graham Thompson, *Globalization in Question* (Cambridge: Polity Press, 1999, 2nd edn). They do not deny it is happening, but point out it has been going for quite some time. Other recent books on globalization include Patrick O'Meara, Howard D. Mehlinger and Matthew Krain (eds), *Globalization and the Challenges of the New Century: A Reader* (Bloomington: Indiana University Press, 2000) and

David Held and Anthony McGrew (eds), *Global Transformation Reader* (Oxford: Blackwell, 2000).

Figures for the slave trade come from Philip Curtain, *The Atlantic Slave Trade* (Madison and London: University of Wisconsin Press, 1969) and L. Bethnell, *The Abolition of the Brazilian Slave Trade* (Cambridge: Cambridge University Press, 1970). The costs of transatlantic travel were computed from data from F. and E. Hyde, *Cunard and the North Atlantic 1840–1973* (London: Macmillan – now Palgrave Macmillan, 1975), from A.L. Bowley, *Wages and Income in the UK since 1860* (Cambridge: Cambridge University Press, 1937) and from the *Annual Digest of Statistics* (London: HMSO, 1996). Migration figures come from Glenn T. Trewartha, *A Geography of Population World Patterns* (London: John Wiley, 1960) and R. Thomlinson, *Population Dynamics: Causes and Consequences of World Demographic Change* (New York: Random House, 1965). *Encyclopedia Britannica* is a good source of information about communications.

11

The Global Environment

The Global Environmental Problem

One thousand years ago, around the year 1000 and just before the Norman invasion of Britain, there were approximately 265 million people in the entire world. It did not matter very much how much mess they made except very locally. Their impact was too small to make much difference. In 1750, just before the Industrial Revolution was getting well under way in Britain the world population is estimated to have been 800 million. Pollution, though severe locally such as in the Thames around London and the Hudson River around New York, had little overall effect on the planet. Fresh fish from the sea were a delicacy except in coastal areas. Deep-sea fishing of cod, for example on the Grand Banks of Newfoundland, had been practised by British, French and Portuguese fishermen since the sixteenth century and their catch, when dried, provided a useful addition to the diet. However, this was never on such a scale that stocks were in danger. A cod swimming in, say, the North Sea could do so largely unmolested and die in whatever is the cod's equivalent of its bed. Parts of Europe had lost their forests due to methods of agriculture that must have had significant local effects on the climate long before the Industrial Revolution. However, the overall pattern of the world's climate remained substantially unaffected by the activities of human beings throughout most of history. There are now over six billion people (that is, 6000 million) and the story is totally different. The inputs and outputs of the human race have enormous impact on the whole global system.

Inevitably this is a global matter. From fish swimming in common waters to acid rain drifting across frontiers, the problems must be considered as features of the globe as a whole. There are some national problems of pollution; some indeed are very local – particular cities may suffer and their sufferings may be assuaged by some form of local collective action. However, many are global. Pollutants are indifferent to national boundaries while scarcities caused by human action are commonly global in their implications.

There is no single problem of the environment. There are several different problems that interact but are separable. What links the problems is that they are the consequence of human activity and impinge on the non-human environment both living and inanimate. Many of the activities would be innocuous if carried out on a small scale. However, given the very large number of human beings they continue on a large scale and, cumulatively, have a great and usually deleterious effect.

The problem of population lies behind much of the problem of the environment with its fears not just of pollution but a continued chronic lack of food. The population at the start of the third millennium is around 6300 million. If it continues to grow at the present rate of slightly under 2 per cent a year, it will be about 8300 million by 2020 and around 11 billion by 2084. In general, poor countries grow faster than rich with no apparent tendency for their economies to grow faster in order to counterbalance this. Precise forecasts are very hazardous. However, short of a nuclear war or a plague of unprecedented proportions, a rapid increase in the world's population over the next century is as near inevitable as anything is in social life. It will bring further serious strains on the environment.

I shall deal with a number of problems in greater detail, the first being that of *global warming*. This has attracted a lot of attention and is sometimes identified as almost the only problem of the environment, which it is not. There is a lot of scientific evidence to suggest that the world is getting warmer primarily because of the side effects of industrial production. This is the so-called *greenhouse effect*. Various gases, particularly carbon dioxide, are released into the atmosphere. Water vapour is significant also. These then trap heat which would otherwise have escaped and raise the temperature of the earth. This will have a number of consequences, some of them unpleasant, such as the rising of the sea-level and the probable increase in violent and destructive storms.

One factor that aggravates global warming is *deforestation,* which is going on in many parts of the world. In particular tropical rainforests in places like Brazil are being cut down both for the sake of the wood and to increase farming land. Plants, including trees, breathe in carbon dioxide and breathe out oxygen. Though there is some planting of trees, the net reduction worldwide (and, for that matter, for most countries individually) is considerable. The fewer trees there are, the more the proportion of carbon dioxide increases in the atmosphere and the more the global-warming process is amplified. Deforestation is also linked with problems of biodiversity. As the terrain on which they live is taken from them, many species become extinct. Even pragmatically from the point of view of human self-interest, this is a worry as one never knows what the use of a plant or animal in some future state of knowledge might be. However, there is also a moral issue, which concerns some people, as to the right of human beings to organize the world in the interests of the human race alone. Clearly this is an issue over which there are strong moral disagreements.

Another problem in addition to that of the ozone layers is the reduction in the *ozone layer*. Around the earth, at a height between 10 and 35 kilometres, there is a layer of ozone that keeps harmful radiation down to levels that the present living inhabitants of the world, human and non-human, can tolerate. This layer is being damaged by the use of chemicals on the earth such as the CFC gases in sprays which, until recently, were thought to be innocuous. The ozone layer has developed holes through which radiation passes in quantities that cause cancer.

Other problems concern the depletion of resources. There are two different problems here. Some resources such as species of fish, for example cod, are reproducible. Cod are mortal and therefore die even without being hunted. They are replaced by offspring like all other forms of life. Fishing in moderation increases the death rate but cod as a species survive. However, at some level of hunting the stocks of cod decrease, which, if continued, would lead to extinction. Many species of animals, which once existed in profusion, such as many forms of whales, have become extinct. Indeed any animal of use to human beings and which it is impracticable to farm is hunted. There is always the danger of overhunting and a number of species are seriously threatened. The second problem is inanimate materials that will be used up after a period of time. Some of these, such as fossil fuels, have deleterious effects on the environment. However, certain fossil fuels such as petrol are crucial to the present way of life. Natural resources of petrol will disappear in the long run though it is not yet a pressing problem. It is widely assumed that there will be a 'technological fix' which will either mean that oil will be synthetically produced at some reasonable cost or that some other form of engine or fuel will be developed. This is, perhaps, a rational attitude, but there is no immediate candidate for replacing, say, the jet engine powered by a product of oil.

These are just some of the more important problems of the environment that are raised by the activities of human beings. They are global problems and can be solved only at a global level, which puts them firmly in the discipline of international relations. It is only comparatively recently that their importance was recognized, and it is still controversial as to how important they are though only a few dismiss them as of no importance. Environmental problems were noticed in the early 1960s and became more prominent in the early 1970s. Once on the fringe, they are now part of the orthodoxy as central issues in the global arena.

Different environmental problems raise different issues though there are some common threads. I shall deal with three of them – global warming, water supplies and pollution in the Mediterranean – to illustrate both problems and successes. They all involve issues in the natural as well as the social sciences, some of which are still controversial. They also raise issues of decision-making in the international arena. Decisions ought to be made about how to control the global environment. Some decisions result in actions that benefit some actors more than others or impose costs on some actors more than others. But these have to be made by the agreement of lots of different decision-makers, if there is no authority to make them collectively, or to enforce compliance with any agreements once made. This is a central problem of international relations and why, given its importance, the environment has now become a central issue in the field.

The Free-Rider Problem

If there is a serious possibility of environmental degradation, then it would seem that we should alter the methods of production to become more ecologically sound and proceed from there. There are obvious short-term costs in this but as the long-term benefits outweigh the costs, there is no fundamental problem involved – or so we might think. Unfortunately there is an underlying theoretical problem which has implications for a great deal of social behaviour but is particularly central to problems of the environment. It is known as the *free-rider problem*.

The problem can be illustrated by a simple example of commercial fishing. Most edible fish have been extensively fished and are in danger of falling below the level at which it will be worth fishing. Indeed many face extinction. The overall level of fishing needs to be reduced to a point where fish can reproduce themselves and the fish stock remains constant over a long period. Thus there is some maximum level of fish that can be harvested in any given year to be consistent with the long-term survival of any species of fish. This is known as the *maximum sustainable yield*. To fish at no more than the maximum sustainable yield implies that there have to be quotas for the fishing industry, imposed ultimately on the fishing boats themselves. There is no serious disagreement about this general proposition and only detailed disagreements about what this level is. The fishing industry knows perfectly well that its long-term survival depends on short-term abstinence in not taking as many fish as is technically possible. However, while this is true of the industry as a whole, it is not true of any particular boat. There are many fishing boats working in European waters. If all the boats but one keep to their quotas but that one boat catches as much fish as it can, it will make no discernible difference to the overall fish stocks. Thus, the boat's owners will be tempted to do just this. By catching as much fish as possible, they will profit but, due to the restraint of the rest, there will be no long-term costs. Unfortunately this logic applies to a second boat, a third and so on. Indeed, whatever the restraint or lack of it by the other boats, it will always be in the interests of any particular boat to defect from the overall agreement.

Reasoning that applies to an individual boat does not apply to the industry as a whole. Suppose all the boats that fish in European waters were owned by a single owner. By looking at the long-term future, clearly the best solution would be restraint. Short-period overfishing might give quick short-term profits but long-term profits are best preserved by present caution. The European fishing industry accepts this broad logic of the situation.

Consumers are, of course, relevant in this. If there is restraint in the catching of fish today it means that current prices will be higher and less fish will be eaten. However, if there is no restraint, the current lower prices will be offset by higher prices in the future and the possible cessation of supplies if overfishing is extreme. The consumer faces the same choice as the producer except (and this is an important exception) that a modification in the consumer's diet is much less of an issue than the whole alteration in the producer's life which, for many, will include leaving their chosen profession. This understandably makes them so much more involved and ready to sense injustices than the comparitively mildly affected consumer.

Perhaps surprisingly, however, in some industries where there is greater concentration of ownership and control, the awareness of long-term costs is not clear. Thus, we know that fossil fuels such as coal and petrol are the culprits as far as global warming is concerned. Nevertheless these industries campaign against any serious attempts to reduce dependency on their products, despite the fact that a significant reduction in consumption of their products (widely estimated at about 50 per cent) is required if global warming is to be halted, much less reversed. Enlightened self-interest would seem to indicate they would be ready, as industries, to join in, even if individual firms and countries look for opportunities to free ride as inconspicuously as possible. The reason for their apparent shortsightedness becomes clear when we look at who in fact will suffer from global warming. The producers of fossil fuels probably will not suffer very much. Any drawbacks will be amply compensated by the good living they will make, either as owners or workers, in their industries. The fossil-fuel industries are concentrated in places like the United States and the oil-producing states of the Middle East, which in relative terms will be less affected by global warming. The potential victims for the most part, are concentrated in non-fossil fuel-producing areas. It appears to be an accident that this should be so, but an unfortunate accident nevertheless.

Fossil fuel is rather different from fish. If the fisheries are overfished then the fishing industry itself will suffer as well as the consumers of fish. In the case of fossil fuels, even after global warming, the industry still benefits. Its members will suffer as consumers, but in general the benefits will outweigh the costs. Thus, these industries are reluctant to forgo present benefits for somewhat uncertain future benefits, particularly when the future benefits will be disproportionately enjoyed by other people.

This raises another issue that makes concerted action to curb global warming difficult. The damage involved in global warming has a very different impact on different groups of people. For some, indeed, it might be beneficial. There would be some pleasurable features if the climate of the south of England became like that of the Northern Mediterranean. However, many people will suffer, such as those living in low-lying coastal areas. Either they will have to move or vast expenditure on coastal defences will be required. In the meantime there may be more floods. Similarly there are parts of the world that are likely to become desert, such as significant parts of sub-Saharan Africa. Where these are poor areas in the first place, the problems will become even more serious. Other areas may not suffer very much and some may even improve. Those groups who pay a disproportionate cost and reap few of the benefits will try and block attempts to combat global warming.

Which groups can promote and which can delay moves to combat environmental problems, such as global warming? What is the role of states in this and what is the role of other groups such as firms, industries as a whole, individuals and pressure groups? Though there are local problems, the central issues are global. As there is no global or world authority, any action has to involve the coordination of actions by international organizations in which states are likely to be significant actors. Thus, it is fundamentally a problem of international relations. I argued above that the free-rider problem is the central problem in environmental issues. The problem is how to restrict production to levels consistent with an environmentally sustainable policy, even though this is smaller than the level the firms would produce in the interests of profit. Thus actors have to act against their own individual self-interest in the short run and possibly in the long run. Unless we have both far-sighted and altruistic actors (which is probably asking too much) we need a state or a state-like body to impose laws and extract compliance from them. One of the state's major roles is to secure compliance in free-rider problems. The policing which is necessary to secure compliance on environmental measures has to come from the state. This means that states must enter into some agreement with other states to control activities that are potentially damaging to its own territorial environment or related sea areas. If a state cannot be persuaded to do so, then firms within its domain will be able to carry on environmentally destructive activities unchecked. Thus the free-rider problem can operate at two levels. First firms within the polity may be tempted to free ride but restrained from doing so by the government. Secondly, states themselves are tempted to free ride if they think that by doing so their national economy will benefit. This double free-rider issue aggravates the problems.

Global Warming

Diminution of the ozone layer and the problem of global warming are two widely-discussed and important issues relating to the environment. We shall look at them a little more closely in this section as some of the problems involved are common to other aspects of the environmental problem.

It is alleged that the world is getting warmer due to the activities of human beings, and in particular the process of industrialization, coupled with quickly expanding populations. So-called *greenhouse gases* are the primary cause of this. The temperature of the earth is partly governed by the balance of the radiation that comes in and escapes. The amount, in either case, is determined by the constitution and quantity of the gases in the atmosphere. If greenhouse gases increase, the earth gets warmer; if they decrease it gets colder. The present forms of life on the earth depend on the greenhouse effect to keep it at the appropriate temperature. However, the difficulties come if the gases vary. Thus, the greenhouse effect in itself is crucial to human life; it is the variations in it which cause the problems. The evidence seems to suggest strongly that the world is getting warmer. Greenhouse gases are increasing, largely due to various forms of economic activity.

The most significant of the greenhouse gases is carbon dioxide, which accounts for a little more than half of the contribution to global warming. It comes mainly from fossil fuel burning and deforestation. Chlorofluorocarbons – more commonly called CFCs – account for about a quarter of the contribution to global warming. These come from various industrial usages, foam blowing solvents (which have attracted a lot of popular attention) and refrigerants. They were virtually unknown prior to the 1930s. In some ways these pose the most difficult problems. Their use is increasing at about 4 per cent a year, much faster than the other greenhouse factors. Further, the expansion of refrigerators, both commercial and domestic, makes an enormous impact on the quality of life. For all other reasons, the expansion of refrigeration, particularly in hot countries, would be a reason for rejoicing. About 15 per cent of global warming comes from methane, the source of which is rice paddies and various forms of fermentation. Nitrous oxide accounts for about 6 per cent and comes from biomass burning, fertilizer use and fossil-fuel consumption. Thus, greenhouse gases are side effects of activities that are not inherently reprehensible; indeed, some are positively desirable from many points of view. Unfortunately, they still pose serious problems for the development of the world economy.

Once the process of greenhouse warming is under way it sets up various *feedback processes*. These processes either speed up global warming – *positive feedback processes* – or counteract the trend – *negative feedback processes*. Global warming increases the amount of water vapour from the seas. Water vapour itself is a powerful greenhouse factor so the warming process is amplified. This is a case of positive feedback. Similarly the warming will melt some of the ice at the polar ice caps. The ice caps reflect a lot of solar radiation and operate as a cooling factor. Thus, the reduction in the size of the ice cap reduces this reflection and therefore increases yet further the global warming. However, there are also negative feedbacks. The increase in cloud cover caused by the increase in water vapour will increase the amount of radiation reflected by clouds and operate as a cooling factor – in other words, as a negative feedback process. The combination of negative and positive feedback processes makes it very difficult to work out what the net effect will be. Unfortunately, it is virtually impossible to measure the respective contributions of the various effects with present techniques or those likely to be available in the foreseeable future. Consequently the degree of global warming which is likely after any period of time is only a set of estimates, which must be within broad ranges. Warming will probably vary regionally. Broadly, close to the equator the effects will be relatively small whereas closer to the poles, the effects will be larger. The impact therefore will vary considerably.

The consequences of global warming are various. First, the sea level will rise, which will put various coastal states in a serious position. Unfortunately, it is an accident that many of the most vulnerable countries are also very poor – Egypt, Mozambique and Pakistan, for example. Bangladesh, already one of the poorest countries outside Africa, will be particularly badly affected. Much of it is low lying and vulnerable to storms and flooding as it is. A rise of one metre in sea level would result in a displacement of ten per cent of the population, which is well over ten million people. Greater increases in the sea level will have correspondingly higher levels of disruption. Rich countries are not immune from the problem. The Netherlands is a particular case in point. The East coast of Britain is already vulnerable to the sea and will become much more so if the sea level rises significantly. However, rich countries are able to do more about it. In the case of Britain the number of people involved is not large and population could move without causing significant social disruption. Further, there are more resources available for sea defence if this is regarded as a more appropriate strategy, though it can be very costly. More seriously, there are a number of small island states that are very low lying, such as the Maldives, which would disappear altogether if the sea level increased by very much. However people try to cope, the effects of the rise in the sea level will be very costly both economically and in terms of social dislocation. Costs will be exacerbated by the likely increase in violent storms as a consequence of global warming, making low-lying coastal areas yet more vulnerable to flooding and sea defence more difficult. However, the costs of higher sea levels will vary significantly from place to place. Countries with low-lying coasts will have a lot of problems. At the other extreme, landlocked states such as Switzerland have nothing to worry about.

Some consequences of global warming may *be* paradoxical. The reduction of the ice caps could set in train a serious alternation in the flow of the ocean currents and divert the flow of the Gulf Stream. The Gulf Stream keeps parts of Northern Europe such as the UK and Northern France much warmer than they would otherwise be. Overall global warming could well bring global cooling to an unpleasant degree for some.

Another major consequence is the displacement of various sorts of economic activity. Thus temperate areas suitable for wheat will become hotter and less suitable, while other areas, which are now too cold, will become more suitable. The central wheatlands of the United States will move northwards to Canada. Similarly Siberia may well become a grain basket. This suggests that the process of global warming will simply shift economic activity. Some areas (and hence certain countries) will gain from this and some will lose. A new, higher level of temperature for the globe need not in itself be worse, but merely different. This is certainly arguable, though the consensus seems to be that the negative aspects of global warming, even if there is some new equilibrium level, outweigh the positive. The cost of moving from one level to another is very high, not just in economic terms but also in terms of social dislocation.

A serious analytical problem in discussing global warming is the high level of uncertainty involved. Though the science of many of the parts of the problem, such as the behaviour of gases, the origin of gases and so on, is well-known, the behaviour of the whole environmental system is not. It is an extremely complex, interdependent system with feedback processes working in opposing directions and with different time lags. It is impossible to make quantitative assessments of many of the different effects. Consequently the behaviour of the environmental system as a whole cannot be determined with any degree of precision. Computer simulations can be made under a wide variety of assumptions. These are, in effect, quasi-experiments. However, we cannot know which assumptions are correct, so we are still peering ahead in a fog of uncertainty. The earth's temperature goes up and down over long periods in any case, irrespective of the activities of human beings. Indeed voices were raised as late as the 1970s fearing a new ice age. The evidence that global warming is going ahead faster than could be accounted for by long-term shifts in the 'natural' temperature of the earth is still ambiguous. Nevertheless, most climatologists regard the evidence of global warming as convincing even if there is no agreement, and can be no agreement, on its scale. There seems to be a near consensus, though, that it is on a sufficient scale to warrant concern. Even if the cause of the present global warming is due to long-term natural causes and the contribution of industrialization to its cause has been exaggerated, this does not alter the problem. Its effects will be just as serious. Further, it can be slowed down by cutting back on the emission of the greenhouse gases just as much as if it were caused by industrialization. That is, the cure can be separate from the cause.

There are doubters, even amongst professional experts, but these are few. The evidence looks convincing. The doubters, of course, provide a lever to those who argue that to expend vast resources on something that may not happen is foolish. We return to this in the final section.

Water

'The wars of the next century will be over water' is the depressing prediction of Ismail Serageldin, former vice-president of the World Bank. Whether or not this turns out to be the case, there is undeniably a problem of water. It is not the total quantity of water which is the issue but where it is located. Nature, rather than the vagaries of the economic and social system, has distributed water very unequally across the world, making for severe shortages in parts, along with excesses in others. Moreover, the demand for water is increasing. Population is increasing, which naturally increases demand both directly and indirectly by its use in industry and agriculture. In 1910, human beings used about 500 cubic kilometres of water. In 2001 it will be 3750. Some forms of water utilization have become more efficient such as in some industrial processes. Indeed water consumption in the USA has fallen from a peak in 1980. However, there are also tendencies the other way. Agriculture uses 70 per cent of water and many forms of agriculture which are being developed today, such as lettuce growing and other forms of market gardening, use a lot of water. Other forms of activity such as tourism are very water-intensive as people from places where water is readily available find themselves in places where water is scarce, but are still anxious to shower and keep cool and clean. The Food and Agriculture Organization (FAO) reports that 15 000 cubic meters of water, which will provide for a hundred rural families for three years, and a hundred urban families for two years, will keep a hundred individual guests in a luxury hotel for only 55 days. The implications of many economic policies for the water supply are often rather casually dealt with.

Water shortages produce a number of international tensions as shortages often do. The water supply has a curiosity of its own. A lot of water is drawn from rivers. Rivers often meander over political boundaries such that states in whose land the water originates have a strong lever over those to whom it flows. Attempts to extract water in the higher reaches mean that there is less lower down. Big water projects involving the building of dams can have catastrophic consequences for those downstream. Thus the Nile, on which Egypt depends for 97 per cent of its water, flows though Sudan, Kenya, Rwanda, Burundi, Uganda, Tanzania and Zaire. Several of these are politically unstable, though a state wracked by instability is unlikely to embark on the sort of large-scale water-extraction projects which could have a devastating effect on the Egyptian economy. Egypt's situation is extreme but the general phenomenon is common. Pakistan is very dependent on the water supplied by the river Indus, two of whose tributaries start in India in the fertile Punjab. The river basin of the Jordan is shared by Jordan itself, Syria, Israel and Lebanon. Turkey controls the head waters of the Tigris and Euphrates on which both Syria and Iraq are very dependent. Clearly tensions can become acute where dependent states feel that not only the economy but life itself is in the hands of the state controlling the head waters. This is unlikely to lead to international harmony unless very sensitively dealt with.

There remains a problem when rivers run through several countries even when states are not so highly dependent on the water. The Rhine runs through Switzerland, Germany and the Netherlands. Any pollution starting in the first two arrives in the Netherlands, which is a concern for the Dutch. Rivers not only supply water but are also a form of transport and a conveyor of rubbish. In all its forms water can prove a source of international friction.

The Mediterranean Agreement

It is easy to be pessimistic about the successes of agreements in the international arena, a world in which self-interest often appears to be a dominant motive. The success of agreements over environmental matters is mixed. However, it would be churlish to overlook the partial success of some agreements. Agreements to limit fishing in various waters may not be perfect but they exist, and have prevented some forms of exhaustion of the fishing stock. A particularly interesting case of a relatively successful set of agreements is that on pollution in the Mediterranean.

In the late 1960s and early 1970s, when awareness of environmental issues was becoming widespread, there was great concern about the Mediterranean. It is almost landlocked, so the water is comparatively static. It is bordered by several industrial states such as Spain, France and Italy who discharge vast quantities of industrial effluent and sewerage into it. Several rivers bearing industrial discharge flow into it. The Mediterranean seemed to be a good candidate for an ecological and environmental catastrophe. The United Nations Environmental Programme (UNEP), set up in 1975, became involved and proceeded with a programme for the Mediterranean known as the Mediterranean Action Plan, which was adopted in 1975 by sixteen governments.

Politically the Mediterranean seems a poor prospect for an agreement on the environment or anything else. It is surrounded by eighteen separate states who are as diverse politically and as mutually hostile as it is possible to be. Israel is one, and there is a host of Arab states including Syria. Greece and Turkey are long-term enemies. At the time the agreements were formed there were two very different communist states: Yugoslavia was a moderate communist regime while Albania was the most old-fashioned and Stalinist of the communist states. Even

Albania finally sent delegates to the conferences, though not at the beginning. There were economically highly-developed states such as France and less-developed Mahgreb states, which are the Arab states on the South West of the Mediterranean. There seemed to be no form of political and international disagreement that was not represented somewhere in the Mediterranean. Coupled with the large number of actors, the hopes seemed slender for an agreement on topics where the free-rider issue was prominent.

Nevertheless, the agreements over the Mediterranean have in fact been quite successful. This needs explaining, as it is not what one would expect. I adopt the explanation of Peter Haas in his magnificent study of the subject. From the beginning there was a desire in the negotiations not to exploit political differences. One of the most difficult problems was that the Arab states did not recognize Israel. The Israelis agreed to keep a low profile in exchange for the Arab states accepting them, though with a ritual statement at each meeting that this did not imply recognition. As the programme developed, procedures arose such that individual states were not pinpointed aggressively for their environmental delinquencies. The analysis and negotiation was kept relatively free of the point-scoring which often goes on in negotiations between states. This was helped by the relatively low profile of the meetings, which were ongoing. They were not the subject of headline news in any country.

Part of the project was research. Though people were aware that there was an environmental problem, the precise characteristics of it were not known and hence the most effective forms of action could not be formulated. As a result of the research, it was discovered for example that about 85–90 per cent of industrial waste came from rivers, so this became a central issue to discuss. In general the care with which the problem was analyzed from a scientific point of view meant that it was taken seriously. Decisions were not reached because they were politically fashionable but in light of serious scientific evidence.

The importance of research was one reason that the less developed countries (LDCs) were willing to participate. The equipment and laboratories were provided by the UN. Countries like France, for example, already had equipment and highly-trained scientists. The LDCs did not but, as a consequence of the project, acquired equipment and their scientists received free training in often elaborate methods of analysis. Thus, they were getting not just the long-term benefits of reduced pollution but the immediate and direct benefits of scientific equipment and know-how. The meetings between the actors were frequent and there was a more or less ongoing process of negotiation and analysis. The scientific representatives of the various countries became the dominant actors. The negotiations moved into the hands of the *epistemic community*, which is a term used to mean the people who are professionally involved in something – in this case environmental science – and who have loyalties to their professional position as well as to the narrow self-interests of their states. In essence, a problem-solving mode developed, if which the need to solve the problem became the dominant motive. This does not mean that the various interests were neglected, far from it, but that they were seen as part of a problem and not the whole of it. Further, the actors involved were not just advocates for their state but participants in the problem-solving mode.

The dominance of the epistemic community in the negotiations led to some interesting switches. Initially the LDCs were rather suspicious of the project. The point, which appears in many environmental contexts, was heard that the rich countries polluted while they were developing but were now prepared to impede the LDCs from doing so, by requiring environmental controls that they had not themselves been required to operate under. However, Egypt and Algeria in particular switched from being sceptics to being enthusiasts for cleaning up the Mediterranean. This can be interpreted as a redefinition of their national interests. The environmentalists, who were members of an international epistemic community, became more prominent in defining the national interests and policies of these countries. It appears that, counter to what one would think, some of the LDCs were more powerfully committed to the environmental goal than some of the richer ones. One explanation is that rich countries have bigger and more efficient bureaucracies and can challenge the epistemic community both in its own terms and from the point of view of narrower national interest. The overworked bureaucracies of the poorer countries are content to let the epistemic community take a problem off their hands.

Global Environmental Policy

The question we shall consider is how people can make decisions that are necessary to eliminate or ameliorate the problems of environmental change. We shall not be concerned about the actual decisions, but rather, assuming such decisions are necessary, the problems that arise in making them. Thus this is a problem in politics and social science, not the natural sciences.

The problems are undeniably difficult ones and would be even if there were a benevolent world dictator to tackle them. They are long-term problems; we are considering issues that have their consequences in fifty or hundred years time when most people currently alive will have died, and when all the people who actually take the decisions will be dead. They differ, though, according to the problem in question. I shall concentrate again on global warming. First, the time lag between the practices that cause global warming and actual warming of the globe is long. Thus there would probably be some global warming in twenty years time even if all the steps against it were taken tomorrow. The same goes for any ameliorative efforts. They will be noticeable only after a considerable period of time. This links with the second point, that there is uncertainty about the degree of global warming. A small minority of sceptics doubt that there is global warming at all. Amongst the majority who accept the reality of global warming it is generally agreed that there is great uncertainty about how severe the global warming will be. Thus, it is unclear what the consequences will be in, say, fifty years time. We are planning very costly activities which may turn out not to have been necessary. It is galling to build a very expensive set of sea defences only to find that it is not needed. Third, many environmental changes are irreversible or are reversible only over centuries. The extinction of a species of animal or plant is totally irreversible. Finally, both the costs and effects of global warming are very different in different parts of the world. Some countries like Bangladesh will be badly affected; others like the United States will only be moderately so. Countries like China and India will be affected, but the costs will fall far short of the benefits of using cheap coal in the much-needed development of their economies.

The problems themselves are inherently difficult and often without an obvious solution. Even if there is a solution, it can be hard to reach it. Most, as exemplified by global warming, involve international decision-making. Even if we look at it as a set of problems that can be solved at the state level, there is no authority to enforce compliance between states. Successful international agreements on the environ-ment imply that governments are both willing and able to enforce compliance with the agreements within their boundaries or, often more awkwardly in the case of fishing and hunting agreements, on their citizens in common waters at sea. Initially I shall assume that governments are willing and able, though this is not always warranted.

The core decision-making difficulty is how to come to terms with the free-rider problem. Even if states were equally affected by global warming, the problem would be hard enough. In one form or another it is encountered in other contexts in international relations such as the sale of arms. In the case of global warming, the problem is aggravated in that some states are much less affected than others.

Free-rider problems have been tackled in relation to certain aspects of the environmental problem with some success, as in the case of the Mediterranean. Also, while improvements could be made, there has been progress in making agreements about overfishing in many parts of the world. There are a number of reasons why these are easier to solve than the global-warming problem. First, the problem is fairly clear-cut and observable. In the case of fishing, it is clear to those currently involved in the industry that fish stocks are in danger. Further, it is also clear that overfishing is a major cause of this. Thus, both the causes and the consequences of overfishing are clear and relatively uncontroversial. There have been plenty of historical precedents for overfishing to reinforce these views. This is also true in many cases of pollution. Second, the time intervals with fishing are short enough for the consequences to be readily imagined by people involved as mattering to them personally. Even if conservation is costly, an uncontrolled industry will clearly come to a halt in a few years. Neither of these conditions hold in the case of global warming which is not obvious in the common experience of most people, although the increased incidence of flooding, which is often put in the context of global warming, has brought this home to many. In the case of pollution and overfishing, the technical solutions are relatively clear. Admittedly there are debates, often acrimonious, over the size of fish stocks. Scientists can normally be found who will be diligent in interpreting the data to suit the policies of their governments and domestic industries. Nevertheless, there is general agreement that fishing must be reduced and usually a compromise is reached in the end. Further there are independent scientists. The broad outline of common action is usually agreed even if the details are contentious. The hope raised by agreements on the pollution of the Mediterranean is that the problems can be taken out of the conflictual interstate and interindustry framework and treated as a problem to be solved by the relevant epistemic communities. It is not clear when epistemic communities become important and how we encourage them. They may simply conceal the genuine conflicts of interest. Global warming, with such vast resources at stake, will be seen as a political problem to be negotiated by political haggling.

It would seem necessary to recognize that countries which will bear a disproportionate burden of the costs without compensating benefits will need some sort of inducement to change. Thus, countries like India and China will require large-scale help if they are to derive energy from non-polluting sources. The LDCs object to global-warming agreements when these impose great costs. They argue that one source of the problem is that, since the end of the eighteenth century, the presently-developed countries have been polluting the atmosphere and have steadily used it as a sink to dispose of their waste material, though admittedly without realizing it until recently. Thus it seems unfair that the LDCs should not do likewise or, if not, be compensated by the developed countries (DCs) who have already benefited enormously through doing just this. Further, this habit of the DCs is by no means over. The contribution of the West to global warming is still considerable. The tons of oil-equivalent used per capita are 7.82 for an American as against 0.4 for an Indian. As Americans are richer, it seems reasonable to suppose that conservation should begin at home. The problems are created when poorer countries increase their pollution levels but the rich countries are in a weak position to complain. This provides a moral argument to add to the more aggressive, pragmatic argument, that some of the LDCs can ignore any agreements and still come out ahead.

There are efforts to try to contain the environmental problem on an international scale by international agreements. Many governments, particularly in Western Europe, are deeply concerned about the environmental problem and are anxious to do something. There is always the free-rider problem. If one country does not cut back on the destructive forms of economic activity while the others do, that country will have an advantage. Similarly there is the problem of poor countries who understandably put their own economic development ahead of fears of long-term environmental damage. Thus, any progress that will be achieved is likely to be done by mutual agreement with all parties agreeing to cut back on destructive activities. The most recent agreement was the Kyoto Protocol signed in Japan in 1997 by 160 countries. This was the result of years of often laborious negotiation. Thirty-eight industrial countries, including the United States agreed to reduce their greenhouse gases on average by 5.2 per cent below the 1990 levels by 2012. The USA agreed to reduce them by 7 per cent and the countries of the European Union by 8 per cent. There is some doubt whether this is enough, but it is a start of significant dimensions. Unfortunately, there are doubts about whether the Kyoto Protocol will be effective as the United States, under the Republican administration which came into power in 2001, is very unsympathetic to environmental issues and has declined to go ahead with the Protocol. As the USA produces about one-quarter of the world's greenhouse gases, this is a significant issue. This withdrawal is the result of pressure from business interests on an administration already strongly sympathetic ideologically to business. They object to the higher costs that would be imposed on them and are happy at the competitive advantage this will give them over the more constrained European industries. This is a very short-run approach. What the long run will look like, we cannot say. However, the present situation with regard to international agreements does not look very cheerful, largely due to the attitude of the United States government under President G. W. Bush.

The political problems of global warming are acute. Finding a solution that overcomes the free-rider problem is difficult. A very different approach finds favour with some economists. It accepts that there are problems of global warming and that these will impose great social and economic costs. However, averting global warming will also involve great costs. It may be more appropriate to accept global warming and use resources to alleviate the effects. Thus a 'Dutch' policy for Bangladesh of building major sea defences would be very expensive but nothing like as expensive as carrying out the policies necessary to reverse global warming. The same can be said for many other compensatory devices. They are costly, but it is costly to avert global warming also. This approach does not appeal to many environmentalists but it should be seriously considered. It has, of course, serious drawbacks, notably that some countries will be very badly affected by global warming (and these are often poor countries) while others are not affected very much. Thus, the less affected parts of the world are going to have to make very large transfers of resources to the more affected parts. It can be easily shown that many countries such as the United States could easily afford it and would profit immensely from doing this, rather than enduring the much larger costs involved in cutting down global warming. However, the history of large-scale transfers of resources, with a few major exceptions, is not encouraging.

It would require a great change in attitude amongst the richer countries.

The worst scenario would be that nothing is done or, perhaps more likely, that a little is done but not enough to make any significant difference. This would leave those countries that are both poor and badly affected to suffer their fate, with inadequate transfer of resources to help them ameliorate it.

Further Reading and Sources

There are many books on the global environmental problem. See, in particular, Norman J. Vig and Regina S. Axelrod (eds), *The Global Environment: Institutions, Law and Polity* (Washington: Congressional Quarterly, 1999); Oran R. Young (ed.), *The Effectiveness of International Environmental Regimes* (Boston: MIT Press, 1999); Mark Imber and John Vogler (eds), *The Environment and International Relations: Theories and Processes* (London: Routledge, 1995); Lorraine Elliott's *The Global Politics of the Environment* (London: Macmillan – now Palgrave Macmillan, 1998). Ian Rowlands faces the political problem directly in *The Politics of Global Atmospheric Change* (Manchester: Manchester University Press, 1995); Malcolm Water, *Globalization* (London: Routledge, 1995). Ismail Serageldin on water is cited in *The Guardian*, 8 August 1995. A brief article by Gwin Prins in *The World Today*, Vol. 56, No. 4 (2000), pp. 5–6, called 'Water, Water Everywhere' was disproportionately helpful for its size. Figures on historical population trends come from R. Thomlinson, *Population Dynamics: Causes and Consequences of Demographic Change* (New York: Random House, 1965). Figures were also taken from the *New Encyclopaedia Britannica* (1995).

12

Moral Issues in International Relations

Introduction: Moral Arguments

War provides us with a startling paradox. Murder is regarded in most societies as a particularly abhorrent crime which normally is punished very severely, often with death. However, the killing of opponents in warfare is widely regarded as noble. The warrior has been venerated in most societies, even relatively peaceful ones. But this seems to involve a contradiction. Both involve the deliberate killing of other people. The only difference is the scale, which might lead us to suppose that warfare would be even more deplored than murder and not the other way round.

This is perhaps the most vivid of the moral dilemmas we face in analyzing war but it is not the only one. In international relations we find some of the most pressing moral problems faced by human beings today. Some are extensions of problems we face in all political situations but some, notably the moral issues raised by war, are particularly conspicuous on the international scene. However, moral problems are rarely clear-cut. We are often faced with conundrums where there seem to be major objections to all courses of action.

We shall consider here two general areas where moral questions are raised. First are the dilemmas and paradoxes raised by the use of war and violence in international relations. Second are questions about our obligations, if any, to people in countries other than our own. In particular are those moral issues raised by the extent of poverty and the great disparity in income and wealth amongst the world's inhabitants. Also important are questions of human rights. This involves asking whether there is an international society in some relevant sense.

First, however, we need to look at the general issue of what constitutes a moral judgement. We make a moral judgement when we say something is good in the sense of virtuous, or bad in the sense of wicked. For example, today there is wide agreement that the institution of slavery is bad. This is a moral judgement that has not always been accepted. Only in the twentieth century has it been possible to assume general agreement with this particular moral position. The moral judgement is different from the purely factual statement that there were about four million slaves in the United States in 1864 when the American Civil War started. The criteria for establishing the number of slaves and for believing in one figure rather than another have nothing to do with moral judgements about whether slavery was right or wrong. The crucial point is that judgements of value cannot be decided by appealing to facts.

The problem is highlighted if we take an issue that is much more morally contentious today, such as biodiversity. There is little doubt that economic development reduces the number of living species. It is not just that an animal is killed or that some plants die; it is that the species as a whole becomes extinct. The threats to biodiversity involve all forms of living matter including plants, fish, mammals, insects and so on. The causes of these reductions in the number of species are numerous. Road-building cuts through the natural habitat of some plants and animals, which might mean the end of the species. Resting places for migratory birds may be built over, putting the bird population at risk. Dams, necessary for hydroelectricity, notoriously disrupt the living species resident in the locality. Herbicides kill off many species of plants and so on.

Though the facts are broadly agreed on, there are profound disagreements between people who accept facts regarding the reduction of biodiversity but have different moral views concerning the elimination of a species. Some people hold that the forced extinction of a species of life, no matter how humble, is morally very grave. Others hold that it is of little or no moral significance. In a conflict between economic growth and biodiversity, the latter will always choose economic growth. The former, at least on occasion, will give biodiversity priority. If the choice is between biodiversity and a luxury casino, many people will choose biodiversity. Others, who had a choice between biodiversity and fresh water for an impoverished community, would give priority to the fresh-water project. In the middle, people will differ. This sort of problem crops up frequently in questions of economic development. Like so many moral problems, there is no clear-cut answer. The crucial point is that even when there is agreement about the factual issues –

and this is rare enough – people often have moral disagreements about what to do.

Unfortunately with phenomena as complex as those dealt with in international relations it is often hard to say what the consequences of any action may be. In this respect, the biodiversity example was an unusual one because, though there are many uncertainties, they are less than in most other areas we cover.

Consider the sale of aircraft to an authoritarian regime. Foreign sales of high-tech equipment are always tempting. The major costs of producing a fighter aircraft are in the design and set-up costs. Once on the production line, the cost of producing more fighters is much smaller (though still high, by most criteria). The more that are built and sold, the more contributions go towards development costs. Thus there are clear benefits in selling as many as possible. Some of the facts are clear-cut. Employment in arms industries will be increased or maintained. Further, employment in related industries will also be maintained. The employment figures can be computed moderately accurately. Similarly the effects on such things as the balance of payments are reasonably well known. The problems get more complicated when we consider the use of the aircraft. Can they be used for internal repression? This should be possible to determine. If the aircraft are for use in defending the country from external threat, what will the consequences be? Will they stabilize the region or make war more likely? Will their acquisition stimulate an arms race in the region and what will be the consequences of that arms race? The sale of arms may give some extra legitimacy to the government and increase the likelihood of it staying in power. If there is a threat to its internal stability, who are the likely successors to the present government and how do we regard them morally? All these questions are factual questions, though ones to which the answers are rarely clear. We could argue about them and agree or disagree about them independently of our views about the desirability of making the arms sale. We could even admit we did not know the answer!

People hold different views about the morality of some course of action even when they agree on the factual side of things which, as we have shown, is often problematic in itself. One approach is to adopt a purely selfish view: what benefits our own state should take priority – the consequences for other states are none of our business. Only if the export of arms causes a war that will harm our own state's interests should we concern ourselves. We are indifferent to a war that does not harm us. Likewise we are indifferent to any internal consequences. It is none of our business whether a state that buys our weapons is authoritarian or not. Second, we might be concerned purely about peace. Hence we sell or not according to whether it is likely to improve the chances for peace but independently of the nature of the regime we sell to. Whether it is authoritarian or not is irrelevant. If we take this view, we still have to consider the costs to our own military industries. Do we just ignore these, and make a decision independently of the internal economic consequences for ourselves? It is unlikely that we will totally ignore such factors, at least if we are government ministers or, indeed, if we are voters in an area which is dependent on the military. In practice, there is likely to be some sort of trade-off. If there is a high chance of war, we will not sell the weapons; if there is only a slight chance, we will give our own industries the benefit of the doubt. While this sounds like a nice compromise, it hides as much as it reveals. People will give very different answers as to where they will trade off these competing principles. Third, we might be concerned about the internal nature of the regime and be unwilling to support repressive regimes. Again we face dilemmas. We may dislike the regime but consider that the likely successor would be worse. Thus regimes in the Gulf have been supported by the West, not for any love for the internal politics of the regimes, but out of fear that they might be replaced by fundamentalist Islamic regimes. We might, of course, even approve of authoritarian governments. They are seen by some, even from democratic countries, as providing a welcome degree of stability and order from more democratic but less predictable regimes. This is unlikely to be explicitly acknowledged in a democratic regime, but arms dealers are rarely political liberals. Thus, we sell the arms to that government, though we might not deal with similarly-placed liberal regimes. On the first two principles, by contrast, we would sell to any regime. These moral principles are by no means exclusive. There are many others we might adopt. However, all involve us in moral debate, whereas the first set of problems includes debates about the facts of the case. These are very different forms of argument but we must use both in discussions about selling arms. What is also clear is that moral debate typically requires trade-offs between different bads and different goods. How much domestic unemployment do we accept in order to increase the stability of some far-flung part of the world? What sacrifices do we make to weaken the power of the military in some other country? Moral problems rarely have clear-cut answers. There is, of course, the final dilemma. We might be willing to forgo some arms sales to some authoritarian regime for good moral reasons. However, if we do not sell the aircraft, someone else will. Hence, we lose the sales and world morality is no further forward. Do we then take a stand on principle, and is the world a better place because we have done so? There is no textbook answer to this dilemma.

This case is typical in its complexity and uncertainty of arguments about what we should do in international relations. Debates are sometimes about the facts of the case, sometimes about the appropriate theory to employ, and sometimes about the morality of the issue in question. It is easy to confuse the different sources of controversy. We must be particularly careful not to let our judgement of what *is* the case be warped by what we would *wish to be* the case, in order to make it easier to hold on to our values.

International Law

While it is a commonplace that law is not the same as morality, nevertheless, within a state, the law sets out a broad framework of what is regarded as acceptable. Admittedly, in our private lives we can do things which we might regard as immoral, such as being emotionally cruel which is perfectly legal, whereas, particularly in some societies, we might feel that many things which are illegal are not immoral, such as expressing disapproval of the government. However, on many issues, for example, murder, theft and so on, there is broad agreement that law and morality coincide. To have a reasonably well-functioning society we have a body of law that people obey and for which there are sanctions on those who disobey. The laws of a society are made by the government. Separate from the government is a system of courts which determines whether people who are accused of breaking the law are guilty or not and, if guilty, what the penalty should be. A lot of courts are involved in *civil cases*, which adjudicate about such things as debts, questions of ownership of property and so on. These are sometimes between corporations and involve vast sums of money. These are not criminal issues, but if someone refuses to obey a civil court then they are punished for *contempt of court*. Legal systems in different countries vary a lot but they broadly involve something like this set of institutions even if, as in Islamic states, the law is regarded as having been given by God and merely administered by the state.

Clearly it is tempting to wonder whether *international law* can be used in a way that parallels domestic law. This might operate as the basis for the practice of some morality, though it would leave many moral problems, including the more serious ones, unaddressed. However, it is equally clear that such international law is problematic. There is no international government either to devise the law in the first place or to be the final source of sanctions if the law is flouted. There is a body of international law but where does it come from and what is its status? Furthermore, to whom does it apply? In particular does it apply to states, individuals or what? Some hold that international law is a minor factor in the international scene as states will always ignore it if necessary. Others argue that it involves a genuine guide to conduct and its significance will grow as its practice increases.

First, we must recognize that for individuals international law is often the law of the place they happen to be in or the place in which their property is located. A British citizen working in Spain is subject to Spanish law including tax laws and so on as well as the criminal law. A child born of Swedish parents in the United States can claim citizenship according to the laws of both states. Laws of citizenship can get very complex if parents are of different nationality and live in a third country, but such problems are resolved. Any disputes are settled by the laws of the country most relevant, though again, this can sometimes be problematic. If an American aircraft is hijacked over Britain, many of the passengers are French and the nationality of the hijackers is unknown, there are many countries in which a trial might reasonably take place. When two Libyan intelligence officers were accused of arranging the sabotage and destruction of an American civil aircraft on 21 December 1989, the legal arrangements were tortuous in the extreme. The aircraft blew up over Lockerbie in Scotland. A number of Scottish people were killed on the ground and, of course, there were victims of many nationalities in the aircraft itself. The Libyan government ultimately released the accused for trial, but with the insistence that it should not be in a place where the guilt of the accused was assumed. Thus, the trial in the end took place in the Netherlands, which is home to the International Court of Justice and had no direct interest in the case, so was deemed to be reasonably neutral. However, it took place under Scottish law and with Scottish lawyers as the event had taken place over Scotland, even though this might be regarded as incidental to the main purpose of the sabotage (Scottish law, it should be stressed, is not the same as English law).

Tax laws become more and more complicated if, as we discussed in Chapter 8, economic activity is spread over many states and the location of money is very problematic. As we discussed earlier, some micro-states make a good living by offering their lightly-taxed banking system as *tax havens* for corporations and individuals wanting to avoid taxation. Nevertheless, there are many issues of the legal arrangements between individuals, and to a less extent corporations, which can be satisfactorily dealt with by normal domestic law even though there is a strong international dimension. This is not true of states themselves in their relations with each other. Most of what is called international law concerns these interstate relationships or the rights of individuals whose nationality is particularly relevant, such as the rights and obligations of diplomats. In fact, there is quite a lot of agreement about what international law is. Treaties between states are at the core of it and if a treaty is properly agreed upon then its violation is regarded as a violation of international law. The other sources of international law are somewhat more vague and rely on, for instance, the writings of 'eminent jurists' which is clearly something open to wide interpretation. Enforcing international law is a problem when there are alleged to be violations. In the case of metropolitan law, a court determines whether there has been a violation of the law and determines the penalties when there has been one. Courts have the ultimate backing of the power of the state in the form of police, prisons and so on. There is no real analogy in the case of international law. There is a *World Court*, also known as the International Court of Justice or ICJ. In principle it has the same role in international law as courts do in domestic cases though without any sanctions. In practice, the World Court can be effective when two countries both want an agreement but disagree over the nature of the agreement, such as over a boundary dispute. They can bind themselves to follow the court's ruling. The court is then acting as an arbitrator. However, parties on the losing side have a bad habit of ignoring rulings that they disagree with, as the United States did in 1986 regarding the mining of Nicaraguan harbours (one of the few times readers of newspapers would have come across any account of the activities of the World Court). The Court ruled against the United States and the USA simply withdrew from that part of the relevant treaty and ignored the ruling. This was what a realist would predict. However, it could be argued that this was against the long-term self-interest of the United States. In general, most countries, and certainly individual people, would be better off if international law were obeyed. In the current state of the world it is obeyed only if other states are willing to enforce it. This they are likely to do only when it is in their self-interest to do so, as when Iraq, led by Saddam Hussein, invaded Kuwait in 1990 and the Gulf War resulted. Otherwise, violations of international law go unpunished. However, states in general might violate international law less frequently if there were a tradition of obeying international law, even when it was in the short-term self-interest of a state to disobey. That is, a *norm* of obeying international law could grow and be of general benefit. However, norms grow only by their practice and are particularly helped when a state clearly does act against its short-term self-interest to support a norm. This is not to suppose that norms will become universal over all aspects of interstate relations. It seems unlikely that any system of norms would have stopped Saddam Hussein from invading Kuwait. However, the violation of a widely-respected norm meant that many countries were willing to join in the opposition to this invasion when it was not in their short-term interests to do so.

International law raises some awkward problems for realists. They agree that the law must recognize that states are the dominant actors and thus interstate law at least tackles the right actors. However, they argue that states will act in self-interest and if this requires breaking a law then they will do so. Law, for a hard-nosed realist who nevertheless sees states as sophisticated actors, is to act as a guide to determining norms for long-term enlightened self-interest rather than moral norms, as the more optimistic observers of the international scene hope. Nevertheless, the sophisticated realist (and the rest of us for that matter) can take solace in the fact that some of international law is observed. It is very rare for laws about diplomats to be broken. In 1980, when American diplomats were kidnapped by Iranian 'students', there was outrage far beyond the United States. Because of the obvious mutual interest in obeying rules about diplomats, the success of international law in this sphere is not too surprising.

It is perhaps more surprising that there has been comparatively little dispute over the ownership of oil deposits under the ocean. This is particularly unexpected as everything seems to be against this. First, oil is very important and all states want to get their hands on it. Second, there have been many disagreements in the past as to how much of the ocean bed a country could claim as its own and, thus, how far from its shores it could claim as being under its jurisdiction. This would seem to be a recipe for conflict, possibly armed conflict, but it has not resulted as such in practice. Perhaps, on the issue of law, the cautious optimists have something to be positive about.

Broadly, international law deals with relations between states, leaving international relations between individuals or other bodies to the various relevant bits of domestic law. There is a significant exception in the *European Court of Justice*. Citizens of member states can take their own governments to court if they think that European law has been broken. Furthermore, people have done so and have won. More significantly, the governments in question accept this and obey the ruling of the Court, as they do if the Court rules against them on any other aspect of European law. Thus, the member states of the EU accept that European law overrides domestic law in some areas. Many governments have not acceded to all the provisions or *articles* of European law but all accept it in general. This is very significant. It is equally significant that this has widespread public support. Indeed, it is not an issue of much public controversy. We can interpret it as saying that the European Union is already some sort of superstate on the grounds that 'real states' would not accept that any law could be above their own. Alternatively it could be interpreted as the beginnings of a genuinely enforceable international law which might be extended to the world as a whole and radically alter the nature of the relationships between states.

Morality and War

The paradox with which this chapter opened has troubled people through the ages. How can one justify war but not murder? Further, suppose we can justify war in some circumstances, what are those circumstances? Which wars are justifiable and which are not?

There are some who argue there is no paradox. They argue that killing is never justified. This includes killing in war just as much as killing on an individual basis. War is murder on a large scale. This view is known as *pacifism*. It is usually held by people as part of a set of religious beliefs, conspicuous among them being members of the Society of Friends who are also known as Quakers. It is not a widely-held view, though those who hold it tend to be conspicuous for their concern with the humanitarian aspects of relief from suffering in war. There are problems associated with this view. Consider the *pacifist's dilemma*. The extreme version of this is the situation that a person is about to kill someone else, say a child, and one could stop this by killing that person. Is it moral to refrain from killing even though by doing so one would save a life? One could extend this by considering the case of someone about to blow up a whole school full of children where the only practicable way of stopping the atrocity would be to kill the would-be perpetrator. A few may still refuse to kill though most people would accept that there are some extreme cases where killing is legitimate. However, if direct killing ever becomes allowable, one has to say where the borderline comes. Most pacifists would argue that it comes at the level of the state in that, even when there is more justice on the side of one state than another, there is rarely, if ever, a simple case of good versus evil. Thus, one should never kill in the service of the state.

One can endeavour to resolve the murder/war paradox by altering the premises. I initially assumed that all killing on an individual basis was wrong. However, while murder is widely condemned, killing in self-defence is not. In many legal systems it is a complete defence and it is widely taken to be an extenuating circumstance, which justifies a mild penalty. Suppose, then, it is justifiable to kill another person in self-defence. It is a modest extension to argue that it is also justifiable to kill in the defence of someone else, a view which would be highly praised if the victim was unable to defend him or herself, such as a child. We can move on and say that, if we are genuinely acting in the defence of a group, then we are entitled to kill. This group can be extended to include the whole society of which we are a member. In this way we can resolve the paradox of killing. We are still treading a delicate path. What does 'self-defence' mean when it comes to a society? For the individual it is normally taken to mean defence against being killed. But defeat in war does not usually mean that all the members of the defeated group would be killed. One has to resort to further arguments such as the destruction of the culture of the society, the integrity of the state or whatever. Clearly the extension of the argument from the legitimacy of individual self-defence to the legitimacy of group defence needs to be handled with care. Nevertheless, there is a path that can be followed.

This justifies wars of self-defence but not expansionary wars, whether these are aimed at gaining some advantage over another state which remains independent or are frankly imperialist, aiming to conquer and to rule. Expansionary wars are harder to justify. Nevertheless, until the last few decades, it was widely thought that such wars needed no justification further than to say that they were in the service of the state. Imperialism was justified in that it seemed self-evident that the spread of Western civilization was a good thing, which was worth a certain amount of suffering. In this more morally cautious age, we are less sure of this.

Another and common approach is associated with realism and is more robust. It is argued that the morality of the group is different from the morality of the individual. The world of states (which is what most of this argument is about) is so different from the world of individuals that it is naive to assume that the state can operate according to the same moral principles. States must exist in a world that is always potentially hostile. The governments, who act on behalf of the states, must have regard for the defence of the continued existence of the state and not just the individuals who live within it. It follows that governments must, if necessary, subordinate other moral principles, such as a reluctance to kill or tell lies, to the general principle that the state must survive. Clearly the argument can be extended, perhaps more convincingly on occasion, to cover wars in defence of a nation (as opposed to a state) or in defence of a religion.

The robust argument can be strengthened in another way. Suppose we take the moral view that killing a human being is in itself wrong but that this must be balanced against other things that might be wrong. Thus, even if, by resisting an invasion, more people are killed than would be the case by allowing the invaders in, there are other goals, such as national independence, which are also of value. The preservation of human life might be a highly-valued goal, but it is not an absolute that never can be traded off against other goals. On this view, then, we could justify warfare in some circumstances such as national self-defence. It would be harder to justify an aggressive war.

This principle also can be used to justify permitting the use of potentially lethal violence at the individual level within societies. However, we can avoid this unwelcome consequence by arguing that societies will be very insecure internally if lethal violence is allowed. The state, in most societies, provides adequate defence for the individual against the violence of others and some, at least, provide for alleviation of injustice. Thus, even if there may be occasional benefits by allowing individual violence, the overall consequences would be very harmful. Most domestic societies are orderly compared with the international system.

By these means, one can justify war while retaining a prohibition on murder, but one has to be very careful about the arguments. The pacifist argument is quite coherent and should be treated with respect. Some people argue that, while warfare can be justified in certain extreme cases, violence is used by states or other political bodies far too readily. Self-defence might be a legitimate reason for fighting. It is much harder to justify the initiation of violence. Even allowing for some ambiguous cases where both sides might have thought they were the victims (the Middle East provides a number of cases of this), this is not normal. People who argue that war is occasionally justified but only very rarely, and far less frequently than wars are fought, are sometimes known as *pacificists* (as opposed to pacifists who object to all war), a term thought to have been introduced by A.J.P. Taylor.

Concern about the moral problems raised by war has a long history. In particular the Catholic Church has had thinkers who have pondered the issue of when war is justified (though very few were pacifists). The so-called 'Just War' tradition has evolved, stemming from the writings of St Augustine. However, it is of interest far beyond the Catholic Church and concerned moralists of war, both secular and of any religious tradition.

Though there are variants, broadly the Just War tradition makes a distinction between two issues. First there are moral issues related to justifying the need for war in the first place. This is referred to by the Latin phrase *jus ad bellum* (the right of going to war). Secondly are the moral aspects of warfare itself known as *jus in bello* (rights in war). In other words, given one is fighting a war, what are the moral constraints on indiscriminate violence? Such a distinction is generally accepted. Further related items would attract general acceptance at least as ideals. A 'standard' *jus in bello* list contains:

1. Prisoners should be properly treated, fed, given medical attention when necessary and properly housed.
2. Non-combatants should not be attacked or killed. When it is inevitable that some civilians will be killed if a military target is attacked, such civilian casualties should be kept to a minimum. (This principle has been violated often both in modern and earlier warfare.)
3. A war should be terminated as soon as feasible. Extreme conditions, such as unconditional surrender, which would prolong a war should not be demanded of an enemy.

The principles of *jus in bello* are more or less incorporated in the *Geneva Convention*, which was signed in 1864 by the major powers of the day, to regulate the conduct of war. In practice, the rights of non-combatants have been systematically violated in most warfare. Possibly the other principles have restrained behaviour, for example over such matters as the treatment of prisoners of war.

As far as *jus ad bellum* is concerned the principles are:

1. The war must be for a just cause (clearly a flexible and emotive term).
2. A related principle is that the comparative justice of the aims of the combatants should be considered. War is rarely an issue of absolute right against wrong. All parties usually have some sort of case. This needs to be recognized.
3. There should be a reasonable chance of winning – glory in war as such should not be valued. War must be purely instrumental to achieve a just outcome.
4. War must be a proportional response to the offence committed by the opponent. Thus the execution, however unjust, of a citizen of one country by the authorities of another state would justify a response, but not a war.
5. A war should be declared by a competent authority. A competent authority is that which is responsible for the governing of the society which is about to be plunged into war. This principle was relatively straightforward in medieval times and indeed in many other times. Who were the legitimate rulers of states was a clear-cut issue. Today this is less clear-cut. Our concepts of legitimate government are much more complex. If we extend the concepts to include 'just revolutions', then it is unclear who has the right to initiate violence. The principle of competent authority derives from a more hierarchical and authoritarian age. The individuals participating in war (or declining to do so) must judge for themselves.
6. War should be used only as a last resort when all other options have been exhausted.

These are rather general principles but they do at least serve the purpose of ordering our thoughts about warfare. Clearly they are principles of defensive war not offensive war. They do not prohibit a state from initiating a war if the reason is very good, but nevertheless the other side must have done something very wrong for it to be legitimate. Even allowing for the very general nature of the terms involved and the large element of subjective judgement, most wars can have a maximum of one combatant who can be regarded as just. The whole tradition incorporates the assumption of being a victim in the situation. If the principles of the just war had been widely held, or were, indeed, widely held today, there would have been very few wars.

Terrorists and Freedom Fighters

The Just War tradition has usually been interpreted as applying to interstate warfare. However, there is nothing in the arguments themselves that restricts it to states. Nor is there any reason to restrict it to warfare as conventionally understood. We could get a closely analogous set of principles that would apply to revolutions. More contentiously we could get a similar set of rules applying to terrorism.

Terrorism is a widespread feature of the modern world. The word 'terrorist' immediately conjures up hostile images for many people. However, as is commonly remarked, the distinction between a terrorist and a freedom fighter depends on which side has our sympathies. In practice, we are often ambivalent about terrorism, condemning it vigorously in our opponents and applauding it in our allies. During the Second World War, there was a great deal of support amongst the Allies for resistance movements in countries occupied by the Germans. For a long time after the war, and still for the generation that remembers that period, resistance fighters were regarded as great heroes. However, they used methods which would be classified as terrorism if used in less sympathetic contexts. Similarly in Palestine in the period before the foundation of the state of Israel, the Zionist 'Irgun' organization, carried out acts of terrorism against the British who were governing the territory temporarily on behalf of the United Nations, under what was known as the *mandate* system. There are many who are understanding about Zionist activitiy in that period but hold very stern attitudes to subsequent Palestinian Arab terrorism. Terrorism is an issue that requires us to think very clearly about the problems involved.

As with a definition of war, we need to define terrorism (or freedom fighting) in terms of what goes on rather than the motives for undertaking it. Without going into fine detail, a terrorist conflict can be defined as an armed conflict in which one set of active participants are not members of an army in the standard sense. The direct military power of the terrorists is small in comparison with the powers of their opponents. They cannot engage the opposing army or police authorities in direct combat. Instead, terrorists seek out 'soft' targets and attack them, often with the primary aim of destroying property. They might also assassinate, by bombing or shooting, people perceived to be part of the governing structure, such as soldiers, police or members of the judiciary, or prominent people within some opposing group. In some cases they may be careful about whether they also kill people who are unconnected with the struggle. In other cases they may be less so. In more extreme cases they might kill people deliberately even if they are not relevant targets with the explicit aim of inculcating fear in a particular population. Thus, Islamicists in Egypt have attacked tourists avowedly in order to discourage tourism which is a major source of income for Egypt. The death toll is often small compared to conventional warfare but the publicity is frequently vivid, as the killing and damage normally take place in an otherwise peaceful situation. This is what causes the terror that gives terrorists their name. It is also what makes them appear particularly horrific to many people.

Are these activities unambiguously wrong no matter how justified the cause, as many argue, or are they indeed simply another way of carrying out warfare which can be justified or not by similar arguments to those used in the Just War tradition? Some might argue that it is justified to kill soldiers or policemen but that care should be taken with bystanders. Unrestricted terrorism would be as unjustified as unrestricted warfare for similar reasons, but terrorism that avoided killing those who were unconnected with the conflict could also be justified for similar reasons.

Again we are faced with sets of moral dilemmas and arguments which need to be thought through carefully.

Nuclear War

The Just War tradition has its origins in Medieval Europe. Not all the conditions of the time apply to the present and, indeed, it is perhaps surprising that it is as applicable as it is. For example, what is a civilian in a modern 'total' war such as the Second World War? Workers in munitions factories were as central to the war effort as combat soldiers.

Conversely, the military personnel were often conscripts and many were reluctant warriors at best. Often the issues are unclear though it is doubtful if they were ever as clear as they appear superficially.

The invention of weapons of mass destruction, particularly nuclear weapons, has created something historically novel which adds a new dimension to the moral problems of war. It is now possible from a technical point of view to eliminate other societies and eliminate life on this planet. In such circumstance can there ever be a Just War? There is no way in which a full-scale nuclear war can avoid killing very many citizens and it would be foolish to pretend to distinguish between combatants and civilians. Many people would regard the actual fighting of a nuclear war as morally wrong. However, the whole institution of nuclear deterrence presupposes the possibility of fighting a nuclear war, albeit a remote possibility. Does this then make nuclear deterrence morally wrong? We now pose the *dilemma of deterrence*. Normally when we use a threat as a deterrent we anticipate that from time to time we will have to use it. If we try to deter burglary with the threat of imprisonment, we suppose that some people will actually commit burglary and some of them will end up in prison. To imprison someone is disagreeable but not inherently immoral and most people feel entitled to apply it on occasion. However, can we say the same about a penalty that is inherently immoral such as the elimination of a whole society? Surely the threat of an immoral penalty is itself immoral. Does this apply to nuclear deterrence? The standard argument for nuclear deterrence is that, though it is threatened, the likelihood of carrying out the threat is so remote that we need not worry about the morality of the act as such. The making of the threat, and the making of it sufficiently firmly, precludes the possibility of having to use it. Thus, in this rather special case, it is moral to make the threat of immoral action, at least if the benefits of doing so, such as the preservation of peace, are moral goals. This is a defensible argument but not one that everyone would accept. The problem needs to be clearly thought through by people on either side of the argument about nuclear weapons

International Societies

We often speak of a 'society' such as 'British society', 'Australian society', 'Dutch society' and so on. At times, we extend this to 'international society' or 'global society'. How legitimate is this extension?

First we have to define society. A simple view, which catches the essence of the concept, is that we feel ourselves to be members of a society when we feel a sense of obligation towards other members of that society. Conversely, we feel that we have rights in the sense that other people have obligations towards us. We recognize other members as people who have some basic similarity to ourselves. We might also feel that our interests are intertwined with other people in the society so, at least for some purposes, our interests are shared. Thus, while we often pursue our own goals and interests, we recognize some degree of restraint in this and acknowledge some obligation to protect the interests of others. Thus, we are involved in a moral debate. We may feel the need to provide education, medical care, protection against the extremes of poverty and so on. When such feelings are broadly shared, we say we have a society. In the case of a family we have a mini-society which works only if there is some sense of reciprocal obligation. Beyond this, we have a weaker sense of obligation. Indeed, notoriously, Margaret Thatcher when Prime Minister said, 'there is no such thing as society', but this is generally regarded as an extreme view.

There are broadly three views concerning international society. First, it is a direct extension of the concept of society to the world as a whole. We see the basic units making up the world as being individual people. We acknowledge individuals, and not groups, to be members of the same society towards whom we have obligations and from whom we have rights. Practically, those closer to home have closer ties and the sense of society might therefore be stronger. Nevertheless, all people are to some degree members of the society. This is often referred to as the *world society* view, or sometimes the *cosmopolitan* view of the world.

Second there is the view that international society consists of a *society of states*. In this view, states are analogous to individual people in that they can form a society in which each recognizes other actors as having rights and obligations, and, in some sense, having equal rights in the system such as those of sovereignty, irrespective of their size or power. This makes states the primary agents, not individuals. These two views have profoundly different implications as far as issues such as human rights are concerned.

The final view is the extreme realist view that there is no society beyond state borders, either of individuals or states. States interact with states purely on the basis of self-interest. If they respect sovereignty, it is because they see it as being in their long-term self-interest to do so. Similarly, there is no sense of obligation by governments, or members of a state, to individuals outside state boundaries. They may give economic aid to stave off a revolution that would harm their self-interest but they would not give economic aid out of any sense of moral obligation. The implications of this view for human rights, or any other principle deriving from a cosmopolitan view, are obvious. This moral view is associated with the realist approach to the international system, though it is not logically implied by realism nor is it accepted by all realists. Realism is a view of how the international system works and, as such, is a theoretical proposition about the nature of the world. It is quite consistent to accept that realism is how things are in fact while deploring it and wishing it were otherwise. Thus, one can be a realist while holding to cosmopolitan moral principles which, one believes sadly, have very limited applicability. The more hardline view is that realism does not merely explain how the world works in fact, but also how it ought to work. I call this point of view *ideological realism*.

If states are the primary agents in the international system, not just from a practical point of view but from a moral point of view, then the preservation of states and the state system becomes the central issue. It follows that sovereignty is the major value in this system. A state is sovereign inasmuch as it can control what goes on within its borders without interference from outside. The view of the ideological realists is that this ought to be the case. Neither other states nor any other actors should intervene in what goes on inside a state. Two things follow. First, attacks on states by other states, are a very serious issue. Members of a state system respond with vigour to aggression, at least if it appears that it will disrupt the state system in any serious way. This is explicit in the Charter of the United Nations and was with its predecessor, the League of Nations. To a lesser extent, it is clear in the activities of states since the Second World War. States will often intervene in conflicts involving aggression even if they tend to do it on a rather selective basis. Second, respect for human rights as a cosmopolitan principle does not apply outside the boundaries of one's own state. If the members of one state are the victims of an oppressive regime, this is no business of anyone other than the subjects or citizens of that state. Other states should be hostile or friendly to that state purely because of its role in the international system, and not because of their feelings about its internal policy.

The idea that sovereignty is the most important principle of international law, and thus that states are its most important subjects, is increasingly a matter of debate. The evolution of a universal concept of human rights and the naming of genocide as a 'crime against humanity' have created a moral framework that potentially conflicts with sovereignty. If human beings are understood to have rights by virtue of their humanity, and not purely as a consequence of citizenship within a state, then international society is forced to grapple with the question of when the principle of sovereignty can be legitimately overridden in the name of protecting human rights. While states have traditionally intervened in other states on behalf of their national interest, there has been an increasingly tendency since the end of the Cold War to advocate intervention for purely humanitarian reasons and particularly to stop genocide. The conflict between sovereignty and humanitarian intervention was most starkly posed by NATO's 1999 bombing campaign against Serbia. Unlike other cases of humanitarian intervention, such as Somalia, where the state had collapsed into anarchy, NATO's act represented intervention in the affairs of a sovereign state. NATO was thus accused of violating international law, which was reinforced by the absence of approval from the Security Council. NATO, and others in international society, accused the Serbs of violating international human-rights law and committing crimes against humanity in the name of ethnic cleansing of Kosovo Albanians.

The Serb violation of international law has taken precedence, given that the Serb leader, Slobodan Milosevic, has been brought before the International War Crimes Tribunal in the Hague with indictments for crimes against humanity in Croatia, Bosnia and Kosovo. This tribunal, and the one for Rwanda, are the first since the Nuremburg Trials following the Second World War. There are, nonetheless, efforts to establish a more permanent International Criminal Court. The Court will come into existence once 60 countries have ratified the Rome Statute, which to date has been ratified by 47. The USA, while a signatory to the Statute, has been strongly opposed to the creation of a permanent court, for fears that it would erode its sovereignty. Both the concept of humanitarian intervention and an international criminal court erode the idea that states are the subjects of international law and free to act with impunity against their own subjects. Human rights are now at the centre of international deliberation.

Human Rights

Individual Human Rights

Human rights are the rights individuals have because they are human. All human beings have them. However, this is not a scientific proposition such as all human beings have lungs; it is a moral proposition which some might deny. What is more important from a practical point of view is that people might disagree as to the nature of these human rights. Historically these concepts are modern. One hundred years ago, only a minority accepted the idea that people of all races and both sexes had equal rights.

Generally, however, people would accept that people have a right to security and some basic level of economic well-being. There is also a general presumption that they have a right to liberty, though many would argue that this comes after the other two because liberty is meaningless without some basic economic well-being. Liberty involves freedom of speech and thus the right to express one's opinions even if they offend people and, in particular, the government and the powerful. It also means freedom from arbitrary arrest and the right to a fair trial. It would usually include the right to participate in the choice of a government. However, there are some liberties which many would argue come at a very early stage in the definition of human rights such as freedom from discrimination because of race or sex. Cosmopolitans believe that these rights should be extended to all people in the world irrespective of the states they live in. However, this implies that states are not the primary guardians of people's welfare, as the ideological realists believe. It would imply that we are entitled to intervene in the activities of other states in order to promote human rights. Thus, in the days of apartheid in South Africa there was a widespread feeling that this was not merely morally wrong but something that the international community could and should do something about.

Collective Rights

The cosmopolitan view involves a classical liberal view of human rights as individual rights. What about the rights of groups such as nations or religions? A widely-accepted principle is that of national self-determination. At the end of the First World War in 1918, many believed that the absence of self-determination was not only wrong in itself, but also caused the anger and frustration which provoked war. President Wilson of the United States was a strong adherent of this view. National self-determination is often presented in broad-brush terms. However morally desirable it is, we pointed out its practical weaknesses in Chapter 2. Almost universally we find that when there is a nation that seeks self-determination, there is a minority nation within it that also wants self-determination. This can work down to the village level. In Cyprus many villages were split between Turkish Moslems and Greek Orthodox Christians. The same was true in what was once Yugoslavia. The right of self-determination is fraught with difficulties however appealing it may seem initially. It certainly has to be linked with further rules about the protection of minorities, which is another important aspect of human rights.

This is generally true of group rights or community rights. Once we endow communities with the capacity for rights we are in danger of conflict between those rights and the rights of other communities. We are also in danger of trading off individual rights for group rights.

The Cynical View of Rights

We frequently hear talk of rights and morality. Political discourse is full of it. But many argue that this is just a cover for the interests of governments or individuals. During the Cold War era, and particularly during the Presidency of Ronald Reagan (1978–86), there was a great deal of rhetorical opposition to human-rights abuses in the Soviet Union. However, the widespread abuse of human rights in Latin America, perpetrated by regimes that the then government of the United States found more congenial, were ignored. On the political left it was considered chic to attack human-rights abuses in Israel while ignoring those of the Arab states. Consistency on moral matters is as rare as it is desirable. If we turn to states' action we get the same. While aggression is generally deplored (ideological realists and cosmopolitans broadly agree on this, though for different reasons), it is normally excused or ignored unless some interests are at stake. Aggression towards a state that is rich in oil, such as Kuwait, provoked a great outburst of moral piety when it was invaded in 1990. For a state rich only in tomatoes, we could expect such piety to be muted.

This should not come as a surprise and the ideological realist would take pride in it. How do we react if we still have some faith in morality and believe it to be a relevant concept in international relations for its own sake, and not as an excuse for doing what we want? Suppose we take human rights seriously. If a government attacks the human rights abuse of one state, but ignores those of another, should we encourage it in its attack or criticize its inconsistency? The inconsistency is not accidental, for the real motive for attacking the offending state is something different and associated with the realist view of state behaviour or *realpolitik*. We can argue that, though the government is being inconsistent and doing what it does for other and perhaps discreditable motives, some good is being done. We cannot hope to do anything about all human-rights abuses in the short run, as the scale of the problem is so large. If something is being done about one manifestation of some problem, this is a net increase in the welfare of the human race even if it falls short of an ideal. Is this different from giving to one famine relief programme because we happened to know about it, but not to another, even though, from the point of view of relieving hunger and distress, they offer the same? What is our attitude to a government that helps with famine relief in one country it wants to keep as an ally, while neglecting famine in another which is less strategically significant?

There are two moral issues involved. First, if we cannot help all the victims of some form of adversity, this does not mean we should not help some. If we cannot help everyone, there need to be principles by which we choose whom to help. Second, do we help an actor such as a government in some enterprise that we think is good (such as famine relief) even though we know or suspect that government of having ulterior motives? This raises an issue that underlies a lot of argument. Do moral judgements of actions depend on the motives of the actor or on the consequences of the act?

Poverty and Wealth

The spread of incomes between rich and poor in the world as a whole is much greater than within any of the industrialized countries such as the USA or Britain. I discussed the disparities of wealth in Chapter 1 (pp. 5–8). The numbers in extreme poverty throughout the world are enormous. 500 million people in the world suffer chronic malnutrition. This is nearly ten times the whole population of Britain and about a twelfth of the world's population. 1.3 billion people live in poverty.

Many people argue that this degree of poverty is a moral affront and that rich countries should help the poor. This can come through government aid or through private organizations such as Oxfam. The help can take the form of enabling their economies to develop and become richer, and of giving direct help in the case of particular catastrophes such as floods and famines. While there is widespread agreement that some help to poorer countries is necessary, it is not universal. The question of economic rights is contentious, even within a domestic society. Some, generally on the political left, hold that there are rights to a reasonable level of economic welfare and that the rich have obligations towards the poor. How broad the degree of equality or inequality of incomes should be, even within a state, is the subject of much political debate. Given the more general disagreement about economic rights, it is correspondingly harder to relate this to the world as a whole. However, if we accept that we have obligations to the poor in our own domestic society, then, from the cosmopolitan perspective which believes in a world society, we have obligations to the poor in the world as a whole. But how far do these obligations extend? Do we give priority to the poor in our own country or do we take a totally cosmopolitan position of treating the world as a single society?

The problem is compounded because of the difficulties in finding the most effective form of aid and the most useful tactics for enabling economies to grow. Many of the poorer economies remain plagued by low productivity after decades of trying to stimulate economic growth. Apart from catastrophe relief, there is often doubt as to the most effective way of giving aid. Often it appears to go to élites leaving the poor just as poor as ever they were. The moral issue of the obligation to give aid is augmented by the obligation to look for the most effective ways of giving aid.

Further Reading and Sources

There is a widespread view that ethical issues in international relations have been neglected until recently but in fact there has been quite a lot of material on the ethics of war, and particularly nuclear deterrence throughout the period of the Cold War. This emphasis on possible nuclear war is hardly surprising nor, indeed, is it reprehensible. However, there has been a more general consideration of moral issues in this period. Michael Waltzer, *Just and Unjust Wars* (New York:

Basic Books, 1977) is a classic and one of my shortlist of books to read for fun. Also on the ethics of war is Michael Dockrill and Barry Paskins, *The Ethics of War* (London: Duckworth, 1979), a useful, interesting and unjustly neglected piece of work.

An excellent analysis of recent thought in normative theory is by Chris Brown, *International Relations Theory: New Normative Approaches* (New York: Columbia University Press, 1993). Another recent book is edited by Terry Nardin and David Mapel (eds), *Traditions of International Ethics* (Cambridge: Cambridge University Press, 1993). Charles Beitz, *Political Theory and International Relations* (Princeton: Princeton University Press, 1979), was an earlier and influential contribution in this same general tradition. Hedley Bull, *The Anarchical Society* (Basingstoke: Palgrave – now Palgrave Macmillan, 2002, 3rd edn), is a leading advocate of an international society of states working out of an older but still flourishing tradition known as the 'English School'.

On the question of humanitarian intervention, see Adam Roberts, *Humanitarian Action in War* (Adelphi Papers, 305) (Oxford: Oxford University Press, 1997); Stanley Hoffman *et al.*, *The Ethics and Politics of Humanitarian Intervention* (Notre Dame: University of Notre Dame Press, 1996); Neeta C. Crawford, *Argument and Change in World Politics: Ethics, Decolonisation and Humanitarian Intervention* (Cambridge: Cambridge University Press, 2002); and Nicholas Wheeler, *Saving Strangers: Humanitarian Intervention in International Society* (Oxford: Oxford University Press, 2000).

On human rights, a central work is R.J. Vincent, *Human Rights and International Relations* (Cambridge: Cambridge University Press, 1987), though also see the earlier work by Richard Falk, *Human Rights and State Sovereignty* (New York and London: Holmes & Meier, 1981). For more recent work by Falk on this topic, see *Human Rights Horizons: The Pursuit of Justice in a Globalizing World* (New York: Routledge, 2001). See also David P. Forsythe, *Human Rights in International Relations* (Cambridge: Cambridge University Press, 2000) and Tim Dunne and Nicholas Wheeler, *Human Rights in Global Politics* (Cambridge: Cambridge University Press, 1999).

Conclusion

International relations is a dramatically changing discipline and will continue to change, probably rapidly. There are three basic reasons for this. First, the world we live in is changing, perhaps fundamentally. Second, a number of issues, such as gender, which were neglected earlier are now widely recognized as important. Third, we know a little more about international behaviour than we used to and we have the methods of discovering more. The first two points are not contentious. The last is more so.

Let us consider the issues in turn. First, it is hard to deny that the world is altering. The Cold War between the Soviet Union and the United States has ended and at least for the moment the nuclear threat seems to have diminished. The world is still not peaceful though the pattern of violence seems to be changing. Ideologies, which at one time seemed to the optimistic liberal to be dying such as nationalism and fundamentalist religion of all sorts, are now vibrant. Many people nowadays hold views that their grandparents thought had passed into the dustbin of history. Other ideologies, which once were vibrant, like communism, now seem to be obsolete, at least in the ways in which they were recently expressed. The process of globalization is making the world a different place. It may be reducing the powers of governments and the role of the state both internally and externally, particularly over economic matters. Whether this is good or bad is open to argument. Indeed the significance of globalization itself is open to dispute. To what extent is it inevitable and to what extent is it something we have chosen? How one evaluates these changes is one of the many disputed areas of international relations, but no one disputes that there are changes.

Second, the range of topics considered as international relations has broadened, in part because of a broader view of what is important and in part because our explanations under the narrower view proved

229

inadequate. Thus, gender issues were there twenty years ago but they went more or less unnoticed even by the feminists of the day. Similarly, international political economy is now widely regarded as an important aspect of international relations. Partly this reflects a change in people's concerns. An increased consciousness of gender issues has pervaded almost every aspect of life over recent decades. It is partly also because there were too many things that were poorly explained purely in terms of the former categories. Many interactions around the world, such as those involved in development, cannot be seen purely as problems in either international relations or economics.

To some extent, then, this is a theoretical change which merges into my third point. The discipline has developed – I use the word 'developed' and not just 'changed' because I see this as an advance. The broadening of theoretical perspectives away from unqualified realism I also see as an advance.

There are other things we know more about now than thirty years ago, even if we know less than we might wish. We know more about international crises, about some of the factors that are linked to the causes of war, and in particular about interstate war. The relationship between democracy and peace is still contested but is unlikely to be totally accidental. We know more about the causes and nature of famines and many other things that are relevant to the discipline. The broadening of the intellectual horizons resulting in the growth of new theoretical positions is partly because of the factual inadequacies of the older views. Thus, there has been progress in our understanding; it is progress which we can suppose will continue as we probe further into the complexities of the international system to find further consistencies, while being sensitive to the idea that these consistencies might change. A theme of this book is that the international system is not just a collection of random occurrences. There are some systematic patterns of behaviour. Further, we can discover them. Though patterns may alter over time we can follow them. Thus, such changes as the process of globalization alter things in ways we can analyze and discover. What matters is the capability of checking a theory of international relations against reality, or what I would refer to as 'the facts', however much this will irritate various philosophers. A successful theory will correspond with the facts. Inasmuch as we are trying to explain what is the case and not what ought to be the case, international relations is an empirical discipline.

Though we might feel that we know more, and are aware of more, than we did thirty years ago, there is no reason to suppose we have reached a state of wisdom where all important and relevant topics have been recognized. In thirty years time our successors will look with amazement and, no doubt, mockery that we managed to ignore some features of the international scene that seem self-evident to them. We are unlikely to be the first generation not to be guilty of what later appears to be foolish oversight.

As we noted in Chapter 7, the postmodernists have pointed out, correctly, that things appear very differently according to the perspective of the observer. An elderly ex-soldier might romanticize about war in a way that a destitute war widow might not. A war of liberation for some might be a war of subjection for others. To yet others it may seem to be a destroyer of their family and livelihood. This is true, but it does not follow, as some postmodernists seem to think, that there is not some basis of objectivity which lies behind it all. There really was a war in the Gulf in 1991 and many people were killed. That people look at it in a variety of different ways and with a variety of interpretations does not alter a certain underlying reality about which most people can agree. Second, while there are different perceptions of 'reality', it is too pessimistic to assume that we can have no understanding of other views, even if these are views held in very different cultures and by people in very different situations. The awareness that there may be many different perceptions of things is salutary and something we should be sensitive to, having ignored it in the past. This is different from saying that there is no underlying factual reality. It is also different from saying that there is no hope of cross-cultural empathy. Human beings have much in common and we can understand, in some limited way, people very different from ourselves. The view that we have no common links seems to me to lead to an irresponsible conservatism. George Bernard Shaw reversed the Christian commandment and said 'Do not do unto others as you would they should do unto you. Their tastes may not be the same.' This is very true, but it does not mean that there is nothing we can do; we can comprehend and therefore allow for other people's tastes.

At the beginning of the book, I suggested that in international relations we posed a set of fundamental problems about some crucial issues of human existence. War and peace, poverty and wealth are fundamental to human happiness and they are central to this discipline.

I have provided a large number of questions but few agreed answers. The discipline is highly contested. We disagree about the moral principles involved – though moral disagreements pervade any discipline that requires choice, whether it is international relations or medicine. We also disagree about the explanations we offer of many things, such as why wars occur. We even disagree about the theoretical principles we can use in finding such explanations. In Chapter 6 we could not talk of *the* theory of international relations agreed on by all practitioners, but only a collection of theories, all of which had their adherents.

The lack of agreement in international relations has its consolations. It leads to intellectual excitement in that everyone, from the very beginning, can participate in the debate about everything, including the fundamentals. However, it can also lead to pessimism. The debate might seem never-ending, leading to an endless argument that fails to help in promoting a happier existence for more people. We can become intellectual Flying Dutchmen sailing in an interminable sea of argument, which may amuse us but will achieve nothing. I have argued that this view is false. We are learning more about how the international system works but this can continue only if we continue to recognize that we are involved with a study of how the world behaves. Ultimately we must look at the world to see if we are correct. It is not a factual study in the sense of being just about a set of facts. It is, however, a factual study in that it will have failed in its purpose if it does not make facts more intelligible. Thus, though the argument is seemingly endless, it is exciting because from time to time it leads to greater understanding of the world and, we hope, a greater understanding of what we can do. It will, or should, show us those elements in the human condition we can alter and those we must endure. It should be a responsible argument about the world and not just a game we play for our own entertainment. While there are no easy answers to these problems, some of our puzzles are soluble.

If this is not so, then we really are in trouble. Few would look at the present state of the world with its poverty, violence and threats of violence with any equanimity. However, if we are to improve its working we must understand how the world works at the moment. This in itself is not sufficient but it is certainly necessary. To get peace, we must understand the causes of war; if we are to reduce poverty we must understand the causes of poverty. It is not sufficient just to find someone to blame. To try to get peace by relying simply on intuition and hope is to follow a desperate remedy. It is rather like giving a sick person a random collection of medicines in the hope that something will work. Systematic knowledge is what we need and this is what many international relations scholars are trying to provide.

I believe this profoundly – but like all else it is contentious and will be contended by many people.

This is the conclusion of the book but not of the argument you were invited to join at the beginning. The argument is a continuing one. All can join in.

Index